Citizen Aid and Everyday Humanitarianism

Citizen Aid and Everyday Humanitarianism brings together, under the umbrella terms of citizen aid and grassroots humanitarianism, interdisciplinary research on small-scale, privately-funded forms of aid that operate on the margins of the official development sector.

The last decade has seen a steady rise of such activities in the Global South and North, such as in response to the influx of refugees into Europe. The chapters in this volume cover a variety of locations in Asia, Africa and Europe, presenting empirically grounded cases of citizen aid. They range from educational development projects, to post-disaster emergency relief. Importantly, while some activities are initiated by Northern citizens, others are based on South–South assistance, such as Bangladeshi nationals supporting Rohingya refugees, and peer support in the Philippines in the aftermath of typhoon Hayan. Together, the contributions consider citizen aid vis-à-vis more institutionalised forms of aid, review methodological approaches and their challenges and query the political dimensions of these initiatives. Key themes are historical perspectives on 'demotic humanitarianism', questions of legitimacy and professionalisation, founders' motivations, the role of personal connections, and the importance of digital media for brokerage and fundraising. Being mindful of the power imbalances inherent in citizen aid and everyday humanitarianism, they suggest that both deserve more systematic attention.

Citizen Aid and Everyday Humanitarianism will be of great interest to scholars and professionals working in international development, humanitarianism, international aid and anthropology. The chapters were originally published as a special issue of *Third World Quarterly*.

Anne-Meike Fechter is a Reader in Social Anthropology at the University of Sussex, UK. Her research focuses on forms of privileged migration and development in Southeast Asia, with a special interest in how mobility, and support for others, interlink in the field of transnational assistance.

Anke Schwittay is a Senior Lecturer in Global Development and Anthropology at the University of Sussex, UK. Her research focuses on representations of development and their links to everyday humanitarianism, as well as the use of design and creativity in global development. Anke is the author of *New Media and International Development: Representation and Affect in Microfinance*.

ThirdWorlds
Edited by Shahid Qadir, *University of London, UK*

ThirdWorlds will focus on the political economy, development, and cultures of those parts of the world that have experienced the most political, social, and economic upheaval, and which have faced the greatest challenges of the postcolonial world under globalisation: poverty, displacement and diaspora, environmental degradation, human and civil rights abuses, war, hunger, and disease.

ThirdWorlds serves as a signifier of oppositional emerging economies and cultures ranging from Africa, Asia, Latin America, Middle East, and even those 'Souths' within a larger perceived North, such as the US South and Mediterranean Europe. The study of these otherwise disparate and discontinuous areas, known collectively as the Global South, demonstrates that as globalisation pervades the planet, the south, as a synonym for subalterity, also transcends geographical and ideological frontier.

The most recent titles include:

Rising Powers in International Conflict Management
Converging and Contesting Approaches
Edited by Emel Parlar Dal

Rising Powers and State Transformation
Edited by Shahar Hameiri, Lee Jones and John Heathershaw

The Spatiality of Violence in Post-war Cities
Edited by Emma Elfversson, Ivan Gusic and Kristine Hoglund

Beyond the Gatekeeper State
Edited by Sara Rich Dorman

Citizen Aid and Everyday Humanitarianism
Development Futures?
Edited by Anne-Meike Fechter and Anke Schwittay

For more information about this series, please visit:
https://www.routledge.com/series/TWQ

Citizen Aid and Everyday Humanitarianism

Development Futures?

Edited by
Anne-Meike Fechter and Anke Schwittay

LONDON AND NEW YORK

First published 2021
by Routledge
2 Park Square, Milton Park, Abingdon, Oxon, OX14 4RN

and by Routledge
52 Vanderbilt Avenue, New York, NY 10017

Routledge is an imprint of the Taylor & Francis Group, an informa business

© 2021 Global South Ltd
Chapter 6 © 2019 Sara Kinsbergen. Originally published as Open Access.

With the exception of Chapter 6, no part of this book may be reprinted or reproduced or utilised in any form or by any electronic, mechanical, or other means, now known or hereafter invented, including photocopying and recording, or in any information storage or retrieval system, without permission in writing from the publishers. For details on the rights for Chapter 6, please see the chapter's Open Access footnote.

Trademark notice: Product or corporate names may be trademarks or registered trademarks, and are used only for identification and explanation without intent to infringe.

British Library Cataloguing in Publication Data
A catalogue record for this book is available from the British Library

ISBN 13: 978-0-367-46488-2
ISBN 13: 978-0-367-55453-8 (pbk)

Typeset in Myriad Pro
by Newgen Publishing UK

Publisher's Note
The publisher accepts responsibility for any inconsistencies that may have arisen during the conversion of this book from journal articles to book chapters, namely the inclusion of journal terminology.

Disclaimer
Every effort has been made to contact copyright holders for their permission to reprint material in this book. The publishers would be grateful to hear from any copyright holder who is not here acknowledged and will undertake to rectify any errors or omissions in future editions of this book.

Contents

	Citation Information	vii
	Notes on Contributors	ix
1	Introduction: Citizen aid: grassroots interventions in development and humanitarianism Anne-Meike Fechter and Anke Schwittay	1
2	Demotic humanitarians: historical perspectives on the global reach of local initiatives, 1940–2017 Bertrand Taithe	13
3	Motivations behind citizen aid: Norwegian initiatives in The Gambia June Fylkesnes	31
4	Development and the search for connection Anne-Meike Fechter	48
5	Don't reinvent the wheel: possibilities for and limits to building capacity of grassroots international NGOs Susan Appe and Allison Schnable	64
6	The legitimacy of Dutch do-it-yourself initiatives in Kwale County, Kenya Sara Kinsbergen	82
7	Beyond crisis management? The role of Citizen Initiatives for Global Solidarity in humanitarian aid: the case of Lesvos Hanne Haaland and Hege Wallevik	101
8	Humanitarianism, civil society and the Rohingya refugee crisis in Bangladesh David Lewis	116

9 Citizen aid, social media and brokerage after disaster   135
   Deirdre McKay and Padmapani Perez

10 Digital mediations of everyday humanitarianism: the case of Kiva.org   153
   Anke Schwittay

   Index   171

Citation Information

The chapters in this book were originally published in *Third World Quarterly*, volume 40, issue 10 (2019). When citing this material, please use the original page numbering for each article, as follows:

Chapter 1
Citizen aid: grassroots interventions in development and humanitarianism
Anne-Meike Fechter and Anke Schwittay
Third World Quarterly, volume 40, issue 10 (2019), pp. 1769–1780

Chapter 2
Demotic humanitarians: historical perspectives on the global reach of local initiatives, 1940–2017
Bertrand Taithe
Third World Quarterly, volume 40, issue 10 (2019), pp. 1781–1798

Chapter 3
Motivations behind citizen aid: Norwegian initiatives in The Gambia
June Fylkesnes
Third World Quarterly, volume 40, issue 10 (2019), pp. 1799–1815

Chapter 4
Development and the search for connection
Anne-Meike Fechter
Third World Quarterly, volume 40, issue 10 (2019), pp. 1816–1831

Chapter 5
Don't reinvent the wheel: possibilities for and limits to building capacity of grassroots international NGOs
Susan Appe and Allison Schnable
Third World Quarterly, volume 40, issue 10 (2019), pp. 1832–1849

Chapter 6
The legitimacy of Dutch do-it-yourself initiatives in Kwale County, Kenya
Sara Kinsbergen
Third World Quarterly, volume 40, issue 10 (2019), pp. 1850–1868

Chapter 7
Beyond crisis management? The role of Citizen Initiatives for Global Solidarity in humanitarian aid: the case of Lesvos
Hanne Haaland and Hege Wallevik
Third World Quarterly, volume 40, issue 10 (2019), pp. 1869–1883

Chapter 8
Humanitarianism, civil society and the Rohingya refugee crisis in Bangladesh
David Lewis
Third World Quarterly, volume 40, issue 10 (2019), pp. 1884–1902

Chapter 9
Citizen aid, social media and brokerage after disaster
Deirdre McKay and Padmapani Perez
Third World Quarterly, volume 40, issue 10 (2019), pp. 1903–1920

Chapter 10
Digital mediations of everyday humanitarianism: the case of Kiva.org
Anke Schwittay
Third World Quarterly, volume 40, issue 10 (2019), pp. 1921–1938

For any permission-related enquiries please visit:
www.tandfonline.com/page/help/permissions

Notes on Contributors

Susan Appe, Rockefeller College of Public Affairs and Policy, University at Albany, SUNY, Albany, NY, USA.

Anne-Meike Fechter, Department of Anthropology, School of Global Studies, University of Sussex, Brighton, UK.

June Fylkesnes, Department for Global Development and Planning, University of Agder, Kristiansand, Norway.

Hanne Haaland, Department for Global Development and Planning, University of Agder, Kristiansand, Norway.

Sara Kinsbergen, Department of Anthropology and Development Studies, Radboud University, Nijmegen, the Netherlands.

David Lewis, Department of Social Policy, London School of Economics and Political Science, London, UK.

Deirdre McKay, School of Geography, Geology and the Environment, Keele University, Keele, UK.

Padmapani Perez, Institute of Arts and Sciences, Far Eastern University, Manila, Philippines.

Allison Schnable, O'Neill School of Public and Environmental Affairs, Indiana University, Bloomington, IN, USA.

Anke Schwittay, Department of International Development and Anthropology, School of Global Studies, University of Sussex, Brighton, UK.

Bertrand Taithe, Humanitarian and Conflict Response Institute, University of Manchester, Manchester, UK.

Hege Wallevik, Department for Global Development and Planning, University of Agder, Kristiansand, Norway.

INTRODUCTION

Citizen aid: grassroots interventions in development and humanitarianism

Anne-Meike Fechter and Anke Schwittay

ABSTRACT
The introduction to this collection brings together, under the umbrella terms of citizen aid and grassroots humanitarianism, interdisciplinary research on small-scale, privately funded forms of aid and development. It notes the steady rise of these activities, including in the Global South as well as North, such as in the context of the recent European refugee crisis. It considers their position vis-à-vis more institutionalised forms of aid; methodological approaches and their challenges; and asks what political dimensions these initiatives may have. It outlines key themes arising from the contributions to the collection, including historical perspectives on 'demotic humanitarianism', questions of legitimacy and their apparent lack of professionalisation, motivations of their founders, the role of personal connections, as well as the importance of digital media for brokerage and fundraising. Being mindful of its critiques and implicit power imbalances, it suggests that citizen aid deserves more systematic academic attention.

Introduction

Over the last few years, forms of aid and development have become visible which are not orchestrated by large donors or aid agencies, but are initiated by ordinary citizens, from the Global North and South.[1] Research on these practices, which we are calling 'citizen aid', is growing, but remains scattered across disciplines. The aims of this collection are therefore to take stock of this emerging area both empirically and theoretically, to flag shared themes arising from a number of different approaches, and to ask what significance citizen aid may have in the wider context of aid and development theory and practice. This introduction will start by mapping the field.

Citizen aid as an 'unstable category'

One reason why studies of these forms of aid are fragmented are the diverse terminologies which are deployed to describe them. Despite this, we propose that they share some distinctive features. Broadly defined, we take citizen aid to refer to projects instigated by individuals who are privately funded and aim to support others in need. The focus on 'citizens' emphasises the agency of ordinary people making ethical decisions about providing assistance to others. Such activities have variously been described as the 'fourth pillar' of development,[2] citizen initiatives,[3] private development initiatives[4] or grassroots international non-governmental organisations (NGOs),[5] or as being carried out by 'independent development volunteers'.[6] With a focus on humanitarianism, they have been labelled 'demotic',[7] 'grassroots humanitarians'[8] or 'everyday humanitarianism'.[9] McCabe and Phillimore flag their existence as 'small-scale civil society actors' who respond to local needs or shared interests rather than policy directives.[10] Their 'action below the radar' thrives in the unregulated space that also characterises citizen aid.[11]

Our aim is not to establish a reified, distinct category of 'citizen aid', which certain practices are deemed to fall into (or not). Instead, rather than creating an object category, citizen aid is more productively employed as a sideways lens, a perspective for recognising forms of intervention and resource distribution which often remain under the radar of established development research and practice. We take a cue here from Lewis and Schuller's helpful notion of NGOs as a 'productively unstable category' that allows for charting similarities and differences across a field of action between aid and activism.[12] While proposed in relation to understanding NGOs, we suggest that in capturing the diversity of activities, citizen aid as an unstable category denotes a set of practices that are dynamic and often temporally limited. They are small-scale and usually operate on the margins of the formal aid and development sector. While some of these initiatives may, over time, incorporate themselves as NGOs, others stay small, downsize or cease to exist, and studying such processes of formalisation or their absence can yield important insights into how citizen aid evolves. For us, citizen aid productively captures the focus on support that citizens extend to each other. Notably, the term 'citizen' does not denote formal national belonging here, but rather a 'global citizenship',[13] in reference to citizens of different nations acting for others, often across borders.[14] These borders follow the changing geographies of development: while most (initial) studies of citizen aid focus on activities originating in the Global North and being implemented in the Global South, recent research is also examining South–South initiatives as well as responses to situations in the Global North. In sum, we adopt 'citizen aid' as a working definition for a diverse and shifting set of mutual support practices funded by private, as opposed to public, means. As evident in this collection, the contributors employ a multitude of terms, and our aim is not to reduce this variety, but to help counter fragmentation and the reduced theoretical visibility and impact that may result from it.

Anecdotal evidence of citizen aid in its current forms has been accruing more recently, though its recognition has not always been flattering, especially when referring to Northern initiatives in the Global South that arguably have been the mainstay of citizen aid. The journalist Linda Polman described such initiatives as 'MONGOs', short for 'my own NGO', referring to aid workers setting up their own projects.[15] More enthusiastically, it was hailed as a 'Do-It-Yourself-foreign aid revolution' by the journalist Nikolas Kristof, focusing on North American college graduates setting up small-scale projects in countries of the Global South.[16] Such promises have not gone unchallenged, partly with reference to being often led by non-development professionals who are initiating piecemeal and small-scale projects based on reactions to needs and situations they sometimes poorly understand. Such projects are not necessarily sustainable or scalable and can do more harm than good. While these critiques are undeniably important, in their wholesale dismissal they foreclose the opportunity to learn about citizen aid as an empirical trend, and where its relevance may lie.[17] More nuanced studies have conceptualised a 'fourth pillar' of development that is sitting alongside, but distinct from, the state, the market and the third sector.[18] Its small-scale private aid initiatives have been studied from a wide range of disciplines, adopting multiple methodologies and regional foci. All of these approaches, in the first instance, aim to raise the visibility of such initiatives through establishing an empirical evidence base. Their theoretical contributions, however, do not coalesce into a unified debate. In the following, we map these approaches to move towards greater cohesion and dialogue.

The most substantial body of work on citizen aid so far has been undertaken with regard to what Clifford calls its 'supply side': that is, taking stock mostly of small-scale charitable initiatives in the Global North which are active in countries of the Global South.[19] For the US, Schnable documents a rise from around 1000 small-scale non-profit organisations registered in 1990 to over 11,000 of them 10 years later.[20] A similar trajectory is identified in the UK, drawing on records of the Charity Commission for England and Wales, which show that in the last 10 years, the number of small charities has grown significantly more than that of large ones.[21] While definitions of 'smallness' vary, Clifford's study covers those with an annual budget of less than £100,000, while in the US context, these are budgets of under $15,000. Studies focusing on continental Europe, examining private development initiatives in The Netherlands, define these as 'small organisations, founded by non-development specialists, run by volunteers and funded by individuals, which are focused on the direct provision of goods or services to individuals and communities overseas'.[22] Estimates put the number of them between 6000 and 15,000 in the Netherlands, with a pronounced period of growth between 1990 and 2009, when data was last collected. 'Small' is here defined as an organisation with 20 or fewer staff, with an average annual budget of around €50,000.[23] Observations of a substantial growth of small international charities are thus corroborated by quantitative data based on national registers, including in Norway and Belgium.[24]

Such a methodological approach that is based on data from sending countries and formal registers inevitably renders insights while also creating blind spots. The material it generates can be taken to indicate the decentralisation or voluntarisation of international development,[25] or alternatively its democratisation, making it accessible to non-specialists or 'amateurs'.[26] Less evident from these 'supply-side' studies is qualitative, in-depth data on how these organisations operate in implementation sites, what people are involved at locations of origin and destination, what relationships exist with local partners and aid recipients, and the nature of activities and their possible impact. To address these questions, some work, including studies in this issue, has begun to study destination sites.[27] Nevertheless, a focus on organisations which are formally registered, often in the Global North, elides one key characteristic of citizen aid, namely its informal and private nature. This often means being set up in an ad hoc way and maintained and funded by small groups of individuals from the Global North and South. The quantitative approach also risks obscuring the role of communities at the destination, and furthers an implicit assumption that citizens there are involved mainly as gatekeepers and beneficiaries. Studying destination sites, while offering limited quantitative material, therefore allows for a more nuanced, qualitative account of citizen aid where it is being implemented. This is the case, for example, with 'independent development volunteers' in Honduras, a network of mainly North Americans aiming to improve the well-being of disadvantaged Honduran citizens;[28] work on brokerage in citizen aid in Cambodia;[29] or the motivation of Norwegian founders who set up projects in The Gambia.[30] This shows that the few designated studies to date that have explored long-term, long-distance transnational citizen aid from the perspectives of sites in the Global South have focused on originators in the Global North. Many citizen aid initiatives disrupt the traditional North–South divisions, however.[31]

This becomes especially evident in studies of 'grassroots humanitarianism', where a focus on the location where citizen aid is carried out is central. By definition, these initiatives revolve around sites of humanitarian emergency and natural disaster, such as the tsunami in the Indian Ocean in 2004, Hurricane Katrina in the US or Typhoon Haiyan in the Philippines in 2013.[32] While some critically observe a 'competitive humanitarianism' in their aftermath,[33] others find them a groundswell of solidarity.[34] They can also become sites of exclusion of local resident survivors by large agencies, who find themselves ignored in their role as first responders, or are subsequently employed as second-class aid workers, showing that citizen aid reproduces many of the conventional development power inequalities.[35] The most recently significant, and indeed fertile, ground for emergent practices of citizen aid and their analysis has been the migration 'crisis' from 2015, which saw increased numbers of refugees arriving in Southern Europe and beyond, fleeing war and violent conflict in the Middle East and sub-Saharan Africa.

Citizen aid practices in the refugee context display particular characteristics, as well as producing different but overlapping theoretical concerns and conclusions than the projects described above. The fact that these perceived humanitarian emergencies were unfolding within Europe facilitated people becoming involved who might not otherwise have done so. Geographical proximity made this more likely, whether this meant travelling from the South of England to informal refugee camps in Calais or further afield to Greek islands, and allowed people to volunteer intermittently, sometimes alongside their paid work. Other factors shaping the popularity of these engagements were the extensive media coverage that framed these events as a historical moment of crisis. They share some key features of citizen aid, namely their often-spontaneous inception, responding to needs as they arise; and their informal, makeshift nature, especially in the early stages. They were driven by 'grassroots volunteers' and typically operated on the margins of the established humanitarian system and separately from mainstream organisations, initially in the absence of formalised, state-sanctioned interventions.[36]

Academic research on such volunteer humanitarians, alongside media attention, has been growing apace, to the extent that research on grassroots interventions with and for migrants and refugees now constitutes a veritable field in itself, despite its disciplinary diversity.[37] Partly due to the political prominence of refugee issues in Europe as well as elsewhere, these grassroots interventions are being associated much more closely with pro-migrant activism and political campaigning.[38] They also tend to be framed as forms of solidarity,[39] more so than citizen aid channeled from the Global North to South. Some of these studies highlight an often-overlooked aspect, namely the grassroots activities of migrants themselves, and of the communities which (more or less) temporarily host them.[40] Despite their evident differences, we argue that both long-distance citizen aid activities and more immediate grassroots humanitarianisms can, and indeed ought to be, considered to occupy places on a continuum of support activities. As contributions to this issue show, informal humanitarianisms may include Bangladeshi citizens intervening on behalf of Rohingya refugees, or survivors supporting each other in the aftermath of a typhoon, and are thus not restricted to a European context. These interventions trigger different theoretical claims, extending to solidarity, activism, governmentality and resistance, to more broadly conceived ideas of shared humanity and social justice. Viewing them in a shared framework of informality and horizontality should sharpen those debates, rather than blunt them.

As evident from even this cursory overview, small-scale private aid activities have grown substantially over the last decade, and have become more visible to the broader public, not least through their self-representation via digital media. The question arises, then, why citizen aid has remained comparatively obscure in academic and policy debates. One reason may be the geographical dispersal of these activities; their small scale, combined with their distributed transnational connections, may keep them out of sight of formal aid and development institutions, and on the margins of its research. It is not coincidental that the most prominent studies cited above are based on charity registers, whereas there exists little reliable data on the number of small-scale aid activities worldwide outside of these. This is compounded by the difficulty of tracking the resource flows of citizen aid, including money, goods and labour, which are channeled by private donors through their networks. According to Hénon, 'data is poor because of low reporting levels, a lack of accountability structures for private donors and an absence of established transparency standards'.[41] In addition to this relative elusiveness, many citizen aid initiatives are reluctant to interface with government apparatuses or formal development institutions and vice versa.[42] While some large development actors have taken note of their existence, initiatives are often dismissed due to – in their view – the initiatives' amateurish nature, rendering them not worthy of development studies' attention. This collection aims to address this oversight by providing a more concerted theorisation around a number of themes that emerge from this collection of papers.

Themes and contributions

Citizen aid activities have thus not just been under-studied, but remain under-theorised. One challenge, we suggest, lies in analytically extracting them from lenses that are fixated on their status as NGOs, or involving volunteers. Research both on NGOs as organisational forms and on volunteering is extensive, but adopting these as sole frameworks risks missing what makes citizen aid distinctive. This is not to deny that many of those projects are registered as NGOs, or that people involved in them deliver voluntary work. Considering them simply as small NGOs, however, loses sight of the fact that they are funded through private donations, and are sustained by personal transnational networks, which channel resources in various forms. Citizen aid initiatives tend to display features of small business start-ups, including an entrepreneurial sense of ownership, agency and the ability to choose their issues, more than is often evident in the literature on NGOs.[43] While citizen aid relies at least partly on unpaid labour, the notion of citizen aiders as 'volunteers' misrecognises its more complicated workings in practice. Many practitioners draw, at least initially, on their own funds, as well as on those of their social networks and other private donations; but they may also engage in paid work to maintain a livelihood, or operate income-generating projects which sustain their non-profit activities. Citizen aid is thus driven by a range of people, some of whom provide their skills and time for free; some are being paid, while founders often use their own resources to set up their projects. The theorisation of citizen aid is therefore not advanced by subsuming it under existing literature on NGOs or volunteers. Instead, the papers in this collection suggest several analytical avenues. A first cluster focuses on their historical origins, the importance of connections, and the motivations of the individuals involved. A second takes as a starting point their relationship to established actors such as governments, development institutions and civil society organisations, while a third considers the role of technology in transnational citizen aid networks.

Origins and motivations

As suggested above, citizen aid and grassroots humanitarianism are not new phenomena. While Schwittay charts the historic rise of everyday humanitarian sentiments, Taithe presents the trajectory of one such grassroots organisation in the North of England, Hudfam, and its proponent Elisabeth Wilson.[44] These activities were already characterised by transnational connections, even though at the time, it was goods rather than people moving between continents. Recipients of these goods were never just that, but collaborators in what frequently turned into long-term relationships. As Fechter argues in her paper, personal relations and connections often provide the motivation and backbone of citizen aid activities.[45] Fylkesnes, in her study on Norwegian founders of aid initiatives in The Gambia, describes how their individual motivations can be seen as a strength of this type of development, as it allows for a sense of ownership, as well as accountability towards beneficiary communities.[46] At the same time, founders' attitudes displayed disinterest in interacting more systematically with larger-scale aid agencies. Appe and Schnable's paper picks up on this evident lack of 'professionalising', and ask what the causes and consequences are for grassroots international NGOs.[47] Such an insistence on autonomy and ostensible 'amateurism' can also account for their at times uneasy interactions with other aid actors.

Relationships to established actors

At their sites of implementation, citizen aid initiatives often relate in ambiguous ways to formal institutions, be they civil society organisations, local government units or professional development actors. With regard to the first, Lewis shows how the personal response of many Bangladeshi citizens to the influx of Rohingya refugees needs to be situated within the country's history, and particularly the 1971 Liberation War, and the ensuing forms of civil society.[48] The paper also illuminates how initial everyday humanitarian responses are becoming formalised and solidified as formal humanitarian organisations and the Bangladeshi government moved to action. This process is not without frictions, partly caused by the apparent amateurish nature of citizens' responses discussed above.

The sometimes-deliberate avoidance of 'professionalisation' also results in complex relationships with development professionals in mainstream organisations, which Haaland and Wallevik analyse through the lens of resistance.[49] The two citizen aid organisations they studied on the Greek island of Lesbos, in the context of the 2015 refugee arrivals, took activist approaches in resisting the establishment's framing of the influx as a short-term crisis. Through an insistence on environmental issues and the responsibility of governments and through collaborating with national and international advocacy networks, both showed the limits of the humanitarian aid apparatus on Lesvos. Their decision to remain on the margins of this apparatus can be understood as a form of resistance to dominant humanitarian interpretations, narratives and practices. This includes a refusal of bureaucratisation that is often also the main reason for keeping local government actors at arm's length, as shown in Kinsbergen's paper.[50] The Dutch citizen aid organisations she studied in Kenya inform local officials of their presence, but do not wish to collaborate with them. The officials themselves, in contrast, argued for a closer and more coordinated relationship, also to avoid the duplication and fragmentation of development efforts. In the Philippine case studied by McKay and Perez,[51] a more distant relationship was desired by both sides. This can lead to a lack of understanding and acknowledgement by local government officials and a conscious effort not to compete with their relief efforts by the citizen aid provider. The latter paper also shows the increasing importance of digital technologies for citizen aid activities.

The role of technologies

Digital technologies are enabling such activities in various ways, by making their work and needs visible to potential supporters and collaborators (and academic researchers). Social media channels coordinate transnational networks of resources, while crowdsourcing platforms aggregate the actions of geographically dispersed individuals to work together on enacting a form of virtual care. In this way, technologies help to build and sustain the connections that are so vital to citizen aid, and shape their work in particular mediated ways. In this sense, they resemble forms of citizen science, which is partly sustained through crowdsourced data, gathered by engaged citizens to contribute to larger projects. As the papers by McKay and Perez and Schwittay show, 'digital humanitarianism' does not eliminate the need for brokers altogether, but it changes who can become involved in development and how. In McKay and Perez's case, focusing on Typhoon Haiyan in the Philippines, the circulation of images, which acted as virtual brokers, enabled a varied set of local and international actors to direct resources to where they were needed. Their analysis draws attention to the work of curating images around particular fundraising appeals and related processes of accountability. Schwittay's paper shows how crowdfunding platforms, such as Kiva.org, aggregate micro-financial contributions from tens of thousands of individuals and mediate their connection to specific causes, organisations and recipients in technological, financial and spatial ways. There are also crisis mapping platforms that came to prominence after the Haiti earthquake, incorporating potentially incommensurate elements of disaster response, building resilience, and witnessing,[52] and platforms such as Department for International Development's (DFID's) Amplify programme that ask individuals to contribute ideas towards finding new solutions to development problems.[53]

Conclusion

In a recent overview, Miriam Ticktin argued that 'anthropologists and others have critiqued humanitarianism for depoliticising structural problems of inequality and domination. Yet, if humanitarianism can be read as an ethico-political project, what might other competing political spaces and movements look like?'[54] We suggest that the contributions in this volume offer an answer of sorts to this question. One of our aims is to document that citizen aid and grassroots humanitarian activities constitute a growing phenomenon deserving of greater empirical and theoretical scrutiny. At the same time, while embracing humanitarian imperatives, they cannot straightforwardly be categorised as political movements – one reason why they may have escaped the attention of Ticktin and others. Our hope is that this volume goes some way to address this, and its contributions outline some of citizen aid's key features.

If, however, we consider both citizen aid and grassroots humanitarianism as 'ethico-political projects', we can ask in what ways these sets of practices are political, and indeed what we mean by 'political'. The case of grassroots humanitarianism in the context of the European refugee 'crisis' is particularly pertinent here, as it presents a compelling case of support acts extended to migrants, which can be subjected to attempts of governmentality by the state(s) where they take place. Humanitarian efforts can become acts of protest and resistance. Activism and advocacy are more obviously live issues among these initiatives than other forms of grassroots humanitarianism. At the same time, to dismiss long-distance citizen aid as merely individualistic and inherently apolitical ignores its potential to disrupt established development practices by making the latter more accessible to a more diverse range of people, in both the Global North and South, outside of policy directives. That does not mean that these initiatives avoid the entrenched hierarchies and inequalities of power, for which formal development has long been criticised. Future research must remain alert to these issues in any configurations of support. It opens up a perspective on aid that recognises a multitude of informal, supportive interactions between citizens, and in that sense forms of more 'horizontal philanthropy'.[55]

One question animating this collection was in what ways citizen aid and everyday humanitarianism may be considered development futures. Rather than replacing the established aid apparatus, these informal practices have come to occupy part of the overall ecosystem of aid, albeit at its margins, and often operate independently of its institutions. The contributions in this volume broaden our conceptions of contemporary forms of aid and development, by taking its informal manifestations seriously. While they may be part of a loosely conceived division of labour, which includes citizens from the Global North and South, their significance lies in encouraging us to recognise the support extended between citizens, beyond and outside of the institutionalised systems which have come to embody 'aid'.

Disclosure statement

No potential conflict of interest was reported by the authors.

Funding

The workshop from which this Special Issue has resulted has been funded by a Research Opportunity Fund and the Department of Anthropology at the University of Sussex, whose assistance is gratefully acknowledged.

Acknowledgements

Our thanks go to the workshop participants and to colleagues at the University of Sussex and Oxford University, whose comments have been immensely helpful in preparing this article.

Notes

1. We use these terms not as a geographical marker but to signal a location of marginality vis-à-vis larger economic and political structures.
2. Develtere and de Bruyn, "Emergence of a Fourth Pillar in Development Aid."
3. Schulpen and Huyse, "Citizen Initiatives for Global Solidarity."
4. Kinsbergen and Schulpen, *Anatomy of the Private Initiative*.
5. Schnable, "Era of Do-It-Yourself Aid."
6. McLennan, "Passion, Paternalism, and Politics."
7. Taithe, this volume.
8. Sandri, "'Volunteer Humanitarianism' across Close(d) Borders."
9. Schwittay, *New Media and International Development*.
10. McCabe, Phillimore, and Mayblin, "'Below the Radar' Activities."
11. Appe and Telch, "Grassroots International NGOs."
12. Lewis and Schuller, "Engagements with a Productively Unstable Category."
13. Baillie Smith and Laurie, "International Volunteering and Development."
14. Isin, *Citizens Without Frontiers*.
15. Polman, *Crisis Caravan*, 8.
16. Kristof, "DIY Foreign Aid Revolution."
17. Algoso, "Don't Try This Abroad."
18. Develtere and de Bruyn, ""Emergence of a Fourth Pillar in Development Aid."
19. Clifford, "International Charitable Connections."
20. Schnable, "Era of Do-It-Yourself Aid," 1.
21. Clifford, "International Charitable Connections."
22. Kinsbergen and Schulpen, *Anatomy of the Private Initiative*.
23. Kinsbergen, *Behind the Pictures*, 58.
24. Haaland and Wallevik, "Citizens as Actors in the Development Field"; Pollet et al., *Accidental Aid Worker*.
25. Schnable, "Era of Do-It-Yourself Aid."
26. Kinsbergen, *Behind the Pictures*.
27. Kinsbergen, Schulpen and Ruerd, "Understanding the Sustainability of Private Development Initiatives," Haaland and Wallevik, "Citizens as Actors in the Development Field."
28. McLennan, "Passion, Paternalism, and Politics."
29. Fechter, "Brokering Transnational Flows of Care."
30. Fylkesnes, Small Streams Make Big Rivers."
31. See eg Prince and Brown, *Volunteer Economies*; and Ho, "Mobilising Affinity Ties."
32. Michel, "Personal Responsibility and Volunteering."
33. Stirrat, "Competitive Humanitarianism."
34. Solnit, *Paradise Built in Hell*.
35. Ong and Combinido, "Local Aid Workers."

36. Sandri, "'Volunteer Humanitarianism' across Close(d) Borders."
37. Borton, "Humanitarian Impulse"; Rozakou, "Solidarity Humanitarianism," Papataxiarchis, "Being 'There'"; Tjensvoll Kitching et al, "Exploring the Role"; Verschragen and Vandervoort, "European Refugee Controversy"; Fleischmann, "Making Volunteering with Refugees Governable."
38. Sandri, "'Volunteer Humanitarianism' across Close(d) Borders"; Verschragen and Vandervoort, "European Refugee Controversy"; Fleischmann, "Making Volunteering with Refugees Governable."
39. Della Porta, *Solidarity Mobilizations in the 'Refugee Crisis'*; Rozakou, "Solidarity Humanitarianism"; Scheibelhofer, "Gender and Intimate Solidarity", Squire, "From Community Cohesion to Mobile Solidarities."
40. Zaman, *Islamic Traditions of Refuge*; Vogt, *Lives in Transit*.
41. Hénon, *Measuring Private Development Assistance*, 17.
42. Appe and Telch, "Grassroots International NGOs."
43. Bebbington, Hickey, and Mitlin, *Development Alternatives*.
44. Schwittay, "Digital Mediations of Everyday Humanitarianism"; Taithe, "Demotic Humanitarians: Historical Perspectives."
45. Fechter, "Development and the Search for Connection."
46. Fylkesnes, "Motivations behind Citizen Aid."
47. Appe and Schnable, "Don't Reinvent the Wheel."
48. Lewis, "Humanitarianism, Civil Society, and the Rohingya."
49. Haaland and Wallevik, "Beyond Crisis Management?"
50. Kinsbergen, "Legitimacy of Dutch Do-It-Yourself."
51. McKay and Perez, "Citizen Aid, Social Media."
52. Givoni, "Between Micro Mappers and Missing Maps"; Kankanamge et al., "Can Volunteer Crowdsourcing Reduce Disaster."
53. Schwittay and Braund, "Participation 2.0?"
54. Ticktin, "Transnational Humanitarianism," 283.
55. Wilkinson-Maposa et al., *Poor Philanthropist*, 76.

Bibliography

Algoso, D. "Don't Try This Abroad: Nick Kristof is Wrong. Amateurs are not the Future of Foreign Aid." *Foreign Policy*, October 6, 2010. http://www.foreignpolicy.com/articles/2010/10/26/dont_try_this_abroad?

Appe, S., and A. Schnable. "Don't Reinvent the Wheel: Possibilities for and Limits to Building Capacity of Grassroots International NGOs." *Third World Quarterly* (2019). doi:10.1080/01436597.2019.1636226.

Appe, S., and F. Telch. "Grassroots International NGOs: Using Comparative Interpretive Policy Analysis to Understand Meanings in Private Development Aid." *Journal of Comparative Policy Analysis: Research and Practice* (2018). doi:10.1080/13876988.2019.1582885.

Baillie Smith, M., and N. Laurie. "International Volunteering and Development: Global Citizenship and Neoliberal Professionalisation Today." *Transactions of the Institute of British Geographers* 36, no. 4 (2011): 545–559. doi:10.1111/j.1475-5661.2011.00436.x.

Bebbington, A., S. Hickey, and D. Mitlin. *Development Alternatives*. London: Zed, 2008.

Borton, J. "The Humanitarian Impulse: Alive and Well Among the Citizens of Europe," 2016. Accessed June 7, 2019. https://odihpn.org/magazine/humanitarian-impulse-alive-well-among-citizens-europe/

Clifford, D. "International Charitable Connections: The Growth in Number, and the Countries of Operation, of English and Welsh Charities Working Overseas." *Journal of Social Policy* 45, no. 3 (2016): 453–486. doi:10.1017/S0047279416000076.

Della Porta, D., ed. *Solidarity Mobilizations in the 'Refugee Crisis': Contentious Moves*. London: Palgrave Macmillan, 2018.

Develtere, P., and T. De Bruyn. "The Emergence of a Fourth Pillar in Development Aid." *Development in Practice* 19, no. 7 (2009): 912–922. doi:10.1080/09614520903122378.

Fechter, A.-M. "Brokering Transnational Flows of Care: The Case of Citizen Aid." *Ethnos* (2019). doi:10.1080/00141844.2018.1543339.

Fechter, A.-M. "Development and the Search for Connection: The Case of Citizen Aid." *Third World Quarterly* (2019). doi:10.1080/01436597.2019.1649089.
Fleischmann, L. "Making Volunteering with Refugees Governable: The Contested Role of 'Civil Society' in the German Welcome Culture." *Social Inclusion* 7, no. 2 (2019): 64–73. doi:10.17645/si.v7i2.1979.
Fylkesnes, J. "Motivations behind Citizen Aid: Norwegian Initiatives in the Gambia." *Third World Quarterly* (2019). doi:10.1080/01436597.2019.1656061.
Fylkesnes, J. "Small Streams Make Big Rivers: Exploring Motivation and Idealism in Norwegian Personalised Aid Initiatives in the Gambia." MA diss., University of Agder, Norway, 2016. https://brage.bibsys.no/xmlui/bitstream/handle/11250/2414518/Fylkesnes%2C%20June.pdf?sequence=1
Givoni, M. "Between Micro Mappers and Missing Maps: Digital Humanitarianism and the Politics of Material Participation in Disaster Response." *Environment and Planning D: Society and Space* 34, no. 6 (2016): 1025–1043. doi:10.1177/0263775816652899.
Haaland, H., and H. Wallevik. "Beyond Crisis Management? The Role of Citizen Initiatives for Global Solidarity in Humanitarian Aid: The Case of Lesvos." *Third World Quarterly* (2019). doi:10.1080/01436597.2019.1656060.
Haaland, H., and H. Wallevik. "Citizens as Actors in the Development Field: The Case of an Accidental Aid-Agent's Activities in Aid-Land." *Forum for Development Studies* 44, no. 2 (2017): 203–222.
Hénon, S. *Measuring Private Development Assistance: Emerging Trends and Challenges*. Bristol: Development Initiatives, 2014. doi:10.1080/08039410.2017.1305444.
Ho, E. "Mobilising Affinity Ties: Kachin Internal Displacement and the Geographies of Humanitarianism at the China–Myanmar Border." *Transactions of the Institute of British Geographers* 42, no. 1 (2017): 84–97. doi:10.1111/tran.12148.
Isin, E. *Citizens without Frontiers*. London: Bloomsbury, 2012.
Kankanamge, N., T. Yigitcanlar, A. Goonetilleke, and M. Kamruzzaman. "Can Volunteer Crowdsourcing Reduce Disaster Risk? A Systematic Review of the Literature." *International Journal of Disaster Risk Reduction* 35, (2019): 101097. doi:10.1016/j.ijdrr.2019.101097.
Kinsbergen, S. *Behind the Pictures: Understanding Private Development Initiatives*. Nijmegen: Radboud University, 2014.
Kinsbergen, S. "The Legitimacy of Dutch Do-It-Yourself Initiatives in Kwale County, Kenya." *Third World Quarterly* (2019). doi:10.1080/01436597.2019.1644497.
Kinsbergen, S., and L. Schulpen. *The Anatomy of the Private Initiative: The Results of Five Years of Research into Private Initiatives in the Field of Development Cooperation*. Nijmegen: CIDIN-NCDO, 2010.
Kinsbergen, S., L. Schulpen, and R. Ruerd. "Understanding the Sustainability of Private Development Initiatives: What Kind of Difference Do They Make?" *Forum for Development Studies* 44, no. 2 (2017): 223–248. doi:10.1080/08039410.2017.1307270.
Kristof, N. "The DIY Foreign Aid Revolution." *The New York Times Magazine*, 2010. http://www.nytimes.com/2010/10/24/magazine/24volunteerism-t.html
Lewis, D. "Humanitarianism, Civil Society, and the Rohingya Refugee Crisis in Bangladesh." *Third World Quarterly* (2019). doi:10.1080/01436597.2019.1652897.
Lewis, D., and M. Schuller. "Engagements with a Productively Unstable Category: Anthropologists and Non-Governmental Organizations." *Current Anthropology* 56, no. 5 (2017): 634–651. doi:10.1086/693897.
McCabe, A. J. Phillimore, and L. Mayblin. 2010. *'Below the Radar' Activities and Organisations in the Third Sector: A Summary Review of the Literature*. Working Paper 29. Third Sector Research Centre. https://www.birmingham.ac.uk/Documents/college-social-sciences/social-policy/tsrc/working-papers/working-paper-29.pdf
McKay, D., and P. Perez. "Citizen Aid, Social Media and Brokerage after Disaster." *Third World Quarterly* (2019). doi:10.1080/01436597.2019.1634470.
McLennan, S. "Passion, Paternalism, and Politics: DIY Development and Independent Volunteers in Honduras." *Development in Practice* 27, no. 6 (2017): 880–891. doi:10.1080/09614524.2017.1339780.
Michel, L. M. "Personal Responsibility and Volunteering after a Natural Disaster: The Case of Hurricane Katrina." *Sociological Spectrum* 27, no. 6 (2007): 633–652. doi:10.1080/02732170701533855.

Ong, J. C., and P. Combinido. "Local Aid Workers in the Digital Humanitarian Project: Between "Second Class Citizens" and "Entrepreneurial Survivors." *Critical Asian Studies* 50, no. 1 (2018): 86–102. doi:10.1080/14672715.2017.1401937.

Papataxiarchis, E. "Being 'There': At the Front Line of the 'European Refugee Crisis." *Anthropology Today* 32, no. 3 (2016): 3–7. doi:10.1111/1467-8322.12252.

Pollet I., R. Habraken, L. Schulpen, and H. Huyse. The Accidental Aid Worker. A Mapping of Citizen Initiatives for Global Solidarity in Europe, 2014. https://lirias.kuleuven.be/bitstream/123456789/466379/3/R1554_The_Accidental_Aid_Worker.pdf

Polman, L. *The Crisis Caravan: What's Wrong with Humanitarian Aid*. New York: Picador, 2010.

Prince, R., and H. Brown. *Volunteer Economies: The Politics and Ethics of Voluntary Labour in Africa*. Melton: James Currey, 2016.

Rozakou, K. "Solidarity Humanitarianism: The Blurred Boundaries of Humanitarianism in Greece." *Etnofoor* 29, no. 2 (2017): 99–104.

Sandri, E. "'Volunteer Humanitarianism' across Close(d) Borders: Volunteers and Humanitarian Aid in the 'Jungle' Refugee Camp of Calais." *Journal of Ethnic and Migration Studies* 44, no. 1 (2018): 65–80. doi:10.1080/1369183X.2017.1352467.

Scheibelhofer, Paul. "Gender and Intimate Solidarity in Refugee-Sponsorships of Unaccompanied Young Men." In *Ludger Pries Und Celine Cantat (Hg.) Refugee Protection and Civil Society in Europe*, edited by Margit Feischmidt, Ludger Pries and Celine Kantat, 193–220. Basingstoke: Palgrave Macmillan, 2019.

Schnable, A. "The Era of Do-It-Yourself Aid: Possibilities and Perils." *Bridge/Work* 2, no. 1 (2016): Article 2. http://scholar.valpo.edu/ilasbw/vol2/iss1/2

Schulpen, L., and H. Huyse. "Citizen Initiatives for Global Solidarity: The New Face of European Solidarity." *Forum for Development Studies* 44, no. 2 (2017): 163–169. doi:10.1080/08039410.2017.1306956.

Schwittay, A. "Digital Mediations of Everyday Humanitarianism: The Case of Kiva.org." *Third World Quarterly* (2019). doi:10.1080/01436597.2019.1625267.

Schwittay, A. *New Media and International Development: Representation and Affect in Microfinance*. Abingdon: Routledge, 2015.

Schwittay, A., and Paul Braund. "Participation 2.0? Crowdsourcing Participatory Development @ DFID." *Information Technologies & International Development* 15 (2018): 1–15.

Solnit, R. *A Paradise Built in Hell: The Extraordinary Communities That Arise in Disaster*. New York: Penguin, 2009.

Squire, V. "From Community Cohesion to Mobile Solidarities: The City of Sanctuary Network and the Strangers into Citizens Campaign." *Political Studies* 59, no. 2 (2011): 290–307. doi:10.1111/j.1467-9248.2010.00865.x.

Stirrat, J. "Competitive Humanitarianism: Relief and the Tsunami in Sri Lanka." *Anthropology Today* 22, no. 5 (2006): 11–16. doi:10.1111/j.1467-8322.2006.00459.x.

Taithe, B. "Demotic Humanitarians: Historical Perspectives on the Global Reach of Local Initiatives, 1940–2017." *Third World Quarterly* (2019). doi:10.1080/01436597.2019.1630815.

Ticktin, M. "Transnational Humanitarianism." *Annual Review of Anthropology* 43, no. 1 (2014): 273–289. doi:10.1146/annurev-anthro-102313-030403.

Tjensvoll Kitching, G., H. J. Haavik, B. J. Tandstad, M. Zaman, and E. Darj. "Exploring the Role of Ad Hoc Grassroots Organizations Providing Humanitarian Aid on Lesvos, Greece." *PLoS Current* 17, no. 8 (2016). doi:10.1371/currents.dis.bd282cd90ade7d4eb63b6bbdb1904d10.

Verschraegen, G., and R. Vandervoort. "The European Refugee Controversy: Civil Solidarity, Cultural Imaginaries and Political Change." *Social Inclusion* 7, no. 2 (2019): 48–52. doi:10.17645/si.v7i2.2260.

Vogt, W. *Lives in Transit: Violence and Intimacy on the Migrant Journey*. Berkeley: University of California Press, 2018.

Wilkinson-Maposa, S., A. Fowler, C. Oliver-Evans, and C. Mulenga. *The Poor Philanthropist – How and Why the Poor Help Each Other*, Cape Town: UCT, 2005.

Zaman, Tahir. *Islamic Traditions of Refuge in the Crises of Iraq and Syria. Religion and Global Migrations*. New York: Palgrave Macmillan, 2016.

Demotic humanitarians: historical perspectives on the global reach of local initiatives, 1940–2017

Bertrand Taithe

ABSTRACT
This article focuses on over 70 years of demotic humanitarianism from a grassroots perspective. Using the archives of Hudfam and Elizabeth Wilson as well as more recent oral history of local nongovernmental organisations in the West Yorkshire region of the United Kingdom, this paper seeks to cast a new light on the complex network of humanitarianism enabled by local groups. The concept of demotic humanitarians will be used here to denote the modest scale of this work, but also the humanitarians' self-perception as local agents of internationalism acting within localised networks. From the creation of Hudfam in 1942 (before Oxfam but in Huddersfield) to the birth of the Christian African Relief Trust or local partnerships with Ghana, this article shows how entangled in other social and political initiatives demotic humanitarians were.

Humanitarians today are observing a 'grassroots' renewal of humanitarian actors, the rise of 'citizen activism' or the simple renewal of humanitarian volunteerism. The camps at the border of recent migration 'crises' in Calais and Dunkirk, in Greece or along the many inroads into Western Europe have given a particular salience to the phenomenon.[1] Outside of the humanitarian system and often ignorant of its dilemmas, practical norms, and Sphere standards or the full range of professionalising drivers of the past 20 years,[2] these new humanitarians seem to many a 'new phenomenon'. Historians can of course recall the mobilisations of the 1980s and 1990s on behalf of the victims of war in the Balkans or the many organisations set up to welcome the thousands of refugees from Viet Nam, Laos and Cambodia.[3]

Yet between the long-lasting survivors of distant crises, such as Save the Children, and new organisations improvising rescue work at the borders of European Union, there are a multitude of vibrant, local, more mundane forms of humanitarianism. This paper seeks to explore this particular configuration of citizen activism and the very localised networks they involve in their own form of global activism. The scholarship of humanitarianism has tended to underplay the significance of the charity market and of its networks, for a range of reasons. Despite the emergence of notions of social entrepreneurship – more attuned with neoliberal market forces[4] – or indeed the Western conviction that a 'vibrant civil society' was the mark of a distinct and vital democratic culture,[5] the scholarship of charities has seldom been connected explicitly with that of humanitarian work.[6] Nevertheless, humanitarianism begins and sometimes ends at home. What I call 'demotic' humanitarianism is anchored in local and vernacular forms arising from charity work combined with often more political forms of solidarity. The term demotic refers specifically to the language and culture of these activities. In its common form the language these mundane actors of humanitarianism use is clearly distinct from the increasingly formal, jargon-prone and technical lingua of a highly regulated sector which defines itself as a 'system'.[7] This higher language of professionalism is not merely an apparatus of technicity; it represents a desire to anchor humanitarian practice in a specific fashion. As Mark Duffield and others have noted, this professionalising driver relies on common assumptions which are either ignored or rejected by demotic humanitarians. While many devote considerable time and energy, deploy professional skills and significantly invest in the field of humanitarian work, they speak only fragments of the professional lingo which might allow them access to state funding.[8] The term demotic thus denotes a positionality in relation to the larger operators of humanitarian aid but also a common tongue intelligible without mediation to the wider public. Importantly, demotic humanitarians barely use the term 'humanitarian' itself and often prefer more familiar cultural references such as charity, rescue or relief work.[9]

Focusing on Huddersfield, a region of middling prosperity, higher than average ethnic diversity and lower than average religious affiliation, this article seeks to set the localisation of demotic participation in humanitarian activities into a longer historical perspective in order to explain its vitality and complexity.[10] Huddersfield had no Oxfam charity shops until the 1990s. This reflected the fact that in this textile town of the West Ridings of Yorkshire, Hudfam has preceded its more famous sibling and retained anachronistic autonomy. Hudfam was created in response to the famine in Bengal. Though it remained a provincial organisation, Hudfam endured from the 1950s, when the Korean War revived its fortunes, until the demise of its leadership in 1991. Independently from this old association, from 1982, volunteers were gathering goods for Africa in schools before forming the Christian African Relief Trust (CART) in 1995. This organization, which still exists today, engaged with the same ethos of volunteering and development. Hudfam and CART stayed resolutely local and demotic throughout their history. These organisations endured thanks to the strength of their local networks, and their history reflects the vitality of their volunteering. Much as Liisa Malkki found about the volunteers of the Finnish Red Cross,[11] these organisations respond to profound desires to volunteer and serve – a 'need to help' which can be documented in the archives and through oral history. Much of the story of Hudfam relies on the archives made public and some private papers and diaries, journalism and memoir writings of a formidable organiser and humanitarian, Elizabeth Wilson. The story of CART, on the other hand, is more inchoate still – the archival sources were gathered for the purpose of this enquiry and much of the interviewing took place in response to my request over a period of three months in the summer of 2017. What both organisations and their humanitarians share is their rootedness and domestic scale. The third organisation under consideration, Ghana Outlook (GO), is more recent still and considerably less structured as a formal organisation, functioning more as a network than as a nongovernmental organization (NGO). It has very few assets and little tangible physical presence in the locality; nevertheless, it illustrates vividly how local networks feed from their exposure to international work. All three organisations are illustrative of locally rooted networks, but they also highlight how, since the 1940s, global issues were mediated and responded to in the provincial 'Global North'. The contextual specificity of this story is what makes it significant: demotic humanitarians are commonplace but they also have a history.

In Britain as in most of Western Europe and North America, most charities remain bound to domestic concerns – a trend which foundations have tended to reinforce.[12] Yet if most charitable activities are small scale and parochial – in the strictest meaning of the word – they have a considerable social and cultural weight associated with a strong sense of 'place'. Cumulatively, the sum of these networks amounts to a thick web of connections. Hudfam raised funding for international relief work in the first instance and, subsequently, for local development projects across the world, some of them directly led by family members of Hudfam leaders.[13] CART was set up to respond in kind and through 'gifts of love' to chronic needs across Africa; more recently it has attempted to engage on its own terms with emergency relief needs. Both were registered with the UK charity commission. By 2016, there were in England and Wales '165,334 charities (and 16,455 subsidiaries) on the register' while the commission claimed to have 'regulated' £70.93 billion pounds of income. To put this in perspective, this charitable market exceeded by nearly a factor of three the international NGO (INGO) humanitarian budget.[14] By 2015, 14,000 charities from England and Wales worked abroad and their share of the budget was around £16.6 billion pounds (which would compare with the 20-odd billion dollars identified by the Active Learning Network for Accountability and Performance in Humanitarian Action (ALNAP) for INGOs of the humanitarian sector in the same period).[15] This figure was for England and Wales only and does not include charities regulated by Office of the Scottish Charity Regulator (OSCR) and the Charity Commission for North Ireland. Furthermore, this only represents the compliant world of charities. Informal groups and organisations which do not claim charity status and tax relief escape any kind of close scrutiny.

The story of Hudfam develops a bridge between post-war volunteerism, links with Quaker work and major international efforts such as the United Nations Relief and Rehabilitation Agency (UNRRA) and the United Nations Relief and Work Agency for Palestine (UNWRA).[16] Through the history of Hudfam and the sociology of CART and GO, one can chart the evolution of a culture of humanitarian volunteering – rooted in sometimes complex engagement with politics, religion and faith – which connects many different groups and extends itself to the wider world. While many of the activities remain small scale or even mundane (staffing a shop smelling of old clothes) or loading a container with goods ('consignment' destined to African 'consignees'), these volunteers contribute to the substance of a largely unreported world of international solidarity. Since the Scottish enlightenment and Tocqueville, via Putnam and other social theorists, the desire to organise in social groups centred on altruistic motives has been the object of specific scrutiny.[17] 'The more the merrier' seems to have been the general understanding of how things ought to be.[18] When countries and nations previously under Soviet rule suddenly opened themselves to Western influence after 1990, Western agencies and donors promoted 'spontaneous' associations in order to revitalise society. The Polish model of social resistance to oppression made this proposition alluring for democratisation processes.[19] As Atlani-Duault showed well, these hopes and soon the ambition to create civil society often fuelled misunderstanding and misplaced efforts.[20] Sociologists of 'civil society' themselves theorised how democratic societies fostered associations and thrived on charitable organisations. They used, as Putnam did, the proliferation of charities and associations as a proxy for the vitality of 'social capital' and trust in a society.[21]

But there is a circularity to their argument which many noted, as it takes a liberal regime to enable NGOs which in turn guarantee the counter-powers necessary to a liberal regime.[22]

If the wider debates on the significance of associative life remain an object of some scholarly contention,[23] there is still much work to be done on what these charities actually represent to those who contribute to their existence.[24] One has to drill through the stories organisers have been telling to understand how their engagement might have related to wider political or ethical concerns. In particular, the debates on 'social capital' relate to broader issues on citizenship and, for organisations concerned with sufferings abroad, internationalism. Hudfam and later CART existed in the period spanning from World War II through the Cold War, and into the war on terror for CART. Throughout these events these small charities navigated constantly renewed regulatory environments and fast-moving representations of the world while remaining rooted in their locality. What made them demotic was their open access to groups of individuals who may not have embarked on any other form of internationally focused collective activism. Provincial housewives, retired and unemployed people, the disadvantaged and poor, and youths who had not yet acquired full citizenship constitute some of the sometimes-transient constituency of demotic humanitarianism. At its heart it feeds from local social opportunities and chance encounters, and from some sharing of cultural and religious values.

Hudfam

The primary sources for the history of Hudfam can be found in the two-volume autobiography of Elizabeth Wilson, which covers the period between 1942 and 1999, as well as fragmentary archives deposited in Huddersfield, folders, hundreds of photographic slides and 19 diaries kept privately.[25] Wilson's autobiography mingles the account of the organisations she supported and to a large extent ran with more complex narratives of her 'encounters on the way'. The Huddersfield and District famine relief committee was created at a meeting of peace-loving activists in the sitting room of a semi-detached house in Huddersfield. The pacifist Vera Brittain was the guest speaker at the meeting. The meeting itself had been organised by Elizabeth Wilson and her husband. Neither was local to Huddersfield; they had met in Cambridge where Elizabeth studied to become a geography teacher while Hugh completed a PhD in chemistry at the university. She came from Richmond and he from Newcastle. After their marriage they relocated to Huddersfield for his work at Imperial Chemical Industries (ICI). Prior to setting up the committee, Elizabeth and her husband had acted on their political and religious convictions and had been involved in refugee work, housing at home a couple of Jewish refugees from Nazi Germany; social work, setting up a nursery school scheme which resembled a little the efforts of Save the Children at the same period;[26] and passive resistance to mass mobilisation. Hugh registered as a conscientious objector and was kept in his role only due to the strategic importance of his research work for ICI.[27] Hugh later was elected as a councillor for Huddersfield and stood for the Labour Party. These bonds with the Labour Party entailed later in life a degree of familiarity with the leadership of the party, Harold Wilson and his wife, and continued correspondence with Barry Sherman, Member of Parliament (MP) for Huddersfield.[28]

The extreme forms of localisation were part of the origins of a large but dispersed network of famine relief funds across the United Kingdom. Hudfam was set up in 1943 to respond to the news of famine in India.[29] What the famine revealed was a crisis of leadership and government. Immediately thereafter another crisis emerged, with the blockade of Athens by the British navy. The event was largely mythologised as the foundation moment of another local organisation in Oxford, one which rested on more elite personnel with a long genealogy of philhellenic liberal sympathies and with a prestigious pedigree.[30] Both the Oxford and the Huddersfield committees existed in relation to a vast efflorescence of over 300 local committees. A Quaker clothes depot in London was taken over by the Oxford committee and clothes from all over the country were sent there, having been collected at local churches and schools. The networks organised clothing depots and pooled large quantities of valuable gifts in depots, the Huddersfield depot being one of the most significant.[31]

Like the Oxfam committee, the Huddersfield branch combined the strengths of various local organisers, labour activists, Quakers and significant figures. The largely honorific mayors of Huddersfield were presidents of the committee ex officio. In practice the fundraising activities were entirely in the hands of women of middle-class origins who used long-established methods with Victorian origins. Police-controlled 'flag day' fundraising involved the deployment of volunteers to collect cash across the city, selling small flags bearing the Hudfam logo. Entire family groups were bonding around this fundraising activity which brought considerable visibility if not large revenues.[32] Flag days were not innovative in themselves and, by the early 1950s, organisers noted the gradual decline of their income which was only revived by appeals in response to major international events.[33] The Korean War thus brought a new lease of life to the organisation and gave new purpose to its house-to-house collections, flag day appeal and Mayoral Christmas appeal. Local Quakers could call on their networks for information since their relief organisation had been particularly active in the Far East since 1944. Unlike most famine relief funds, Hudfam refused to end its activities at the end of World War II, and also refused to merge entirely with the soon much more organised and powerful Oxfam, even though it benefited from its patronage, influence and campaigns.[34]

Unlike Oxfam, Hudfam did not intend to develop projects of its own. It sent money out rather than people and it represented world crises secondhand rather than through deployment in the field. Consequently, it could choose and discriminate among many causes. As a charitable clearing house, it exercised considerable due diligence, an approach to disbursing money we will see replicated in other demotic organisations of a comparable size. Hudfam activists were particularly attuned to the great United Nations (UN) campaigns that started to punctuate the development agenda of the 1950s and thus stood clearly in responsive mode when facing a compelling top-down internationalist agenda. In 1958 it acted as the local organiser of the World Refugee Year.[35] As Peter Gatrell has shown, this global movement took stock of the long-term consequences of unresolved displaced persons stranded in Germany and of the new arrival of political refugees from the Hungarian insurrection of 1956 or the Communist takeover in China.[36] In Huddersfield the fundraisers started to sell Chinese goods crafted by refugees detained in camps in Hong Kong, heralding thus the onset of fair trade in Oxfam, an initiative attributed to Elizabeth Wilson.[37]

Huddersfield was a long way from events but its networks and religious groups could echo forcefully the causes orchestrated from New York and Geneva. In 1962–1963, Hudfam dutifully supported the UN Freedom from Hunger campaign.[38] Hudfam opened its own charity shop in 1963, considerably later than the ones set up by Cecil Jackson Cole on behalf of Oxfam, as explored by Jessica Field.[39] The charity shop was set up to retail bric-à-brac, donated objects and fair-trade goods produced by refugees, and to distribute pamphlets and information material. It also served as the headquarters and meeting room of the organisation. In this respect the charity shop complemented forms of sociability which might be served in other locales. Due to its close association with a number of religious groups, Hudfam's groups gathered around food and activities. From 1960 onwards, the charity set up its frugal Lenten lunches. In the early 1960s Hudfam split its giving into two separate funds. One was specific to causes chosen and discussed by its members; the other (about two-thirds) was sent directly to Oxfam. In return, Oxfam recognised the existence and relevance of Hudfam and Elizabeth Wilson stood on its committees.[40]

Through its fundraising and charity shop Hudfam developed the type of demotic activism described by Putnam as the cornerstone of civil society. Culturally many of these activities borrowed from the religious register established in later Victorian Britain by the Salvation Army, while fundraising also created notional membership in charity work through consumption.[41] As Matthew Hilton has shown, the age of the Welfare State, often portrayed as antagonistic to the charity culture of yesteryear, in fact nurtured an associative revival.[42] The diaries of Elizabeth Wilson reveal political connections through the Labour Party and church networks as well as a web of educational connections with schools – fostered in part by her husband's role on the local council. The politics of these networks were nevertheless often unspoken, and her arrest for pacifist activism, in the name of Quakerism rather than Campaign for Nuclear Disarmament (CND) activism, as she was keen to argue, led to a backlash within her networks.[43] Despite its success the charity ran its course as a social network; in 1991 it came to the conclusion that it had failed to renew itself and, facing increasing rents, the elders of Hudfam decided to close the shop. Oxfam, by then the largest commercial operator of charity shops in the country, moved into the town, opening its own charity shop and rebranding the depot. On the face of it, the history of Hudfam is a minor footnote to a major story, that of a large INGO which grew to become part of what Stephen Hopgood has described as a monopolistic world market.[44]

Yet there is much more to the story of Hudfam. In particular, the demotic nature of the activism enables us to explore in more depth the profound connections between humanitarian activism and other forms of activism and spirituality. The role of individuals is intrinsic to any study of grassroots activism and, though limited to her role as a 'Fartown mother' (Fartown being a district of Huddersfield which has since become heavily associated with immigrant populations),[45] a key individual like Elizabeth Wilson can inflect not only the work done by a small organisation but also the manner in which it is recalled. The archives she left behind are exceptional in terms of volume, quality and diversity. Most recently, Peter Wilson was able to source hundreds of her photographs, which will undergo digitalisation and indexing. In a sense, that made her profile original and unusual; yet by remaining focused on her domestic arrangements, provincial networks and domestic life, she also retained key features of demotic humanitarianism. Working as a bridge between Hudfam and Oxfam, she brought back from Oxford information, pamphlets and development ideas that she was keen to disseminate in slide show fundraisers and public talks. Yet these rarely took her very far from her locality. Nevertheless, she could also make first hand visits and explorations of humanitarian work abroad.[46] Elizabeth Wilson inherited money at a stage when her activism took a much more diverse and active form. When the Algerian war of independence reached its apex in 1958, Wilson could afford to visit the humanitarian aid which reached camps in

Morocco and Tunisia.[47] At that stage, the Algerian National Front (FLN) had begun a campaign of parallel diplomacy which entailed obtaining endorsement from humanitarians.[48] While major humanitarian groups uneasily engaged with the consequences of recognising the existence of an undeclared war led by one of the five permanent seat holders of the UN Security Council, free-spirited militants such as Wilson could devote their own resources to fact finding. In 1967 Wilson reiterated the role, acting as local correspondent to the local newspaper, the *Huddersfield Daily Examiner*, to report on the refugees of the Six-Day War or on development work in India.[49] As the main traveller and journalist of Hudfam, Elizabeth Wilson was vital in making the link between the mundane fundraising activities of the organisation and the delivery of concrete relief work abroad.

This multifarious activism was combined with her concern for non-Western religious philosophies, setting up what she called her 'Hindu networks' and gradually shifting from her fascination with female mystics to Zen Buddhism and Japanese flower arranging.[50] Between two journeys in support of international causes, Wilson worked with the local council and school authority to develop a more inclusive approach to compulsory religious education. Huddersfield was then a very active textile town, and much of its immigrant workforce originated from South East Asia.[51] Wilson got involved in the social dimensions of welcoming the spouses and children of textile workers and, through her links with the council, contributed to devising a comprehensive educational religious curriculum which included Hinduism and Islam.[52] Her interest in India was fuelled by her own travels across the country.[53] Once again acting as a correspondent for the local newspaper, Wilson went to India in 1966 and 1971–1972.[54] Her son John set up a dispensary in the tribal region of Nilgiri Hills in India.[55]

Each trip proved a spiritual exercise in its own right.[56] Discovering meditation and practices of nonviolence in the land of Gandhi proved irresistible to Wilson, but it also conflated the developmentalist agenda which fundraising campaigns promoted, notably through the major Oxfam campaigns of the 1960s, with Indian perceptions of foreign meddling. The discrepancies between modernist goals and spiritual personal relationships gave her a specific viewpoint on humanitarian work. She corresponded with Indian activists for three decades, beginning in 1965.[57] She visited schools in India but also, and, perhaps more importantly, received visitors from India: activists, students and humanitarians who reciprocated by visiting British schools in her area.

Elizabeth Wilson's theology proved surprisingly flexible and reflected a complex quest for God.[58] Her closest religious denomination remained throughout her life the Quaker faith she had joined in adulthood. This anchorage was going through some changes of its own, and over the period 1940–1999 her Quaker faith evolved on its own path of ecumenical liberalism. Following this personal engagement with a religious group, Wilson, by then battling occasional bouts of severe depression, developed a lifelong engagement with psychoanalysis. Sociologists and anthropologists of activism have seldom scrutinised the more inner recesses of the psyche, favouring instead religious motivations[59] or desire to be useful and participative in order to overcome the solitude of modern life.[60] Wilson exhibited both traits, combining social pleasures such as her folk dancing group which ran for 44 years, her political discussion groups or silent prayer meetings with a very individualistic take on the world.[61] Throughout the 1970s and 1980s, her engagement could thus take specific psychological forms and was included among other vicarious forms of anticipation and dreaming. She encountered the work of Karl Jung in the 1940s, somewhat early for this particular strand of psychoanalysis in the UK,[62] and applied his work to the reading of her dreams not, as

Freud would have it, as the solipsistic duel of ego, id and superego, but as the expression of human universals. Even asleep, the middle-aged Huddersfield woman could be tied to universal values and internationalism.[63]

This idiosyncratic approach to internationalism is not, however, as exceptional as it may look. Just as Hudfam began its terminal decline as the project of the generation of World War II, unable to renew its core membership and refresh its leadership, new organisations emerged in the same area, reflecting new forms of activism.[64] While much of the debate on the revival of associative activism has focused on militant political forms, socialist solidarity and grassroots contestation of Thatcherite policies, the demotic forms of humanitarianism in the Huddersfield locality focused on in the remainder of this article were shy of expressing openly any clear political views, and their archives retained a restrained charitable focus on inequalities.[65]

Northern views on Africa: CART and GO

CART and GO, created in 1982 and 2000, respectively, were set up by local activists. For the current secretary of CART, her charity emerged in the aftermath of Biafra when the events she refers to more specifically referenced the 1980s response to the famine in Ethiopia.[66] For Richard,[67] the founding secretary of GO, the origin was a combination of reading a Scout magazine while resting from an outdoor injury. The origins of both organisations are not explicitly grounded in historical events but in what they described as a general sense of global inequality combined with a desire to exploit local resources and energy.[68] This particular focus on using latent forces and enthusiasm among the young and existing organised groups dominates the accounts given of both organisations. CART volunteers were recruited from a variety of backgrounds, primarily Christian in the first instance and through church groups of various Protestant denominations, but soon included a range of individuals, some without explicit faith, and one Muslim, who could gather in the charity depot and its shop in the poor neighbourhood of Lockwood. GO gradually evolved from an activity on behalf of a local Boy Scout group, the Penistone Venture Scouts,[69] to include a collaboration between fire services in the North of England and Ghana, organised by a Ghanean activist, Joseph Achana.[70] The organisation then blossomed as a network under the inspirational leadership of a Ghanean activist who 'could talk to a little boy in England and to the president in Ghana … [after his death] we hit rock bottom'.[71]

CART was set up first, and it sought to deliver concrete aid to meet neglected needs. Unlike more sophisticated organisations which concerned themselves with the development agenda, CART organisers wished to bring a pared-down response directly to beneficiaries following a trail of contacts and exchanges they could explicitly document and report back on in minute detail. Set up explicitly as a 'gift in kind' organisation, it imitated the parcel delivery services of humanitarian organisations like the Red Cross or the remittances of CARE in the 1940s. Much like the organisation studied by Farré and Wieters,[72] CART developed a specifically logistical approach to humanitarian aid. Gathering goods, loading them and sending them became central activities to the organisation's community spirit. Its communication strategy was circumscribed to the locality and to schools where it ran shoebox gift package schemes. Over its 37 years of experience, the charity developed its own professional ethos. The monthly gathering to load a container became an activity in its own right when 'everything we do makes sense'.[73] The volunteer group which gathers on a Saturday morning is not necessarily the same one that runs the administration or the inevitable charity shop. Armed with a 'shopping' list, the volunteers carefully pack the container so that all the desired objects are included in the order in which they are meant to be unloaded and prepared for distribution. The container is then shipped to an African country taken from a rota of beneficiaries. On arrival the container goes into the hands of local intermediaries chosen by the consignee who then has to deliver to a list of vetted recipients and produce detailed evidence of how the delivery has taken place. Consignees often originate from personal contacts between churches. Throughout the process, the charity documents what recipient people desire (through a wish list) and how they will obtain access.

The products themselves are the object of a specific custodianship. In a small rooftop room, computing volunteers assemble serviceable machines from salvaged parts. Most gifts to CART are sold on while specific goods are set aside in the compound of the charity set in a small industrial landscape. The giving is contingent on local circumstances, as witness the sudden flood of school furniture gathered when New Labour school reforms led to the updating of school facilities across the local authority.[74] The charity shop reflects the same engagement with material values and purpose. It serves primarily a local customer base, and bric-à-brac and old clothing are barely granted the status of vintage goods in the socially deprived neighbourhood of Lockwood. Though their status is uncertain in the shop, the goods that make it into the container have acquired a new purpose. Their destination is clearly mapped and identified. Specific individuals are named recipients and custodians. Of course, such a system relies on trust and on checks and balance. Volunteers who have made the journey to Africa have engaged with the recipients at a personal level.[75] CART visitors were often received with hospitality they thrived to reciprocate, when, less commonly, African visitors came to Northern England.[76] The contrast of facilities and wealth is a constant feature of all travel accounts and newsletters. The needs that the charity engages with are essentially material rather than spiritual or educational, and throughout the interviews my informers reminded me of the skills that their partners had demonstrated in shaping their own organisations. Several clearly engaged with a discourse of accountability and efficiency which has long run through the humanitarian sector, and reflected on the formal demands made by the Charity Commission in this respect.[77] In contrast with some of the debates key to the 'system' humanitarians, words such as 'beneficiaries' and 'accountability' were not granted any transformative qualities[78] – the logistical focus of these organisations and their absolute reliance on partnerships and leadership from Africa dominated the description of their work.[79]

Though CART manages at most one container per month, and GO's heyday of sending entire teams of volunteers to build 10 schools is over, both remain active and influential in their own webs of solidarity. CART's founders have long since retired, and the board that succeeded them has distanced itself from the overflowing generosity that denoted 'true' humanitarian solidarity, moving to something more attuned to the pitfalls of custom duties, fraudulent appropriation or indeed the likely impact of gifts on the local market. Informed by visits and dialogues with recipients, the leadership of CART takes a very careful approach which is explicitly neither naïve nor jejune. Indeed, it then acts as advisor or mentor to many smaller groups which are keen to exploit its logistical platform to dispatch goods to Africa. Though very small by international standards, with an annual turnover of no more than £165,000 in 2017 and with 120 declared volunteers, 159 supporting schools and a board of seven trustees, CART is a relatively large player in a very niche activity.[80] Smaller fundraisers and organisations thus constantly knock on its door to offer goods or initiatives which might chime with its mission statement. Schools and churches sometimes borrow space in the container. Beyond these happenstance networks, CART also benefits from its school networks, all of which dutifully deliver goods every year. The critique of sending gifts to Africa and their distorting effects on the local garment industry, for instance, are not lost on CART's decision makers, and they focus instead either on foodstuff in periods of genuine food scarcity or on goods which are unattainable locally.

As demotic humanitarians, most of the volunteers keep a very humble profile. Some stress that CART work did them good, following a crisis of faith or depression (eg 'it gave me a purpose'), but are keen to emphasise that their commitment remains purely professional: 'it's not social – it's just work here'.[81] What Malkki calls the need to help, or the immediate returns on activist investment, was clear in all the interviews I conducted. They reflect the sense of reward that Wilson expressed in her diaries. More fundamentally, they explicitly acknowledge the transactional nature, at a very personal level, of humanitarian work – even if it remains work. Another interviewee reflected on the humility that came from having been abroad, meeting people and marvelling at their 'resilience'.[82] It is difficult to know whether this stress on resilience reflects the current humanitarian jargon or whether, as is more likely, it echoes professional terminology common among teachers and social workers in the United Kingdom. The visit of Ugandan religious figures cemented this commitment which was originally rooted in meetings that had taken place when my informant's eldest daughter had volunteered in their country.

GO, an organisation with an income of £17,000,[83] is another prime example of a serendipitous encounter in which a generally well-meaning individual met a 'gatekeeper' – in this case a Ghanean travel agent in Barnsley. Through her, Richard met Joseph Achana in How, Ghana. The relationship between the micro-charity activists and the Ghanean 'beneficiaries' ultimately revolved by 180 degrees when the Ghanean activist became the main actor in Yorkshire fundraising. His charisma and gentle manners – 'his presence' – brought funding and support to the micro-organisation.[84] At the time of the interview it was very clear that GO founder Richard was still grieving for the loss of his friend and mentor. Nevertheless, he made it very clear throughout the interview that the debt of gratitude had to follow a reverse path from the one commonly expected for foreign aid, or what Monika Krause calls the 'commodification of beneficiaries'.[85] The beneficiaries were, clearly, the good people of Penistone near Barnsley and Huddersfield who attended a memorial service in Achana's honour in Penistone.

Joseph Achana was, by the time of his death in June 2012, the executive director of GO, but he was also a member of the Ghanean Rotary Club, a regular speaker in Rotary Club meetings in West Yorkshire, and a prize-winner of humanitarian awards.[86] A truly international figure, Achana had other partners besides his Yorkshire friends, and he notably collaborated with the Salvation Army, Rotary International, American Cultural Solutions, and GlobeMed, a medical student volunteer organisation from the USA.[87] Achana was quite literally a civic organiser and activist channelling and guiding the delivery of aid, but also shaping its strategy. Over the years Achana had become far more than the fabled 'gatekeeper' anthropologists and field operators tend to describe with some scorn; he had also profoundly transformed the organisations that dealt with him and had taken a leading role in West Yorkshire.

With small and demotic humanitarian efforts, the issue of the relationship with beneficiaries is not one of scale or logo recognition but one of trust.[88] The donor and recipients are entangled in bonds of trust and trusteeship which can break down when doubts arise: 'we had question marks ... there were discrepancies'.[89] Humanitarian aid is set in a reinvented neighbourliness. This is borne out by the narrowing of income disparity between donors and recipients. There is still a marked difference but not an incommensurable one, and though the travels highlight difference they also establish proximity.

The travels that occupied much of the latter period of Elizabeth Wilson's life were still not entirely routine, but all the volunteers I met had made one or several journeys to the lands targeted by their relief work. These travels became the object of personal photographic albums but also fed newsletters and webpages or women's institute lectures.[90] In all circumstances the travels are portrayed as enriching ventures. My informers were aware that their travels located them on the margins of the world they observed. They noted that sacrifices had been made to accommodate them in austere circumstances. Though they all noted the difficulties of travelling, the routine tediousness of the fufu diet or the poverty of their surroundings, they used this form of tourism to explore the full extent of their own inadequacies.[91] Much like how Elizabeth Wilson used her journeys as a more general metaphor for the run of her lifework, 'the way' being if not quite the 'Dao' at least an exploration of her deep self, more contemporary demotic humanitarians undertake their travels with a view to transforming themselves and their families.[92] This motivation is probably one of the most widely shared traits among volunteers and key actors, but it is also a form of mediation for those whose involvement remains more marginal. Much as Wilson travelled the world on behalf of her donors and peers in Hudfam, the CART leadership reports back on and vouches for the meaningfulness of more menial tasks in loading the container.

In all these cases the issue of secularisation fails to loom large. The spiritual quality of charity work is defined in marginal ways, as well as the core belief. Some of the members of CART do not imagine themselves Christians at all, others only loosely; some firmly ground their charity work in faith.[93] Elizabeth Wilson's musings along the way are thus not an eccentric trajectory but perhaps more of a common path. Something she would have figured as a Jungian universal, perhaps. As Annie Collovald has shown, the management of volunteerism takes many secular, spiritual and religious forms.[94]

Though the evidence would seem at first glance steeped in very small-scale narratives, I contend that the macro-economic figures this article begun with set the scene for a considerable yet under-studied engagement with the wider world. My local evidence does not support the Putnam claims of a sudden collapse of civil society in the face of growing consumerism and secularism in the 1980s and 1990s when many of these new micro international organisations emerged. Yet there is undoubtedly something modest and self-limiting in the work of demotic humanitarians since the 1990s, in contrast to the broader aspirations of pacifist and developmentalist activists like Elizabeth Wilson. Rather than tackling great political themes of the age – world poverty, refugees and nuclear disarmament they have engaged with setting up basic maternity ward facilities, schools, a chicken hatchery,[95] access to water or firemen's training in car accident rescue work. The issues they contend with are those of marginal gains in the broader picture of development and humanitarianism. Though the people of CART and GO reflect the realities of global exchange networks, and though they undoubtedly respond to the growing racial and social diversity around them, they also remain intrinsically bound to their provincial context. The superimposing of old and new forms of collective and individual action which remains the preserve of small groups of individuals reveals a capacity to reinvent the world – quite literally defining afresh relationships with distant sufferings and offering solutions which still capture the imagination and enable local responses and participation.[96] Yet CART and GO organisers have fewer connections with large INGOs or international humanitarianism than Hudfam had through Wilson herself. They do not interact with the shapers of international public opinion. The language of provincial humanitarians has become increasingly demotic and it is further disconnected from the more hieratic lingo of increasingly bureaucratised international actors in the humanitarian sector. As this paper has argued, this chasm opened up from both sides. The development of professional terms and notions of highly technical cultures in INGOs responded to a desire to mimic forms of government-sponsored developmentalism, while the increasingly demotic language of provincial organisations reflected their desire to occupy an increasingly depoliticised space of international collaborations rooted in human exchanges and local sociability. This disjuncture between the local and the international is something humanitarians working at the international level have themselves encountered and sometimes regret.[97]

Disclosure statement

No potential conflict of interest was reported by the author.

Acknowledgements

I am grateful to my colleagues who commented on earlier versions of this paper, and the editors of this special issue, Eleanor Davey, Peter Gatrell and Marie-Luce Desgrandchamps. I am especially grateful to Peter Wilson who has shared private archives with me, as well as the staff of CART and GO for their willingness to share so much with me. I am also grateful for the readers' extremely useful and detailed comments which showed their intimate knowledge of issues, debates and localities.

Notes

1. Sandri, "Volunteer Humanitarianism," 65–80.
2. Walker and Purdin, "Birthing Sphere," 100–11; and Walker, "What Does It Mean."

3. Taithe, "Cradle of the New Humanitarian System," 335–58.
4. Fowler, "NGDOs as a Moment in History," 637–54.
5. Wright, "Generosity vs. Altruism," 399–416.
6. Taithe, "Humanitarian History?," 90–101.
7. Davey, Borton, and Foley, *History of the Humanitarian System*.
8. See Macrae, et al., *Uncertain Power*.
9. For a broader discussion of charity boundaries see Roddy, Strange, and Taithe, "Charity-Mongers of Modern Babylon," 118–37. Also see Fiori et al., *Echo Chamber*, for a critique from within of the humanitarian system and of its management language.
10. Haigh, *Huddersfield, a Most Handsome Town*; and Scott, "West Pakistanis in Huddersfield," 38–43.
11. Malkki, *Need to Help*.
12. Jung, Harrow, and Phillips, "Developing a Better Understanding," 409–27.
13. Wilson Archive, Blue folder, in particular the work of John Wilson, "Towards Self-Sufficiency: New Project with Indian Aboriginal Tribes" (Oxfam publication, no date).
14. Charity Commission, *Annual Report and Accounts*, 4.
15. Taylor et al., *State of the Humanitarian System*.
16. Reinisch, "Internationalism in Relief," 258–89; Salvatici, "Help the People to Help Themselves," 428–51; and Rosenfeld, "From Emergency Relief Assistance to Human Development," 286–317.
17. Foley and Edwards, "Paradox of Civil Society," 38–52; and Putnam, *Bowling Alone*.
18. The main critique of this approach to NGOs has been its normative quality focusing on how NGOs ought to be a guarantor of democratic development. See Mercer, "NGOs, Civil Society and Democratization," 5–22.
19. Ekiert, and Kubik, *Rebellious Civil Society*.
20. Atlani-Duault, *Au Bonheur des Autres*.
21. Edwards and Foley, "Civil Society and Social Capital," 124–39.
22. Fukuyama, "Social Capital, Civil Society and Development," 7–20; and McLaverty, "Civil Society and Democracy," 303–18.
23. Hilton, "Politics Is Ordinary," 230–68.
24. Weinbren, "Supporting Self-Help," 75–96; and Hall, "Social Capital in Britain," 421–2.
25. E. Wilson, *Encounters on the Way*.
26. Baughan, "Every Citizen of Empire Implored," 116–37.
27. Interview with Peter Wilson, November 16, 2018.
28. Wilson Archives, Blue folder, correspondence with Barry Sheerman, August 23, 1999; May 12, 1998.
29. Brennan, "Government Famine Relief in Bengal, 1943," 541–66.
30. Gill, "Now I Have Seen Evil," 172–200; Black, *A Cause for Our Times*; and Ermisch, *Children, Youth and Humanitarian Assistance*.
31. Norris, "Trade and Transformations," 128–43.
32. Interview with Peter Wilson, November 16, 2018.
33. Kirklees Archives (KA), Hudfam papers, KC1030/1/5 1973-1990 Flag Day accounts.
34. Hudfam thus organised the annual Oxfam conference in March 1964; and Wilson Archives, Blue Folder.
35. KA, Hudfam papers, KC1030/1/1 Huddersfield Refugee week 1957; famine relief committee annual reports for 1945–1990.
36. Gatrell, *Free World*, 141–56.
37. Anderson, *The History of Fair Trade*, 25.
38. Bocking-Welch, "Imperial Legacies and Internationalist Discourses," 879–96.
39. 6 Queen Street (until 1991).
40. She took a lesser role in Hudfam from 1966 onwards but remained active in Oxfam's council of management and on the Asia grant committee of the executive committee. Bodleian Library, Oxfam PRG/1/2/1.
41. Field, "Consumption in Lieu of Membership," 979–97.
42. Hilton, "Ken Loach and the Save the Children Film," 357–94; and Jones, "British Humanitarian NGOs."

43. There was some reporting that she had been expected to be named a Judge of the Peace. See Blue folder private archives, letter from the Sheriff court in Argyll, August 18, 1962; *Huddersfield Daily Examiner,* August 29, 1962, 'Mrs Wilson was named for Bench.'
44. Hopgood, "'Saying No' to Wal-Mart?," 98–123.
45. "Fartown Mother Goes to Gaol," *Huddersfield Daily Examiner* clipping, Wilson Archives, blue folder, August 16, 1962.
46. Wilson Archives, India and Assam 1966 black notebook; India 1971 red notebook; and Red Notebook, Lebanon 1975.
47. Wilson Archives, visual material, slides, Morocco 1958.
48. Gatrell, *Free World,* 56–9; Oneydum, "Humanize the Conflict," 713–31; Connelly, *A Diplomatic Revolution.*
49. Wilson Archives, Blue folder, "Aftermath in Agadir," *Huddersfield Daily Examiner,* December 14, 1961; "Scene that Catches at Heart and Leads to World beyond," *The Huddersfield Daily Examiner,* February 15, 1965; "I Have Known Poorer People in Huddersfield," *The Huddersfield Daily Examiner,* February 26, 1965; "A Leper Colony Run by a Hard Working Idealist," *The Huddersfield Daily Examiner,* March 5, 1965; "Suddenly the Sun Caught the Peaks of Kanchenjunga," *The Huddersfield Daily Examiner,* April 8, 1965; "Lepers Afraid to Enter Hospital If They Get There," *The Huddersfield Daily Examiner,* March 26, 1965; and "Vietnam Self-Help and Rehabilitation," *The Huddersfield Daily Examiner,* 16 October 1973.
50. Wilson Archives, Blue folder, 4 Certificates in Ikebana, Sogetsu School, 1974 (February 1974; February 1974; August 1974; October 1974); Diary visit to Japan 1974; Red book, 9.5–16 cm. Women mystics. No date.
51. The work of Duncan Scott (cited above) is here essential reading to understand the make-up of this town in transition. Hopkinson, "A Sociological Tableau of Inter-Ethnic Relations in Huddersfield," 25–36.
52. KA, Hudfam papers, Elizabeth Wilson, KC1030/2/1 1960s–70s Education Including Religious Education.
53. Wilson Archives, Bordeaux notebook, 9.5–15.5, India, Bangladesh, 1971/72 Amritsar. Fully annotated; Red notebook, 9.5–16 cm, loose cover, India 1971/72, India, Bangladesh, Nepal, Jellunda, Amritsa, Bangalore, Madras.
54. E. Wilson, *Encounters on the Way,* 25–40.
55. Wilson Archives, red notebook, 10–16 cm, visit to India and her son John, January 1978.
56. E. Wilson, *Encounters on the Way,* 39–42.
57. Ibid., 37.
58. Her theological readings were considerable and showed a strong interest in contemporary theologians as well as the lives of seventeenth-century divines. Red book, 9.5–16 cm. Women mystics. No date, 1960s?
59. Siméant, 'Entrer, Rester en Humanitaire," 47–72.
60. Malkki, *Need to Help,* 138–43.
61. E. Wilson, *Encounters on the Way,* 9–10.
62. Casement, "A Brief History of Jungian Splits," 327–9.
63. KA, KC1030/3/2 further encounters 1999, unpublished manuscript.
64. Much 1980s activism took a more openly political form, as shown in Payling, "Socialist Republic of South Yorkshire," 602–27.
65. Crowson, "Introduction: The Voluntary Sector in 1980s Britain," 491–8.
66. Interview with Vanessa, June 19, 2017.
67. All informants of this study will be referred to by the first name only or by a pseudonym depending on our agreement at the time of interview.
68. R. A. Wilson and Brown, *Humanitarianism and Suffering*; and Ambroise-Rendu and Delporte, *L'Indignation: Histoire d'une Émotion.*
69. "Good News from CART," 3.
70. Interview with Richard, July 5, 2017. The British fire service sent five engines and equipment for rescue work.
71. Ibid.
72. Farré, *Colis de Guerre*; and Wieters, *NGO Care and Food Aid.*

73. Interview with Liz, July 1, 2017.
74. Hill, "New Labour's Education Policy," 73–86.
75. For some the travelling to Africa predated and qualified volunteers for management roles in CART. Interview with Brigitte, June 26, 2017.
76. Father Heston and his wife Joyce thus spent two weeks visiting West Yorkshire and local schools.
77. Retzl, "Audits and Accountability," 39–48.
78. On this see: Hilhorst, "Being Good at Doing Good?," 193–212.
79. In this respect they reflected the depoliticisation that has been noted in relation to humanitarian logistics more broadly: Tomasini and Van Wassenhove, 'Pan-American Health Organization's," 437–49.
80. Charity commission Return; Founding groups list provided by CART, June 2017.
81. Interview with Brigitte, July 1, 2017.
82. Interview with Liz, July 1, 2017.
83. Charity Commission. GO has four trustees and no declared volunteers.
84. Interview with Richard.
85. Krause, *The Good Project*, 49–53.
86. Kristiansen, "Social Networks and Business Success," 1149–71.
87. http://globemed.org/2012/07/25/remembering-joseph-achana/, accessed November 24, 2017.
88. Abu Sa'da, *In the Eyes of Others*.
89. Interview with Brigitte, June 23, 2017. The breakdown applied to a consignee in Liberia.
90. Interview with Liz, July 1, 2017.
91. Interview with Brigitte; interview with Liz, July 1, 2017.
92. Liz, for instance, went to Malawi after her daughter; interview with Liz, July 1, 2017.
93. Interview with Brigitte, June 23, 2017.
94. Collovald, *L'humanitaire ou le Management des Dévouements*.
95. See for instance the Winter 2013 CART Newsletter.
96. Arrowsmith, *To Asia in Peace*.
97. Borton, "The Humanitarian Impulse."

Archival sources

Bodleian Library, Oxfam PRG/1/2/1.
CART papers list. "Good News from CART." CART photocopied newsletter. 1(1), 2000.
Charity Commission. Data for Financial Year Ending 31 March 2019, Ghana Outlook. Accessed June 11, 2018. http://beta.charitycommission.gov.uk/charity-details/?regid=1091636&subid=0
Charity Commission Return. Data for Financial Year Ending 31 March 2018, Christian African Relief Trust. Accessed October 11, 2018. http://beta.charitycommission.gov.uk/charity-details/?regid=803686&subid=0.
Oral history conducted in June 2017 among CART staff.
Oral history conducted in July 2018 among GO staff.
Oral history conducted with Peter Wilson, October 2018–March 2019.
Private Elizabeth Wilson papers and diaries, accessed November 24, 2017, accessed and digitized in December 2018. http://globemed.org/2012/07/25/remembering-joseph-achana/
West Yorkshire Archives, Kirklees Archives, KC1030, Hudfam Papers, Elizabeth Wilson, KC1030.

Bibliography

Abu Sa'da, Caroline. *In the Eyes of Others: How People Perceive Humanitarian Aid*. New York: Humanitarian Outcomes – NYU Centre for international Cooperation MSF, 2012.
Ambroise-Rendu, Anne-Claude and Christian Delporte, eds. *L'Indignation: Histoire d'une Émotion, XIXe–XXe Siècle [Indignation: The History of an Emotion, 19th–20th Century]*. Paris: Nouveau Monde Editions, 2008.

Anderson, Matthew. *The History of Fair Trade in Contemporary Britain*. Basingstoke: Palgrave, 2015.

Arrowsmith, Pat. *To Asia in Peace: Story of a Non-Violent Action Mission to Indo-China*. London: Sidgwick & Jackson, 1972.

Atlani-Duault, Laëtitia. *Au Bonheur des Autres [In the Name of Others]*. Paris: Armand Colin, 2009.

Baughan, Emily. "'Every Citizen of Empire Implored to Save the Children!' Empire, Internationalism and the Save the Children Fund in Inter-War Britain." *Historical Research* 86, no. 231 (2013): 116–137. doi:10.1111/j.1468-2281.2012.00608.x.

Black, Mary. *A Cause for Our Times: Oxfam, the First Fifty Years*. Oxford: Oxfam, 1992.

Bocking-Welch, Anna. "Imperial Legacies and Internationalist Discourses: British Involvement in the United Nations Freedom from Hunger Campaign, 1960–70." *The Journal of Imperial and Commonwealth History* 40, no. 5 (2012): 879–896. doi:10.1080/03086534.2012.730840.

Borton, John. "The Humanitarian Impulse: Alive and Well among the Citizens of Europe." September 2016. https://odihpn.org/magazine/humanitarian-impulse-alive-well-among-citizens-europe/

Brennan, Lance. "Government Famine Relief in Bengal, 1943." *The Journal of Asian Studies* 47, no. 3 (1988): 541–566. doi:10.2307/2056974.

Casement, Ann. "A Brief History of Jungian Splits in the United Kingdom." *Journal of Analytical Psychology* 40, no. 3 (1995): 327–342. doi:10.1111/j.1465-5922.1995.00327.x.

Collovald, Annie. *L'humanitaire ou le Management des Dévouements: Enquête sur un Militantisme de 'Solidarité Internationale' en Faveur du Tiers-Monde. [Humanitarianism or the Management of Volunteerism, Enquiries among Militants in Favour of the Third World]*. Rennes, France: Presses Universitaires de Rennes, 2002.

Connelly, Matthew A. *A Diplomatic Revolution: Algeria's Fight for Independence and the Origins of the Post-Cold War Era*. Oxford: Oxford University Press, 2002. doi:10.1086/ahr/108.5.1566.

Crowson, N. J. "Introduction: The Voluntary Sector in 1980s Britain." *Contemporary British History* 25, no. 4 (2011): 491–498. doi:10.1080/13619462.2011.623861.

Davey, Eleanor, John Borton, and Matthew Foley. *A History of the Humanitarian System: Western Origins and Foundations*. HPG Working Paper. London: Overseas Development Institute, 2013.

Edwards, Bob, and Michael W. Foley. "Civil Society and Social Capital beyond Putnam." *American Behavioral Scientist* 42, no. 1 (1998): 124–139. doi:10.1177/0002764298042001010.

Ekiert, Grzegorz, and Jan Kubik. *Rebellious Civil Society: Popular Protest and Democratic Consolidation in Poland, 1989-1993*. Ann Arbor, MI: University of Michigan Press, 2001.

Ermisch, Marie-Luise. "Children, Youth and Humanitarian Assistance: How the British Red Cross Society and Oxfam Engaged Young People in Britain and Its Empire with International Development Projects in the 1950s and 1960s." PhD diss., McGill University, Montreal, 2014.

Farré, Sébastien. *Colis de Guerre: Secours Alimentaire et Organisations Humanitaires (1914–1947) [War Food Parcels and Humanitarian Organisations (1914–1947)]*. Rennes, France: Presses Universitaires de Rennes, 2014.

Field, Jessica A. "Consumption in Lieu of Membership: Reconfiguring Popular Charitable Action in Post-World War II Britain." *VOLUNTAS: International Journal of Voluntary and Nonprofit Organizations* 27, no. 2 (2016): 979–997. doi:10.1007/s11266-014-9460-3.

Fiori, Juliano, Fernando Espada, Jessica Field, and Sophie Dicker. *The Echo Chamber: Results, Management and the Humanitarian Affairs Agenda*. London: Humanitarian Affairs Team & Humanitarian and Conflict Response Institute. 2016. https://gsdrc.org/document-library/the-echo-chamber/

Foley, Michael W., and Bob Edwards. "The Paradox of Civil Society." *Journal of Democracy* 7, no. 3 (1996): 38–52. doi:10.1353/jod.1996.0048.

Fowler, Alan. "NGDOs as a Moment in History: Beyond Aid to Social Entrepreneurship or Civic Innovation?" *Third World Quarterly* 21, no. 4 (2000): 637–654. doi:10.1080/713701063.

Fukuyama, Francis. "Social Capital, Civil Society and Development." *Third World Quarterly* 22, no. 1 (2001): 7–20. doi:10.1080/713701144.

Gatrell, Peter. *Free World: The Campaign to Save the World's Refugees, 1956–1963*. Cambridge, Cambridge University Press, 2011.

Gill, Rebecca. "'Now I Have Seen Evil, and I Cannot Be Silent about It': Arnold J. Toynbee and His Encounters with Atrocity, 1915–1923." In *Evil, Barbarism and Empire*, edited by Tom Crook, Rebecca Gill, and Bertrand Taithe, 172–200. London: Palgrave Macmillan, 2011.

Haigh, Hilary, ed. *Huddersfield, a Most Handsome Town: Aspects of the History and Culture of a West Yorkshire Town*. Huddersfield, UK: Kirklees Cultural Services, 1992.

Hall, Peter A. "Social Capital in Britain." *British Journal of Political Science* 29, no. 3 (1999): 417–461. doi:10.1017/S0007123499000204.

Hilhorst, Dorothea. "Being Good at Doing Good? Quality and Accountability of Humanitarian NGOs." *Disasters* 26, no. 3 (2002): 193–212.

Hill, Dave. "New Labour's Education Policy." In *Education Studies: Issues and Critical Perspectives*, edited by Derek Kassem, Emmanuel Mufti and John Robinson, 73–86. Maidenhead: Open University Press, 2006.

Hilton, Matthew. "Ken Loach and the Save the Children Film: Humanitarianism, Imperialism, and the Changing Role of Charity in Postwar Britain." *The Journal of Modern History* 87, no. 2 (2015): 357–394. doi:10.1086/681133.

Hilton, Matthew. "Politics Is Ordinary: Non-Governmental Organizations and Political Participation in Contemporary Britain." *Twentieth Century British History* 22, no. 2 (2011): 230–268. doi:10.1093/tcbh/hwr002.

Hopgood, Stephen. "'Saying No' to Wal-Mart? Money and Morality in Professional Humanitarianism." In *Humanitarianism in Question: Politics, Power, Ethics*, edited by Michael Barnett and Tom G. Weiss, 98–123, Ithaca, NJ: Cornell University Press, 2008.

Hopkinson, Joe, "A Sociological Tableau of Inter-Ethnic Relations In Huddersfield: The Duncan Scott Archive At Heritage Quay." *Postgraduate Perspectives on the Past* 2, no. 1 (2016): 25–36. doi:10.5920/ppp.2016.213.

Jones, Andrew, "British Humanitarian NGOs and the Disaster Relief Industry, 1942–1985." PhD diss., University of Birmingham, 2014.

Jung, Tobias, Jenny Harrow, and Susan D. Phillips. "Developing a Better Understanding of Community Foundations in the UK's Localisms." *Policy & Politics* 41, no. 3 (2013): 409–427. doi:10.1332/030557312X655594.

Krause, Monica. *The Good Project*. Chicago: The University of Chicago Press, 2014.

Kristiansen, Stein. "Social Networks and Business Success: The Role of Subcultures in an African Context." *American Journal of Economics and Sociology* 63, no. 5 (2004): 1149–1171. doi:10.1111/j.1536-7150.2004.00339.x.

Macrae, Joanna, Sarah Collinson, Margie Buchanan-Smith, Nicola Reindorp, Anna Schmidt, Tasneem Mowjee, and Adele Harmer. *Uncertain Power: The Changing Role of Official Donors in Humanitarian Action*. London: Overseas Development Institute, 2002.

Malkki, Liisa. *The Need to Help: The Domestic Arts of International Humanitarianism*. Durham, NC: Duke University Press, 2015.

McLaverty, Peter. "Civil Society and Democracy." *Contemporary Politics* 8, no. 4 (2002): 303–318. doi:10.1080/1356977022000038908.

Mercer, Claire. "NGOs, Civil Society and Democratization: A Critical Review of the Literature." *Progress in Development Studies* 2, no. 1 (2002): 5–22. doi:10.1191/1464993402ps027ra.

Norris, Lucy. "Trade and Transformations of Secondhand Clothing: Introduction." *Textile* 10, no. 2 (2012): 128–143. doi:10.2752/175183512X13315695424473.

Oneydum, Jennifer Johnson. "'Humanize the Conflict': Algerian Health Care Organizations and Propaganda Campaigns, 1954–62." *International Journal of Middle East Studies* 44 (2012): 713–731.

Payling, Daisy. "'Socialist Republic of South Yorkshire': Grassroots Activism and Left-Wing Solidarity in 1980s Sheffield." *Twentieth Century British History* 25, no. 4 (2014): 602–627. doi:10.1093/tcbh/hwu001.

Putnam, Robert. *Bowling Alone: The Collapse and Revival of American Community*. New York: Simon & Schuster, 2000.

Reinisch, Jessica. "Internationalism in Relief: The Birth (and Death) of UNRRA." *Past & Present* 210, no. Suppl 6 (2011): 258–289.

Retzl, Kenneth J. "Audits and Accountability in Non-Governmental Organizations." PhD diss., University of Nevada, 2012.

Roddy, Sarah, Julie-Marie Strange, and Bertrand Taithe. "The Charity-Mongers of Modern Babylon: Bureaucracy, Scandal, and the Transformation of the Philanthropic Marketplace, c. 1870–1912." *Journal of British Studies* 54, no. 1 (2015): 118–137. doi:10.1017/jbr.2014.163.

Rosenfeld, Maya. "From Emergency Relief Assistance to Human Development and Back: UNRWA and the Palestinian Refugees, 1950–2009." *Refugee Survey Quarterly* 28, no. 2–3 (2009): 286–317. doi:10.1093/rsq/hdp038.

Salvatici, Silvia. "'Help the People to Help Themselves': UNRRA Relief Workers and European Displaced Persons." *Journal of Refugee Studies* 25, no. 3 (2012): 428–451. doi:10.1093/jrs/fes019.

Sandri, Elisa. "'Volunteer Humanitarianism': Volunteers and Humanitarian Aid in the Jungle Refugee Camp of Calais." *Journal of Ethnic and Migration Studies* 44, no. 1 (2018): 65–80. doi:10.1080/1369183X.2017.1352467.

Scott, Duncan. "West Pakistanis in Huddersfield: Aspects of Race Relations in Local Politics." *Journal of Ethnic and Migration Studies* 2, no. 1 (1972): 38–43. doi:10.1080/1369183X.1972.9975171.

Siméant, Johanna. "Entrer, Rester en Humanitaire: des Fondateurs de MSF aux Membres Actuels des ONG Médicales Françaises [Becoming and Remaining a Humanitarian: From MSF Founders to Current Members of French Medical NGOs]." *Revue Française de Science Politique* 51, no. 1 (2001): 47–72. doi:10.3917/rfsp.511.0047.

Taithe, Bertrand. "The Cradle of the New Humanitarian System? International Work and European Volunteers at the Cambodian Border Camps." *Contemporary European History* 25, no. 2 (2016): 335–358. doi:10.1017/S0960777316000102.

Taithe, Bertrand. "Humanitarian History?" In *The Routledge Companion to Humanitarian Action*, edited by Roger Mac Ginty and Jenny Peterson, 90–101. London: Routledge, 2015.

Taylor, Glyn, Abby Stoddard, Adele Harmer, Katherine Haver, Paul Harvey, Kathryn Barber, Lisa Schreter, and Constance Wilhelm. *The State of the Humanitarian System*. London: (ALNAP) Overseas Development Institute, 2012.

Tomasini, Rolando M., and Luk N. Van Wassenhove. "Pan-American Health Organization's Humanitarian Supply Management System: De-Politicization of the Humanitarian Supply Chain by Creating Accountability." *Journal of Public Procurement* 4, no. 3 (2004): 437–449. doi:10.1108/JOPP-04-03-2004-B005.

Walker, Peter. "What Does It Mean to Be a Professional Humanitarian?" *The Journal of Humanitarian Assistance* 14 (2004). Accessed September 12, 2018. https://sites.tufts.edu/jha/archives/73

Walker, Peter, and Susan Purdin. "Birthing Sphere." *Disasters* 28, no. 2 (2004): 100–111. doi:10.1111/j.0361-3666.2004.00246.x.

Weinbren, Daniel. "Supporting Self-Help: Charity, Mutuality, and Reciprocity in Nineteenth-Century Britain." In *Charity and Mutual Aid in Europe and North America since 1800*, edited by Bernard Harris and Paul Bridgen, 75–96, London: Routledge, 2012.

Wieters, Heike. *The NGO Care and Food Aid from America 1945–80*. Manchester: Manchester University Press, 2017.

Wilson, Elizabeth. *Encounters on the Way*. York, UK: William Session, 1998.

Wilson, Richard Asby, and Richard D. Brown. *Humanitarianism and Suffering: The Mobilization of Empathy*, Cambridge: Cambridge University Press, 2009.

Wright, Karen. "Generosity vs. Altruism: Philanthropy and Charity in the United States and United Kingdom." *Voluntas: International Journal of Voluntary and Nonprofit Organizations* 12, no. 4 (2001): 399–416. doi:10.1023/A:1013974700175.

Motivations behind citizen aid: Norwegian initiatives in The Gambia

June Fylkesnes

ABSTRACT

Little is known about citizen aid initiatives originating in Norway, and they are not recognised as part of the official Norwegian development aid. Citizen aid initiatives are personal and small, and by themselves they do not raise large sums of money, nor do they individually have a large-scale development impact. But collectively, their influence on sponsors in Norway and on aid beneficiaries in the Global South might be substantial. Through qualitative interviews, this study explores the motivations of Norwegian founders of citizen aid initiatives, who run small development projects in The Gambia. The study finds that they are motivated by the very characteristics of these citizen aid initiatives which set them apart from formal development organisations. These include the initiatives' small size, which allows for a personal closeness to and control over the projects. These features are often interconnected with motivations stemming from the founders' personal experiences. The study finds that, inasmuch as the founders see the need for beneficiaries to be supported, they also experience a need to help themselves. The founders' identities, as helpers and givers, are both formed and continually reinforced by their personal involvement in this specific type of aid work.

Not much is known about citizen aid initiatives and there is still no consensus on how to define them,[1] or on what to call the phenomenon,[2] which makes research into this type of aid initiatives challenging. This part of the aid landscape is generally not on the radar of development studies, and is rarely on the agenda of policymakers, mainly due to an overriding focus on larger, more established development organisations and channels of development aid.[3] Official aid is generally provided through three channels: bilateral, multilateral and 'civilateral' aid (traditional, established non-governmental organisations – NGOs),[4] but the world of development aid is larger and more complex than these three channels.[5] Develtere and De Bruyn[6] point to 'the fourth pillar', which Kinsbergen and Schulpen[7] call 'the philanteral aid channel', and it is under this fourth category that citizen aid initiatives fall. Traditionally, citizens have not been seen as proactive when it comes to development aid, but rather as recipients, supporters or donors,[8] whilst the more prominent actors have been located in aid agencies and NGOs. However, this view is called into question by the important and active roles that citizens can and do have in development.[9] More research on citizen aid initiatives is important and necessary, as by overlooking this area of development aid one is not seeing the full picture and, indeed, exactly what is missing is not even known.[10]

Citizen aid initiatives form a heterogeneous group in terms of what they do, how they organise their work and where they work, and they can be loosely organised and run on an ad-hoc basis or be more structured with a permanent set-up. However, citizen aid initiatives also share many traits which allow them to be categorised as part of the same phenomenon. Kinsbergen[11] states that citizen aid initiatives are, *inter alia*, distinguished from more established NGOs by their small scale, by their focus on direct support and direct giving, by being based on volunteering work, and by not receiving funds from the government aid budget. In Norway, larger, more established NGOs often receive substantial sums from the Norwegian state towards their development work, whilst citizen aid initiatives do not, as they most often do not meet the criteria for such disbursements. Kinsbergen[12] acknowledges that it is difficult to define 'small scale' in regard to citizen aid initiatives,[13] and this is also true in the Norwegian context. Citizen aid initiatives are not regulated by laws in Norway, so just how many citizen aid initiatives exist is unknown. It is not mandatory for the initiatives to register their activities anywhere, and they are not required to produce annual reports with budgets and accounts. However, for the six citizen aid initiatives described in this article, 'small scale' means that none of the initiatives had any paid employees in Norway, and the initiatives' incomes were mainly based on regular donations from between 20 and 700 sponsors, as well as from various *ad hoc* fundraising activities, such as flea markets and waffle sales and by selling Gambian artefacts in Norway. Some initiatives also received *ad hoc* funds and *pro bono* services from companies, and some had involved local schools to raise funds through various education-related activities.

This paper aims to understand the motivations of the people behind six Norwegian citizen aid initiatives operating in The Gambia. Why did they start their initiatives and what makes them continue their work? This article argues that the very organisational characteristics of citizen aid initiatives are motivational to the founders. It further argues that these features are inseparably intertwined with the founders' personal, internal drivers of motivations, such as their beliefs, feelings and emotions, and their identities.

The paper starts by briefly situating citizen aid initiatives in the Norwegian development aid context. Structural characteristics of citizen aid initiatives is then described; a short discussion on altruism, the 'warm glow' effect and identity follows. The six Norwegian initiatives are then introduced, and examples are used to illustrate the interconnection between the very structures of the initiatives and the internal, personal drivers of motivation of the founders.

Citizen aid initiatives as continuity and change in Norwegian development aid

An individual interest in development aid is not new in Norway but has roots in missions and faith-based organisations.[14] In the nineteenth century, Norway had the world's highest proportion of missionaries abroad compared to its own population, and this missionary work can be viewed as the forerunner to modern development aid in Norway,[15] which also includes citizen aid initiatives. Several missionary societies were established in Norway in the mid-nineteenth century, based on local associations operating throughout the country.[16] These associations indirectly linked ordinary Norwegian citizens to people overseas through religious-based development work. Today, Norway is much more secular and local missionary associations are only marginally important in linking Norwegian citizens to the outside world.

In an increasingly globalised world, Norwegians now make direct contact with people in the South through their own travels. Indeed, many features of globalisation are changing Norwegian civil society and possibly contributing to an increase in the citizen aid phenomenon, which seems to have grown with more North–South tourism, overseas volunteering, philanthropy and individualism.[17]

Through globalisation, specific governance structures have been introduced into organisational work[18] and have contributed to the NGO sector becoming more bureaucratic and expert driven.[19] The bureaucratisation and professionalisation of the NGO sector have closed doors for ordinary citizens who wish to actively engage in development processes, whilst citizen aid initiatives offer an opportunity to be hands-on, active aid agents without having to worry about aid impact, outcome analysis and power relations, and without having the expertise required by most of the established development organisations.[20]

Structural characteristics and motivation

Travelling and social media

Many citizen aid initiatives are the results of seemingly coincidental encounters, often during a holiday, between a would-be initiator and a person or a situation in a country in the South.[21] In some cases, when the tourist returns home, s/he has developed a desire to help – a need to 'do something'.[22] Many tourists, of course, do not develop this urge or do not act on the feeling that 'I should do something', but this article exemplifies why some decide to take matters into their own hands and start a citizen aid initiative. During their travels, many tourists who later start their own aid initiative will have made contact with a local individual who later might manage and coordinate the aid project at the beneficiary end, often in the absence of the founders.[23] Haaland and Wallevik[24] question how random some of these encounters really are and draw attention to 'recipient entrepreneurs'.[25]

The founder is likely to regularly travel to the country where the initiative is running a project, and close contacts can be further developed and maintained across continents via the internet and social media, which allow for easily available updates about the project developments. Travels and online technologies can thus bridge the psychological and geographical gap between founders and supporters in the North and coordinators and beneficiaries in the South.[26]

Concrete projects and folk-to-folk aid

Social media is used by citizen aid initiatives to raise funds through individual donations from friends, relatives and extended social networks, and to some extent from corporate sponsors.[27] People are attracted to support citizen aid initiatives as their projects often are concrete, direct and tangible,[28] such as building schools, wells, lavatories or health clinics. Many citizen aid initiatives also offer one-to-one child sponsorships, which brings the beneficiary closer[29] to the donor. The imagined connectedness to a 'world out there'[30] can become less abstract by applying the 'logic of the one'[31]: focus on *one* child, or on *one* smaller, concrete project. Whereas larger NGOs in Norway are becoming further removed from ordinary citizens through bureaucratisation and professionalisation, citizen aid initiatives can offer direct folk-to-folk aid as an alternative.

The supporters are often impressed by the visible results and the speed with which citizen aid initiatives realise their projects.[32] The concrete, direct and tangible projects and the child sponsorships are attractive to sponsors, but they might also serve a purpose for the founders. These types of development projects might allow for oversight and control to be exercised by the founder in the North, though managed by a coordinator in the South.

Low or no administration cost

As most citizen aid initiatives are not run by trained development professionals, they may lack the knowledge and experience of what works and what does not work in development cooperation and thus may end up repeating NGOs' earlier mistakes.[33] However, it is possibly the very 'de-professionalisation' and 'de-bureaucratisation' in citizen aid initiatives that make the initiatives attractive, to both founders and funders. Citizen aid initiatives often boast of their low or non-existent administration costs,[34] an organisational feature which might be particularly prominent in, though not unique to, such initiatives in Norway.[35] This does not mean that citizen aid initiatives operate without any form of organisation or administration, but rather that this is not accounted for in monetary terms. However, exactly what the initiatives mean by 'administration' is not clear. There seems to be an accepted assumption in the Norwegian public that the lower the administration cost, the more efficient and effective the aid project,[36] although there is no consensus on what 'efficient and effective aid' is.[37] It could be that citizen aid initiatives use the 'no or low administration cost' to distinguish themselves from larger NGOs, as a reaction or protest to the increasing bureaucratisation and professionalisation that is occurring in the NGO sector[38] and to which citizen aid initiatives might offer an alternative.

Good Samaritans, identity and motivation

One important question concerning citizen aid initiatives is also an open-ended critique: Are good intentions enough? Tvedt calls Norwegian development assistance 'a regime of goodness',[39] in which citizens have been conditioned to see themselves as 'Norwegian Samaritans'.[40] He claims that national efforts, such as telethons, have formed the Norwegian collective psyche and identity, and that Norwegians accept as a fact that 'we are world champions of goodness'.[41] In this 'regime of goodness', Tvedt argues, legitimacy, distribution of resources and the interpretation of the world are based on self-defined, but not qualified, premises of 'being good', not on balanced, facts-based debates and analyses of what aid can and has achieved.[42] The 'regime of goodness' analysis is evidenced in citizen aid initiatives, where development interventions often are built on emotional, personal encounters with poverty[43] and not, for example, on formal needs assessments and evaluations.

Some good acts are carried out with a disregard for oneself, whilst others can be done with self-interest in mind. Altruism can be defined as an unselfish regard for the welfare of others and as a sacrifice for others without consideration of personal gains.[44] Doing good for another person with an ulterior motive has traditionally been viewed as the opposite of altruism.[45] de Jong[46] argues that altruism and self-interest are not necessarily binary opposites, but that they sometimes overlap and exist simultaneously. Some good acts are performed with a conscious acknowledgement that altruism is not the sole reason for the behaviour and that people feel good when they help and give,[47] and feel their contribution makes a difference in other people's lives.[48] This psychological reward has been labelled the 'warm glow':[49] the gratitude and recognition that people receive when doing good, the enjoyment of making someone happy, and the feeling of being relieved of guilt by being a giver. de Jong argues further that it is not productive to distinguish between motivation and outcome in development, as one can perhaps be considered selfish and the other altruistic, and yet they exist at the same time.[50]

Lichtenberg[51] claims that people do what they think is good because it is part of who they are – part of their identity – and because it is the right thing to do. Lichtenberg[52] argues further that identity is closely connected to people's values and beliefs, their norms and morals, and their understanding that doing good is the right thing to do. And Malkki asserts that beyond altruistic motives, 'the gift *of* the self to an imagined other, [is] also a gift *to* the self'.[53] Giving and helping can be viewed as being both selfless and self-interested, and giving and helping can be part of identity formation and consolidation, and self-transformation.[54] Malkki,[55] in her book *The Need to Help*, questions who 'the needy' really is. Her conclusion is that *both* the giver/helper and the recipient/beneficiary of aid are the needy. The need to help, Malkki states, often reflects the needs of the benefactor as much as it does the needs of the recipient. However, one need does not necessarily diminish the other, and the different needs are not necessarily contradictory, but rather complementary. By alleviating one's own neediness, an aid worker or a donor becomes part of something that is greater than him/herself.[56] Haaland and Wallevik[57] point to the seeming paradox that in an increasingly individualised world, there is a need to work towards something that is larger than oneself. Starting and running a citizen aid initiative might be enabled by increased individualism, as well as providing the means for engagement beyond the individual – in a collective world outside oneself.

Research methods and context

This study is based on qualitative interviews undertaken in 2016 with founders of six different Norwegian citizen aid initiatives which all had aid projects in The Gambia. Five of the interviewees were women and one was a man. The aim of the study was to gain a better understanding of the founders' motivations for starting and running a citizen aid initiative. Although all of the interviewees are referred to as 'founders' in this article, one of the persons interviewed had not taken part in the start-up of the relevant aid initiative but had been an active volunteer and a member of the board for over 15 years. The interview with her thus did not cover the motivation for *starting* a citizen aid initiative but focused on her reasons for *joining and staying involved* in the work.

The Gambia is one of the smallest but also one of the most densely populated nations in Africa, with just over 2 million citizens.[58] The Gambia is ranked in the 174th place out of a total of 189 countries on the 2018 Human Development Index,[59] which the United Nations

Development Programme (UNDP) produces every year. UNDP has also estimated that around 55% of the Gambian population is multidimensionally poor[60] and approximately 10% of the population lives below the poverty line.[61] The economy of the country relies mainly on tourism, agriculture and remittances.[62] For decades, The Gambia has been a favoured holiday destination for many Norwegians.[63] The flight from Europe to The Gambia takes just a few hours, the country has a well-developed tourist industry, and it offers warm winter sun and great beaches. In the Norwegian press, The Gambia has been promoted as a 'Africa for beginners',[64] despite having been governed by a dictator for 22 years until 2017.[65] As noted, many citizen aid initiatives are started after a holiday during which the would-be founder experienced an emotional, face-to-face encounter with poverty, and one could thus expect to find Norwegian citizen aid initiatives in The Gambia.

The first citizen aid initiative considered for this study was brought to my attention by a friend. The citizen aid initiative ran a school in The Gambia. An initial online search revealed several Norwegian initiatives operating in the country. The Gambia was of particular interest to me, as I have family ties to the country. A research decision was made to contact the founders of seven Norwegian citizen aid initiatives that were working in The Gambia. Six of them agreed to participate in the study. Only citizen aid initiatives located in Eastern Norway were contacted, to allow for face-to-face interviews. The initiatives were thus chosen by a purposive sampling method. The interviews with the founders were semi-structured and were conducted face-to-face in an informal setting in four towns in Eastern Norway in the first quarter of 2016, except for one interview which was conducted within the same time frame, but via email and a Skype video conversation.

The initiatives in this study

The selected initiatives shared many traits, but there were also differences, for instance in sizes and modes of intervention. All of the initiatives were the result of holiday trips to The Gambia, and they were engaged in various education projects. The modes of operation on the Norwegian side were quite similar for the six projects, but their modes of intervention in The Gambia differed.

(1) One initiative was larger than the other initiatives in the study. It had built a large school which it also managed; it sponsored around 1500 pupils, and had around 700 individual, regular sponsors in Norway. The initiative was governed by boards both in The Gambia and in Norway and was registered with the Brønnøysund Register Centre (the Norwegian government register for businesses, associations and citizens). It is not compulsory for associations, such as citizen aid initiatives, to register, but they can do so voluntarily.[66] This specific citizen aid initiative was the largest one in this study, had operated for the longest period of time, and was apparently the most structured initiative in the study's cohort. The initiative spent minor funds on administration costs, whereas the other initiatives prided themselves in not doing so at all.

(2) At the other end of the organisational spectrum was a citizen aid initiative operated by one individual alone, Alfred. He would solicit support for his development projects from his social and professional networks, and he alone would plan how best to spend the funds he raised. The initiative was not registered with the Brønnøysund Register Centre and did not have a board. The main activity for the initiative was to support a school it had built, as

well as to sponsor several pupils' tuition fees, whose sponsorships depended on their individual educational merit. The funds raised in Norway also supported the sponsored children's families, where food items and other essentials were provided to them on an *ad hoc* basis.

The four other initiatives in this study were more similar to each other. They were registered with the Brønnøysund Register Centre, had boards in Norway consisting of close family and friends and had coordinators in The Gambia. Despite having a board in Norway, the project operations and decisions were *de facto* handled by the founders alone. Funds were raised mainly from extended social networks and through other activities, such as waffle sales, flea markets, and the sale of Gambian artefacts in Norway. Nevertheless, their modes of intervention differed.

(3) One initiative had built a nursery school and managed everything regarding the school, from repairs of the building to hiring and paying the teachers, to caring for all the needs of the pupils.

(4) Another initiative had also fundraised and built a nursery school *building* but had not developed a plan for the management of the nursery school once it had been built. This resulted in conflicts between the initiative and the headmaster and teachers. For instance, the initiative wanted to be involved in managerial decision-making processes at the nursery school, although it did not have sufficient funds to support the running of the school. The management of the nursery school was eventually taken over by the Gambian government, which, according to Ingrid, the initiative's founder, is unusual in The Gambia where all nursery schools are privately owned and run without much official intervention. This incident exemplifies that development processes do not take place in a vacuum but are connected to local and national structures.[67] It also highlights that good intentions do not necessarily guarantee good outcomes. In this specific case, though, the Norwegian initiative continues to be involved in the Gambian nursery school, although not in managerial decision-making processes. The initiative sponsors some pupils' tuition fees, it raises funds for smaller building repairs and improvements, and it sponsors the school kitchen to ensure a heavily subsidised daily warm meal for the pupils.

(5) Another initiative in this study mainly functioned as a facilitator between sponsors in Norway and pupils at a few, select schools in The Gambia. On the Norwegian operational side, the fundraising activities and the structures of the initiative were comparable to those of the other initiatives in the study, but the development intervention differed.

(6) The last citizen aid initiative in the study ran a children's home, had refurbished two schools, provided fees for some pupils and had given a micro loan to a group of women who had started their own café. In 2016, the initiative had plans to build a school, and as of 2019 the work has begun.

Motivations for starting and running a citizen aid initiative

As very little is known about citizen aid initiatives in Norway, a primary purpose of this study was to start at the origins, namely with the start-up of a citizen aid initiative. By interviewing initiative founders about their aid projects and their motivations for engaging in this type of work, it transpired that both the way citizen aid initiatives are structured and the internal, personal drivers, such as the feelings, emotions and sense of identity of the founders, often overlapped as motivational for the founders.

Travelling and transformations

Some of the very characteristics and features of the citizen aid initiatives served as motivational factors for the interviewees. When asked whether they could have worked as volunteers in Norway, applying their desires and needs to be useful there rather than abroad, the interviewees stated that it was a coincidence that the projects ended up in The Gambia. Nevertheless, they also acknowledged that they were driven by the continued opportunity to travel to The Gambia which their initiative allowed them to do. They were excited about the adventure, the 'otherness' and the different culture they would encounter there. And, having spent some time in The Gambia initially, they had become attached to *that* country. Kinsbergen[68] describes a 'fun factor' as a motivational driver: the work is serious but can also be enjoyable. Synne, a woman in her 50s who had started her aid initiative a few years earlier, described how she sometimes felt pulled in different emotional directions by her work. She enjoyed the work – 'it is fun, and I have something to do' – but sometimes she would think 'this is just a nonsense project', because to have real development impact 'you should be big, right?'. She would then remind herself that without her initiative, without her efforts, 15 children would not attend school, and 'someone has a less terrible life because [I] helped them'. The fun factor, along with the seriousness of her involvement, acted as a motivation for her to do the work. Birgit, a woman in her 60s who had been involved in several citizen aid initiatives in The Gambia for more than 20 years, said she laughed and joked and had a lot more fun when she was in The Gambia compared to Norway. For her, it was motivational that the specific aid work offered her the opportunity to travel to and be happier on 'The Smiling Coast', which The Gambia sometimes is colloquially referred to. Malkki[69] states that 'travel has been sought as a chance to feel differently, to be differently embodied, differently gendered, differently classed, or just to be *otherwise*'. Travelling allowed the aid initiatives' founders to have more fun, and it allowed for self-transformation. The opportunity to leave their everyday lives behind, to go somewhere else and become someone else – a happier version of themselves – was a motivation, and it was linked to their identity formation. The travels which the citizen aid initiative structures allow for can affect the identities and personalities of the founders, and both can be motivational for the citizen aid work.

Up close and personal: ownership and control

A common feature among the initiatives was that most of their incomes were based on private Norwegian sponsors who wanted to directly support 'their own' child. Little thought seemed to have been given by the founders to the larger community impacts of personal support between one sponsor and one specific child – for example, how this might this affect a neighbour's child who is not sponsored, or how it might change community dynamics. For the child sponsors and the initiative founders alike, the 'logic of the one'[70] appeared to be of overarching concern: the sponsoring of the *one* child, or the focus on the *one* school. The 'logic of the one' fuels the sense of personal closeness to a project, and makes it easy to visualise what the aid money is spent on[71] in a manner that is not utilised or perhaps even possible in larger development NGOs. This direct, concrete, singular focus of the citizen aid projects functioned as motivation for the initiatives' founders in this study, much in the same way that sponsors are drawn to the citizen aid initiatives due to this focus.

The set-ups of the initiatives allow for a closeness to every aspect of the aid projects, which the mainstream NGOs do not offer. The personal involvement of the initiatives' founders in their projects enables them to control most aspects of their development intervention, from deciding what funds should be spent on to where, how and when. Indeed, most of the interviewees explicitly stated that they were partly motivated to do the work they do because they were in control of the projects and the funds. The interviewees also expressed a sense of ownership of the projects they were involved in. Birgit explained, when discussing the lack of interaction and cooperation between various citizen aid initiatives in The Gambia, that most founders would find it important to build their *own* schools and put their *own* logos on them. Synne stated: 'I need to have full control and do what I think needs to be done'. This statement also reflects the broader relationship the founders had with the Norwegian and international development discourses: they did not think development debates were relevant to them because their initiatives were too small for such big ideas. In addition, the founders felt that they themselves best knew how to carry out *their own* development project.

Power, control and ownership

The issues of control and ownership, however, raise questions about participation and sustainability in these aid projects. From the interviews it emerged that stakeholder participation was mostly limited to the inputs of the project coordinators in The Gambia and, for one initiative, the board in The Gambia. When Astrid, a woman in her 50s who had established her own initiative just a few years earlier, was asked about the planning process of her aid project, she stated: 'it was my clear impression that, when the coordinator found the village, there was a need for a nursery school there'. To a certain extent, the local coordinators had influential roles in the initiatives, but did they represent the community where the aid project was started? Although the coordinators themselves were not end beneficiaries of the aid, they nevertheless benefitted from being employed by the aid initiative. The influence that the coordinators had, for instance, on where a school was built, what the priority for the next investment should be and so forth, transformed the coordinators into active aid agents or 'recipient entrepreneurs',[72] or what others have called 'development brokers'.[73]

It is difficult to ascertain the balance of the power relationship between the founders and the coordinators; however, the ultimate decision-making power lies with the founder who controls the money. The lack of stakeholder participation could possibly affect the sense of project ownership among the beneficiaries, which in turn could affect project sustainability. The initiatives in this study were dependent on the efforts of the founders, without whom there would not be an aid project. The pivotal roles of the founders left the citizen aid initiatives and the projects vulnerable, should the founders no longer want or be able to continue the work. For example, since the interviews were undertaken in 2016, one founder has passed away. The initiative has been continued by his daughter, but this solution was not guaranteed. On the one hand, the very personal investments that the initiatives' structures allow the founders to make in their projects, coupled with the control and sense of ownership that these bring, motivate them both to start and to continue their aid work. On the other hand, such personalised projects are fragile, and this can also be viewed as the Achilles' heel of citizen aid initiatives.[74]

Administration costs

The founders in this study took pride in spending very little money or nothing at all on organisational administration costs in Norway. That no funds are spent on administration was highlighted on the websites and Facebook pages of all the initiatives. The focus on spending as little money as possible on administrative matters might be connected to a general sense among the Norwegian public that official development aid often ends up in the hands of corrupt state leaders, is embezzled *en route* to beneficiaries or is spent on organisational administration in Norway.[75] Most of the interviewees supported this notion, although none could think of concrete examples of aid money mismanagement. Birgit vaguely stated 'you hear about this all the time', and said that her initiative gets a lot more work done per krone[76] than does NORAD,[77] because none of the funds her initiative raises go to 'administration costs, corruption and embezzlement and such nonsense'. According to Eggen,[78] 'effective aid' in its simplest form means that for every *krone* spent, the best possible results are achieved. But what are the best possible results? As most citizen aid initiatives do not engage in discussions about what aid is or should be, and do not discuss what the best development result are, their effectiveness claim can be questioned.

Nonetheless, the initiative founders showed pride and seemed inspired and motivated by spending every *krone* on their projects abroad. By not using funds on administration in Norway, the founders voluntarily invested their own time and energy into every organisational aspect of their projects. This personal engagement ensured a tight control over the initiatives and furthered a sense of ownership. Thus, the particular organisational feature of no or low administration costs became intertwined with the founders' sense of ownership and control of the project, which was a motivation for them to start and run the initiatives.

Good Samaritans, interdependency and identity

Contrary to Tvedt's theory about the Norwegian 'regime of goodness'[79] and the 'Norwegian Samaritan',[80] and despite the positive Norwegian public attitude towards development aid,[81] this study found that interviewees did not attribute their interest in development work to a 'goodness socialisation process' through their upbringing or education. Some of interviewees explained that certain personal life experiences had been 'wake-up calls' for them, such as losing a loved one or going through illness, and that this has made them rethink the meaning of life. Some stated that as their children moved away from home, they needed something worthwhile and rewarding to do – to have someone to care for. The involvement in a citizen aid initiative connected them to something that was bigger than themselves,[82] and this might have given their lives more meaning and purpose. The interviewees reported that rather than being influenced by the media, their upbringing or their education, their desires to 'do something' stemmed from 'something' inside themselves. For most of them, the urge to 'do something' followed from the personal encounters with poverty they experienced whilst on holiday in The Gambia. Some of the founders also believed themselves to innately be the kind of person who cares for and serves others – that this was part of their identity. Others, however, were surprised that they had gotten personally involved in and stayed committed to their aid work in The Gambia. For them, their identity as a helper, as someone who does good, was developed as part of their engagement in the citizen aid initiative.

Dependency was a recurring theme during the interviews, and it was discussed in connection with control and ownership and the initiatives' sustainability and fragility. It was clear that the Gambian beneficiaries to some extent became dependent on the work and the funds from the aid projects. However, it was surprising to find that this very dependency was not viewed as something negative by the founders. Rather, they were motivated and inspired by this, and it drove them to continue the work. The interviews revealed an interdependency: the founders themselves had become almost as dependent on the citizen aid initiative work as the beneficiaries had, although for very different reasons. Margot, the woman who volunteered for, but had not started, one citizen aid initiative, said: 'once you start this type of work, you cannot just stop'. Birgit also said that even though she felt tired and overwhelmed by the amount of work running an aid initiative entailed, she could not just quit, as the work had become a part of her life and of who she was – a part of her identity. Similarly, Astrid stated that she would never stop working with the nursery school she had built, as it had become an integral part of who she was as a person. The continued engagement of the interviewees in their aid initiatives further developed and consolidated their identities as helpers and givers.

Selfless and self-interested aid

Although the initiative founders experienced an internal urge to help, the 'warm glow' effect was also an important motivational factor for them. The co-existence of altruistic and selfish motives for helping can be identified, supporting de Jong's claim that this is indeed a false binary.[83] The interviewees were asked: 'What do *you* get out of being involved in your initiative's work?'. Everyone found this direct question very difficult to answer. It is hard to ascertain why, but it could be that the founders perceived their own help as altruistic, that their assistance was purely for someone else's needs and not for their own. It could also be that they found it embarrassing to acknowledge that they personally gained something from another person's poverty. Nevertheless, the respondents stated that their aid work was 'very rewarding' but found it problematic to say in what ways this was the case. Some stated that just seeing a child smile and be happy was a reward, and others said that they were inspired by knowing that someone else's life was better because of their intervention. Astrid was very direct and said: 'it gives me a good feeling'. Altruistic intentions and selfish rewards might not diminish the outcomes of an aid intervention, which is also what de Jong argues: that it is perhaps not necessary to distinguish between altruistic and self-interested motivations and outcomes in aid interventions.[84]

The personal encounters with poverty influenced the founders' perceptions of the Gambians as those who were needy. However, they often had not conducted a thorough analysis of what the needs in The Gambia consisted of, or what the people in The Gambia themselves would say their needs were. For instance, was the need for a nursery school the greatest need in the country, or did the initiative choose start a project that was 'easy' to invest in and manage from Norway? The perceived need for help in The Gambia must be seen in relation to the needs of the founder – the inherent, possibly guilt-driven, urge to 'do something'. That this 'something' might not have been based on an assessment of the self-identified needs of the beneficiaries might suggest that for the founders the need *to* help was as important as the need *for* help at the beneficiary level.

Concluding remarks

This article has argued that the founders of citizen aid initiatives help and give partly due to internal factors: they believe it is the right thing to do and their biographies tell them so. The founders might have believed that their citizen aid work was based on altruism, but it also emerged that the 'warm-glow' effect was in play. In addition, the study found that the founders' identities were tied to being helpers and givers and that these particular identity traits were continually reinforced and consolidated by this specific aid work. This article has also argued that the specific features of citizen aid initiatives acted as motivating factors for the founders. Some of the initiative structures that were highlighted were the tangible project investments and the use of social media, which ensured a feeling of closeness to the projects. The study further showed that the allowance the initiative structures gave the founders for ownership and control of their project was an important motivational factor for engagement in this particular type of aid work. It proved difficult to draw lines between the internal motivations and those tied to the structures of the initiatives, as these were interconnected and overlapping.

A citizen aid initiative, in many cases, is permeated by and revolves around the personal involvement of the founders. This personal involvement can be seen as the strength of citizen aid initiatives, but it might also be one of their main weaknesses, as a project's sustainability may not be secured beyond that one person's involvement. Research from the Netherlands has shown that the motivation of founders and supporters greatly influences the sustainability of a project's development intervention.[85] The same study recommended that citizen aid initiatives rely less on 'internal drivers', such as personal motivation, and more on 'external drivers', such as organisational and contextual factors, for the development intervention to be sustainable.[86] More research is needed to see whether citizen aid initiatives take on this recommendation. And if they do, will they still be defined as 'citizen aid initiatives' or will they become a different aid phenomenon altogether?

Disclosure statement

No potential conflict of interest was reported by the author.

Acknowledgements

This paper was developed following the workshop on 'Citizen Aid and Everyday Humanitarianism' at the University of Sussex, in April 2018, and is based on my master's thesis submitted to the University of Agder, in June 2016. Thanks to the participants at the Sussex workshop for their comments to the draft paper. Many thanks in particular to Anne-Meike Fechter for reading and commenting on the paper several times.

Notes

1. Kinsbergen and Schulpen, "Anatomy of the Private Initiative," 6.
2. Citizen aid initiatives are, *inter alia*, also known as personalised aid (PAID) initiatives, private initiatives (PIs), private development initiatives (PDIs), private aid, my own NGO (MONGO), grassroots international non-governmental organizations (GINGOs), citizen aid, do-it-yourself (DIY) aid, home-made aid, independent development volunteers, and so on.
3. Fechter, "Do-It-Yourself-Aid."
4. Develtere and de Bruyn, "Emergence of a Fourth Pillar in Development Aid," 912–3.
5. Pollet et al., "Accidental Aid Worker," 7.
6. Develtere and de Bruyn, "Emergence of a Fourth Pillar in Development Aid," 913–4.
7. Kinsbergen and Schulpen, "From Tourist to Development," 49.
8. Schulpen and Huyse, "Citizen Initiatives for Global Solidarity," 165.
9. Ibid.
10. Fechter, "Do-It-Yourself-Aid."
11. Kinsbergen, "Behind the Pictures," 57.
12. Ibid.
13. This paper uses 'citizen aid initiatives' to describe the same phenomenon which in the Netherlands is called 'private development initiatives' (PDIs).
14. Gullestad, *Misjonsbilder: Bidrag til norsk*.
15. Engh, "Conscience of the World," 65, 67.
16. Eldstad and Rasmussen, "Kristendommens historie i Norge."
17. Haaland and Wallevik, "Citizen as Actors in the Development Field," 205.
18. Tranvik and Selle, "Rise and Fall of Popular Mass Movements."
19. Enjolras and Strømsnes, *Scandianvian Civil Society and Social Transformations*.
20. Haaland and Wallevik, "Citizens as Actors in the Development Field," 205; and Schulpen and Huyse, "Citizen Initiatives for Global Solidarity," 163.
21. Kinsbergen and Schulpen, "From Tourist to Development," 57.
22. Pollet et al., "Accidental Aid Worker," 16.
23. Kinsbergen and Schulpen, "From Tourist to Development," 58.
24. Haaland and Wallevik, "Citizens as Actors in the Development Field, 208.
25. See also Lewis and Mosse, *Development Brokers and Translators*.
26. Kinsbergen, Tolsma, and Ruiter, "Bringing the Beneficiary Closer," 63.
27. Mathers, "Mr. Kristof, I Presume"; and Pollet et al., "Accidental Aid Worker," 37.
28. Kinsbergen and Schulpen, "From Tourist to Development," 12.
29. Kinsbergen, Tolsma, and Ruiter, "Bringing the Beneficiary Closer."
30. Malkki, *Need to Help*, 130.
31. Ibid., 96–7, 102.
32. Haaland and Wallevik, "Hva er Lurt og"; and Kinsbergen and Schulpen, "From Tourist to Development," 54.
33. Develtere and De Bruyn, "Emergence of a Fourth Pillar in Development Aid," 918; Kinsbergen and Schulpen, "From Tourist to Development," 56; and Pollet et al., "Accidental Aid Worker," 37.
34. Haaland and Wallevik, "Hva er Lurt og."
35. Fylkesnes, "Small Streams Make Big Rivers," 78.
36. Eggen, "Virker Bistand? Noen Spørsmål"; and Haaland and Wallevik, "Hva er Lurt og."

37. Schulpen and Huyse, "Citizen Initiatives for Global Solidarity," 168.
38. On increasing bureaucratisation and professionalism in civil society in Norway, see for instance Tranvik and Selle, "Rise and Fall of Popular Mass Movements"; and Enjolras and Strømsnes, *Scandianvian Civil Society and Social Transformations*.
39. Tvedt, "Utviklingshjelp Og Det Nasjonale."
40. Tvedt, *Den Norske Samaritan*.
41. Ibid., 10 (my translation from Norwegian.)
42. Tvedt, "Utviklingshjelp Og Det Nasjonale," 62, 64.
43. Haaland and Wallevik, "Bistanden Ingen har Oversikt."
44. Lichtenberg, "About Altruism"; and Lichtenberg, "Is Pure Altruism Possible?"
45. Lichtenberg, "Is Pure Altruism Possible?"; and de Jong, "False Binaries. Altruism and Selfishness," 24, 26.
46. de Jong, "False Binaries. Altruism and Selfishness," 27.
47. Lichtenberg, "Is Pure Altruism Possible?"
48. Kinsbergen, Tolsma, and Ruiter, "Bringing the Beneficiary Closer," 62.
49. Andreoni, "Philanthropy," 1220.
50. de Jong, "False Binaries. Altruism and Selfishness," 28.
51. Lichtenberg, "About Altruism"; and Lichtenberg, "Is Pure Altruism Possible?"
52. Lichtenberg, "Is Pure Altruism Possible?"
53. Malkki, *Need to Help*, 10 (emphasis in original).
54. Lichtenberg, "Is Pure Altruism Possible?"; and Malkki, *Need to Help*, 42–3.
55. Malkki, *Need to Help*, 8.
56. Ibid., 9.
57. Haaland and Wallevik, "Citizens as Actors in the Development Field"; Haaland and Wallevik, "Flyktningkrise, Global Solidaritet og."
58. World Bank, "World Bank in The Gambia."
59. UNDP Human Development Reports, "Table 1. Human Development Index."
60. Multidimensional poverty goes beyond income as a measurement for poverty and looks at three key dimensions where people are left behind: Health, Education and Standards of Living. UNDP Human Development Reports, "2018 Global Multidimensional Poverty Index."
61. Poverty line as PPP $1.90/day. UNDP Human Development Reports, "Gambia. The Human Development."
62. World Bank, "World Bank in The Gambia."
63. Reiseguiden.no.
64. See for instance Holmlund, "Paradis og Slum"; Glesnes, "Afrikansk for Nybegynnere"; and Hagen, "Turist i Gambia."
65. Daramy, "Letter from Africa: Torture Revelations."
66. Brønnøysundregistrene.
67. Haaland and Wallevik, "Citizens as Actors in the Development Field," 217.
68. Kinsbergen, "Behind the Pictures," 144.
69. Malkki, *Need to Help*, 43 (emphasis in original).
70. Ibid., 96–7, 102.
71. Kinsbergen, Tolsma, and Ruiter, "Bringing the Beneficiary Closer"; and Malkki, *Need to Help*.
72. Haaland and Wallevik, "Citizens as Actors in the Development Field," 208.
73. See for instance Lewis and Mosse, *Development Brokers and Translators*.
74. Kinsbergen and Schulpen, "From Tourist to Development," 58–9.
75. See for instance Bolle, "Norske Bistandspenger var med"; "Administrasjon sluker Innsamlede Midler"; Haugen, "Clinton Foundation Fikk 410"; Salvesen and Dahl, "Norsk Bistand til Alle"; Salvesen, "Vet ikke om 30-milliarders"; and Skevik, "Avslører Millionsvindel Med Norsk."
76. Norwegian currency.
77. NORAD is the Norwegian Agency for Development Cooperation.
78. Eggen, "Virker Bistand? Noen Spørsmål."
79. Tvedt, "Utviklingshjelp Og Det Nasjonale."
80. Tvedt, *Den Norske Samaritan*.
81. OECD-DAC, "OECD Development Co-Operation."

82. Haaland and Wallevik, "Citizens as Actors in the Development Field; and Haaland and Wallevik, "Flyktningkrise, Global Solidaritet og."
83. de Jong, "False Binaries. Altruism and Selfishness."
84. Ibid., 28.
85. Kinsbergen, Schulpen, and Ruben, "Understanding the Sustainability of Private Development Initiatives," 223.
86. Ibid, 244.

ORCID

June Fylkesnes http://orcid.org/0000-0002-5849-0052

Bibliography

"Administrasjon Sluker Innsamlede Midler i Røde Kors." *Dagens Næringliv*. January 21, 2010. https://www.dn.no/samfunn/administrasjon-sluker-innsamlede-midler-i-rode-kors/1-1-1424534

Andreoni, James. "Philanthropy." In *Handbook of the Economics of Giving, Altruism and Reciprocity*, edited by Serge-Christophe Kolm and Jean Mercier Ythier, Vol. 2, 1201–1269. Amsterdam: Elsevier, 2006.

Bolle, Tor Aksel. "Norske Bistandspenger var med på å Betale Sjefsleilighet." *Bistandaktuelt*, January 26, 2016. https://www.bistandsaktuelt.no/nyheter/2016/kjopte-leilighet-med-bistandspenger/

Brønnøysundregistrene. Accessed January 15, 2019. https://www.brreg.no/home/

Daramy, Ade. "Letter from Africa: Torture Revelations Transfix The Gambia." *The Guardian*, June 6, 2019. https://www.bbc.com/news/world-africa-48525284

de Jong, Sara. "False Binaries. Altruism and Selfishness in NGO Work." In *Inside the Everyday Life of Development Workers: The Challenges and Futures of Aidland*, edited by Anne-Meike Fechter and Heather Hindman, 21–40. Sterling, VA: Kumarian Press, 2011.

Develtere, Patrick, and Tom De Bruyn. "The Emergence of a Fourth Pillar in Development Aid." *Development in Practice* 19, no. 7 (2009): 912–922. doi:10.1080/09614520903122378.

Eggen, Øyvind. "Virker Bistand? Noen Spørsmål til Avklaring." *NORAD*, 2013. http://www.noradbloggen.no/2013/12/virker-bistand-noen-sporsmal-til-avklaring/

Eldstad, Hallgeir, and Tarald Rasmussen. "Kristendommens historie i Norge." *Store Norske Leksikon*. June 13, 2016. https://snl.no/Kristendommens_historie_i_Norge#-Pietisme,_misjon_og_religi%C3%B8s_sosialisering

Engh, Sunniva. "The Conscience of the World?: Swedish and Norwegian Provision of Development Aid." *Itinerario* 33, no. 2 (2009): 65–82. doi:10.1017/S0165115300003107.

Enjolras, Bernard and Kristin Strømsnes, eds. *Scandinavian Civil Society and Social Transformations: The Case of Norway*. Cham: Springer, 2018.

Fechter, Anne-Meike. "Do-It-Yourself-Aid: Alternative Funding for Rights Work?" *Open Democracy*, April 21, 2015. https://www.opendemocracy.net/openglobalrights/annemeike-fechter/doityourselfaid-alternative-funding-sources-for-rights-work

Fylkesnes, June. "Small Streams Make Big Rivers: Exploring Motivation and Idealism in Norwegian Personalised Aid Initiatives in The Gambia." Master's thes., Universitetet i Agder, 2016. http://hdl.handle.net/11250/2414518

Glesnes, Gjermund. "Afrikansk for Nybegynnere." *Asker og Bærum Budstikke*, March 7, 2007. https://www.budstikka.no/reise/reise/afrikansk-for-nybegynnere/s/2-2.310-1.3423806

Gullestad, Marianne. *Misjonsbilder: Bidrag til norsk selvforståelse: Om bruk av foto og film i tverrkulturell kommunikasjon*. Oslo: Universitetsforlaget, 2007.

Haaland, Hanne, and Hege Wallevik. "Bistanden Ingen har Oversikt Over." *Vårt Land*, January 28, 2013.

Haaland, Hanne, and Hege Wallevik. "Citizens as Actors in the Development Field: The Case of an Accidental Aid-Agent's Activities in Aid-Land." *Forum for Development Studies* 44, no. 2 (2017): 203–222. doi:10.1080/08039410.2017.1305444.

Haaland, Hanne, and Hege Wallevik. "Flyktningkrise, Global Solidaritet og Hjemmelaget Bistand." *Vårt Land*, September 30, 2015.
Haaland, Hanne, and Hege Wallevik. "Hva er Lurt og hva er Lureri med Bistanden?" *Fedrelandsvennen*, December 9, 2013. http://www.fvn.no/mening/synspunkt/Hva-er-lurt-og-hva-er-lureri-med-bistanden-2519658.html
Hagen, Jørgen Aune. "Turist i Gambia." *NRK*, January 7, 2005. https://www.nrk.no/kultur/turist-i-gambia-1.1428726
Haugen, SteinOve. "Clinton Foundation Fikk 410 Millioner Bistand Fra Norge." *Dagbladet*, May 6, 2015. https://www.dagbladet.no/nyheter/clinton-foundation-fikk-410-millioner-bistand-fra-norge/60667757
Holmlund, Arvid. "Paradis og Slum i Kontrastenes Rike: Tusener av Nordmenn til Gambia igjen." *VG (Verdens Gang)*, February 1, 2008. https://www.vg.no/reise/i/7l7QEB/paradis-og-slum-i-kontrastenes-rike-tusener-av-nordmenn-til-gambia-ig
Kinsbergen, Sara. "Behind the Pictures. Understanding Private Development Initiatives." PhD diss., Radboud University Nijmegen, 2014. http://www.ru.nl/cidin/general/recent_publications/@932559/sara-kinsbergen-2014/
Kinsbergen, Sara, and Lau Schulpen. "From Tourist to Development Worker. Private Development Initiatives in The Netherlands." *Mondes en Développement* 161, no. 1 (2013): 49–62. doi:10.3917/med.161.0049.
Kinsbergen, Sara, and Lau Schulpen. "The Anatomy of the Private Initiative." Radboud University Nijmegen, 2010. http://www.ncdo.nl/sites/default/files/46_The%20Anatomy%20of%20the%20Private%20Initiative%20-%20Kinsbergen%20&%20Schulpen%20-2010.pdf
Kinsbergen, Sara, Lau Schulpen, and Ruerd Ruben. "Understanding the Sustainability of Private Development Initiatives: What Kind of Difference Do They Make?" *Forum for Development Studies* 44, no. 2 (2017): 223–248. doi:10.1080/08039410.2017.1307270.
Kinsbergen, Sara, Jochem Tolsma, and Stijn Ruiter. "Bringing the Beneficiary Closer: Explanations for Volunteering Time in Dutch Private Development Initiatives." *Nonprofit and Voluntary Sector Quarterly* 42, no. 1 (2011): 59–83. doi:10.1177/0899764011431610.
Lewis, David, and David Mosse. *Development Brokers and Translators: The Ethnography of Aid and Agencies*. Bloomfield, CT: Kumarian Press, 2006.
Lichtenberg, Judith. "About Altruism." *Philosophy & Public Policy Quarterly* 28, no. 1/2 (2008): 2–6. doi:10.13021/G8PPPQ.292009.106.
Lichtenberg, Judith. "Is Pure Altruism Possible?" *The New York Times*, October 19, 2010. https://opinionator.blogs.nytimes.com/2010/10/19/is-pure-altruism-possible/
Malkki, Liisa H. *The Need to Help: The Domestic Arts of International Humanitarianism*. Durham, NC: Duke University Press, 2015.
Mathers, Kathryn. "Mr. Kristof, I Presume?: Saving Africa in the Footsteps of Nicholas Kristof." *Transition* 107, no. 1 (2012): 14–31. https://www.jstor.org/stable/10.2979/transition.107.15
OECD. OECD *Development Co-operation Peer Reviews: Norway 2013* Paris: OECD Publishing, 2014. doi:10.1787/9789264196315-en.
Pollet, Ignace, Rik Habraken, Lau Schulpen, and Huib Huyse. "The Accidental Aid Worker. A Mapping of Citizen Initiatives for Global Solidarity in Europe." Radboud University Nijmegen, 2014. https://repository.ubn.ru.nl/bitstream/handle/2066/134916/134916.pdf?sequence=1
Salvesen, Geir. "Vet ikke om 30-Milliarders Bistand Virker." *Aftenposten*, January 25, 2016. https://www.aftenposten.no/norge/politikk/i/Mn3r/Vet-ikke-om-30-milliarders-bistand-virker
Salvesen, Geir, and Siri Gedde Dahl. "Norsk Bistand Til Alle De Mest Korrupte." *Aftenposten*, December 2, 2011. https://www.aftenposten.no/norge/i/9vr4E/Norsk-bistand-til-alle-de-mest-korrupte
Schulpen, Lau, and Huib Huyse. "Citizen Initiatives for Global Solidarity. The New Face of European Solidarity." *Forum for Development Studies* 44, no. 2 (2017): 163–169. doi:10.1080/08039410.2017.1306956.
Skevik, Erlend. "Avslører Millionsvindel Med Norsk Bistand." *Verden Gang (VG)*, November 8, 2011. https://www.vg.no/nyheter/utenriks/i/0Pvdo/avsloerer-millionsvindel-med-norsk-bistand
Tranvik, Tommy, and Per Selle. "The Rise and Fall of Popular Mass Movements: Organizational Change and Globalization—The Norwegian Case." *Acta Sociologica* 50, no. 1 (2007): 57–70. doi:10.1177/0001699307074883.

Tvedt, Terje. *Den Norske Samaritan: Ritualer, Selvbilder Og Utviklingshjelp*. Oslo: Gyldendal, 1995.
Tvedt, Terje. "Utviklingshjelp, utenrikspolitikk og den norske modellen." *Historisk tidsskrift* 85, no. 1 (2006): 59–85. doi:10.18261/issn.1504-2944.
UNDP Human Development Reports. "Gambia. The Human Development Indicators." Accessed April 15, 2019. http://hdr.undp.org/en/countries/profiles/GMB
UNDP Human Development Reports. "Table 1. Human Development Index and Its Components." Accessed April 15, 2019. http://hdr.undp.org/en/composite/HDI
UNDP Human Development Reports. "The 2018 Global Multidimensional Poverty Index (MPI)." Accessed April 15, 2019. http://hdr.undp.org/en/2018-MPI
World Bank. "The World Bank in The Gambia." Accessed April 15, 2019. https://www.worldbank.org/en/country/gambia/overview#1

Development and the search for connection

Anne-Meike Fechter

ABSTRACT
The stated purpose of development is often characterised by the motivation to 'help' – that is, to intervene in the lives of others in supportive ways. This paper argues that this perspective has obscured how development activities are also animated by its twin desire to 'connect'. While this holds significance for development more broadly, it becomes particularly evident in a mode of assistance that has gained prominence more recently. These are privately funded, small-scale projects led by individual founders, here described as 'citizen aid'. Based on ethnographic research among citizen aid initiatives in Cambodia, the paper argues that the relevance of 'connecting' has been insufficiently recognised so far. It explores different aspects of what participants mean by 'making a connection', including face-to-face contact, direct experience of aid activities, and their tangible efficacy. It also finds that establishing interpersonal relationships across national, ethnic and cultural differences, while potentially challenging, is a key motivation for those involved. Finally, the paper argues that acknowledging the desire to connect questions notions of the 'distant stranger' as the archetypical humanitarian object, highlighting the wish for familiarity and closeness as potentially just as important for motivating and directing assistance to others.

The stated purpose of development is often characterised as the motivation to 'help' – that is, to intervene in the lives of others in ways that make a positive difference to them. This paper argues that this perspective has paid insufficient attention to the extent and the way in which development activities are also animated by its twin desire to 'connect'. In this case, it means the wish to establish personal relations with those who are the objects of intervention. While this holds relevance for development as a whole, it becomes particularly evident in a mode of assistance that has grown and gained prominence more recently. These are privately funded, small-scale projects led by individual founders, here described as 'citizen aid'. Based on ethnographic research among such initiatives in Cambodia, the paper outlines how the relevance of 'connecting' forms the backbone of these activities. It highlights some of the features of the relations that are envisaged and enacted and, finally, sketches the implications that this search for connection might have for development practice more generally.

The term 'connections' is, of course, notoriously slippery. As an emic term, it is an apposite starting point for analysis. It warrants systematic scrutiny insofar as it is frequently invoked by research participants themselves. This does not necessarily render it suitable as an analytical lens, at least not without some caveats. While both Cambodians and foreigners involved in citizen aid spoke of the importance of 'connections' for what they were doing, the term was not neutral, but held multiple meanings for them. This paper sets out to identify some of these, being mindful of the imbalances of power that it can mask. As Pedwell has warned, 'the risk of a focus on intimacy, proximity and "face-to-face" encounters in […] international development praxis is that attention is directed towards individuals as if they could be extracted from structural relations', and as such risks 'obscuring analysis of the transnational circuits of power in which "subjects who feel" are differentially embedded and produced'.[1] The foreigners who come to Cambodia with the purpose of intervention, from the Global North and neighbouring countries, are in many ways privileged – not least in the way that their transnational mobility affords them the opportunity to actively pursue such 'connections' in countries other than their own. This does not mean, however, that the balance of power is entirely skewed in their favour. Citizen aid as discussed here is carried out by both foreign and Cambodian 'do-ers', although what kind of connections they seek in this context, and how they matter for them, differs. The paper thus aims to also be attentive to how differently positioned practitioners are able to fulfil their desire for 'connection'.

In a broader view, the notion of 'connection' refers to establishing personal relations. The debate to which this paper contributes examines the ways in which such social relations, or relationships, matter for aid and development. Even though one might assume that development, a profoundly humane project at its core, is necessarily underpinned by relations between people, their theoretical visibility is uneven. As a productive approach, I propose here to understand development as 'practices of responsibility and care'.[2] As Raghuram, Madge and Noxolo argue, adopting a postcolonial lens through which to view these practices draws attention to them as 'forms of existing and evolving relationalities' and, most importantly, leads us 'to interrogate the deployments of these terms in the context of past and present inequalities'.[3] Rather than being wary of focusing on relations between individuals as losing sight of structural power imbalances, it is possible, following Barford, that 'a more public and emotionally engaged appreciation of connectivity and relationality could diminish the conceptual, and ultimately socio-economic, distances between people'.[4] Through interrogating the ethnographic material in this manner, the paper will probe some of these possibilities.

From this broader view follows an imperative to understand the role of social relations in aid. One way in which this has been acknowledged is how relationships matter for aid implementation.[5] This perspective draws attention to the instrumental value that relationships have for aid delivery and effectiveness. With a focus on institutions, Eyben argues that 'the quality of relations within and between organizations in the web of aid is crucial for organizational performance'.[6] This concerns relations between practitioners within the 'aid bureaucracy'[7] in both formal and informal capacities.[8] Further contributions include how friendships between differently situated aid workers, such as local and international staff, matter for capacity building.[9] Mawdsley, Porter and Townsend[10] emphasise the importance of face-to-face encounters to improve mutual understanding and trust between Northern and Southern non-governmental organisation (NGO) partners. These accounts examine social relations among aid practitioners themselves, and their role in enhancing aid effectiveness.

While such recognition has been necessary and overdue, it leaves out of view the possibility that relationships are essential to development processes, not merely for operational purposes, but as a key motivating factor from the outset. This paper aims to explore how the 'desire for development' and the 'search for connection' are linked in less formal and privately funded modes of assistance, and what these insights in turn contribute to how relationships in aid are being theorised. There is a broad acknowledgment in the literature that relationships matter for aid. Erica Bornstein, in her account of charity practices in urban India, claims that 'only [...] through a relational prism, does humanitarian activity make social sense'.[11] The acts of charity she is exploring are, at least partly, driven by the 'impulse of philanthropy'.[12] Liisa Malkki provides a differently orientated reading by foregrounding not the 'desire for development'[13] but the 'need to help'.[14] This means casting the helpers – in her case, Finnish people working or volunteering for the Red Cross – as those who are in need, searching for purpose, for companionship or for ways out of what they consider the mundane realities of their lives in Finland.

The relevance of relations is acknowledged in both Bornstein's and Malkki's works. In Bornstein's account of charity in Delhi, she identifies a 'relational empathy' that is at stake.[15] More specifically, this means that in contrast to forms of liberal altruism based on individual autonomy, what matters in the Indian context is the forging of kin-like relations. In a more tangential manner, Malkki emphasises that 'connections' are an important – if not the most important – aspect of helping others. For many of the elderly volunteers at the Finnish Red Cross for example, the making of connections was of vital concern.[16] Such a connection could be with a child for whom they had knitted a soft toy, even if this was an imagined connection across a geographical distance.

A more comprehensive proposal of how the desires of helping and connecting are intertwined is provided by Heron's work on Canadian women development workers in sub-Saharan Africa.[17] Her analysis is also grounded in the assumption that development is a relational experience.[18] In fact, she observes a 'disappearance of altruism' from participants' narratives once in situ, and instead a focus on establishing relationships with local people. A key question is thus how the two desires are linked.[19] In Heron's reading, central to the desire for development is that it offers 'new dimensions of identity formation for Canadian women development workers'.[20] Drawing on Ann Stoler's[21] work on the making of bourgeois identities through the colonial project, Heron argues that the development encounter is instrumental in constituting white identities. There is, however, 'a constant tension for us in these connections born of our need for African people to be "different" and our simultaneous desire for the kind of pure meeting across and beyond difference'.[22] The wish for relations is further complicated, she notes, by the fact that 'seeing African people as fully equal, that is, "just like us", however, is risky because it erodes the ethical basis for our presence "there"'.[23] Relationships with aid beneficiaries are thus imagined and practiced in particular ways to justify development interventions. All these accounts articulate, more or less explicitly, the importance of relationships in development. The search for connection among some development actors thus warrants a more comprehensive discussion than has occurred so far. Based on research on forms of aid which fundamentally revolve around a person-to-person connection, this paper aims to provide a fuller, more nuanced exploration of what participants mean by 'connection', and how it matters for development practices. In order to examine this, the paper draws on the case of small-scale private aid activities, where having a personal connection with the recipients of aid matters greatly for individual project founders, supporters and donors.

Research context

The material presented here was gathered during fieldwork conducted between 2013 and 2015 and in 2018, in several sites in Cambodia, as part of a wider project on alternative actors in aid.[24] Specifically, research was carried out among private aid initiatives, referred to as 'citizen aid'[25] (see also the introduction to this volume). 'Citizen aid' is understood here as small-scale activities and projects set up and run by individuals, aimed at assisting others. They are typically funded by private donors, and are often facilitated by the founders' transnational social networks. Founders includes foreigners and Cambodians, who often work in close collaboration with each other. The small scale of the initiatives is defined here as involving 15 or fewer staff or volunteers. While some of these projects are registered as NGOs, they typically operate on the margins of the formally established aid sector. Their activities comprise educational after-school programmes; food, health or disability support; vocational training programmes; or income generation through handicraft production. The ethnographic material was gathered from engagement with over 30 private aid projects. Research participants were actively involved in citizen aid, including Cambodian and foreign project founders, local partners, supporters and, to a limited extent, beneficiaries. Participant observation, informal conversations over repeat visits, and semi-structured interviews were carried out with 45 individuals. Their nationalities included Cambodian, Japanese, Singaporean, Malaysian, Australian, North American, and several European countries. The participants' ages covered a wide spectrum, ranging from people in their mid-twenties to those who were retired, in their late sixties. With regard to gender, participant numbers were about evenly balanced between women and men, among both foreign and Cambodian nationals. They included those of Southeast Asian ethnicities, white and mixed, across all countries of origin. Participants included college graduates, those in full-time employment in their home countries, self-employed people across all ages, and those who had taken early retirement. While some relied on other sources of income, such as property or savings, others were engaging in income-generating activities while pursuing citizen aid projects.

It is important to note that while some projects were set up by foreigners and others by Cambodians, most intensely relied on collaboration between the two. While some of the foreigners resided in Cambodia on a long-term basis, others stayed there for periods between a few weeks and a few months per year. Fieldwork was carried out in the capital Phnom Penh, and in two provincial towns. In addition to observation at project sites, methods included attending fundraising and networking events, and drawing on material and debates as they were presented via the projects' social media communications. They entailed engagement with occasional project visitors and volunteers, and extended to donors, those whose main involvement took the form of providing resources, but who were less directly involved with the day-to-day activities of the projects. The paper highlights the crucial roles of Cambodian founders, partners and facilitators in these projects. One aspect which this paper does not address is the Cambodians who are being targeted, and their experiences with these private aid initiatives, as they lay outside the scope of the original research project. While the perspectives of beneficiaries of citizen aid are clearly important, there is, as yet, insufficient research attentive to their perspectives.[26]

What does it mean to 'make a connection'?

Establishing the sense of a 'personal connection' between donors and a cause, or a group of beneficiaries, is a well-recognised challenge for large international NGOs. Specifically, individual donors may feel that the promise of connection, such as that presented through campaign materials, is tenuous, and often not realised to an extent that they find meaningful or rewarding. This apparent disconnect between donor and beneficiary in large-scale, state-funded or formalised modes of aid is one reason why small-scale aid initiatives – citizen aid – appeal to potential supporters, and even motivate people to found their own projects. Going further, I propose that the significance of 'connection' is not limited to an instrumentalist incentive for fundraising or a tool for aid effectiveness, but can be understood as a desire which is sought to be fulfilled through acts of assisting others. This does not mean that one excludes the other, but it offers an expanded perspective on how connections or relationships and acts of giving are interrelated. A fundamental question is what people mean when they invoke their desire for 'connection'. The following sections begin to unpack some of these meanings.

A helpful distinction arising from the material may be between what could be called 'thin' and 'thick' connections, the latter being sought after in the sense of providing a holistic, immersive experience. In the first instance, a key element identified was being physically present in a place, at events, and having face-to-face contact with those involved. The desire for 'being there' resonates with its perceived lack in formalised aid work.[27] This was illustrated by Adam, an Australian in his late twenties, who ran an education-focused project. He observed that

> in fact most of our supporters are looking for small organisations [to sponsor]: they say they used to give money to the Red Cross, but they have such big operations, big cars, they don't want that. People really want to do the work themselves, in a hands-on environment. They want to be part of it, to build that house, to know the students who are benefitting.

Variously described as 'being there' or 'being part of the process', physical presence and participation were cited by many as essential to 'making it real', and to bringing about a 'connection' – with the people, a place or a process – that they were looking for. This wish was for a 'connection' that was as little mediated as possible. As Laura, who runs a small education project, says, 'what our supporters are looking for is direct, first-hand experience of the situation'. In this sense, people who are engaged in citizen aid as supporters, founders or volunteers are looking for relationships imbued with physicality and authenticity – displaying some resonance with what the Kiva fellows, as described in Schwittay,[28] seek in their personal visits.

'Making a connection' thus indicates a desire for being actively, directly and effectively involved in acts of supporting others. This was also illustrated by Patrick, who runs an after-school club in a disadvantaged community on the outskirts of a provincial town, which he had co-founded with his Cambodian project partner, Khean. Patrick talked about one of their supporters from Northern Europe, who raised funds among his work colleagues for a number of bicycles to be distributed among families in their community. As Patrick pointed out, it was not sufficient for him to send over the money, but

> he came over [to Cambodia] because he wanted to meet the people and learn about the culture. He bought and delivered the bicycles himself, he wanted to be part of the process. So he knows, this mum doesn't have to walk far any more to the market – it's very concrete.

In this case, Patrick attributed their supporter's decision to travel and organise the delivery of the bikes in person to his wish for connection. On another occasion, Patrick and Khean were supporting the construction of basic houses for families in Khean's home village. In a similar fashion, some of their overseas supporters chose to come along and help because, as Patrick put it, 'they wanted to be part of it, to build that house, to know the students who are benefitting'. Being physically present and immersed, combined with a sense of their tangible efficacy, was a significant incentive.

This was also evident in a related project, named 'Food for Life'. Its main activity consisted of distributing hot meals on a weekly basis to marginalised families and elderly Cambodians without recourse to other assistance. Their meal-preparation sessions were often well attended by a mixture of tourists, resident foreigners and some young Cambodian volunteers. Asked about what attracted them to this initiative in particular, Rob, an older Australian who frequently helped out, explained that he and his wife 'want to do the work ourselves – this is a hands-on environment. The best bit is at the end, when we get to distribute them to the families who are waiting for us'. The activities of the organisation encapsulated two of the aspects of 'connection' mentioned above – that is, providing an immersive experience and establishing contact with fellow human beings in a supportive manner, in this case through the act of food provision to some of those living on the margins of Cambodian society.

Another example was provided by Borey, a young Cambodian working in the hotel sector. He explained that he often encountered hotel guests who wanted to make a donation, so for this purpose he took them to a rural area he was familiar with:

> they want to do something to help; they bought school uniforms, fish, rice, and took it out to the village. They are back in the States with their careers now, but they told me that that was a special moment for them.

By taking them to the village, the tourists said, Borey had 'made it real' for them. Such quests for 'realness' or authenticity have been widely documented and critiqued within tourism studies.[29] It is nevertheless worth noting that in the context of development, this desire plays a more substantial role in engaging networks of supporters than is often acknowledged, or indeed achieved. With this in mind, Borey actively sought out and valued interactions and connections with international visitors. He tended to give up his free time to facilitate donations to communities he considered deserving. He was providing visitors with a 'real' experience, and, one might argue, a sense of connection. While their visits, and indeed donations, were at the discretion of the tourists, it was in Borey's control to let them materialise, and to decide who would receive them. Uneven power balances, as discussed at the outset, were therefore not a straightforward distribution between privileged visitors and disadvantaged residents, but played out in more nuanced ways.

As discussed by Schwittay,[30] the appeal of a unique person-to-person connection for aid donations has long been recognised by NGOs. While early forms of child sponsorship are emblematic of this,[31] this has more recently been extended to, for example, microlending through organisations such as Kiva. It is also reflected in campaign materials by large NGOs, which seek to present possible beneficiaries in a personal, intimate style, often with curated quotes and biographies. As the case of Kiva demonstrates, these can be perceived as 'thin' connections, insofar as supporters are aware that, for administrative reasons, their donation or loan may not be received exactly by the person they were presented with on the platform or campaign website. As Schwittay suggests, one way of addressing this relative distance is to become a 'Kiva Fellow', in order to establish face-to-face contact with loan recipients.[32] I suggest that when those involved in citizen aid speak of 'making a connection', they aspire not to managed, distanced and to some extent fictive connections, but rather to those of a 'thick' quality – that is, holistic and immersive, as mentioned above.

Such desire for 'thick' connections was illustrated by Patrick's and Khean's experiences in their after-school club for marginalised youth. As an initial fundraising strategy, they set up scholarships for named children, but realised that they were not particularly popular among supporters, compared with other forms of fundraising. As Patrick explained, the most effective modus was indeed for supporters to have personal knowledge, either of young individuals through visiting, or through personal acquaintance with Patrick or Khean as the founders; or through following regular updates on particular children's progress posted on the project's website. The person-to-person approach in itself was therefore not sufficient to get people involved; it had to be someone known to the supporter or donor, even if that extended to just the project founders. The following examples illustrate some of the ways in which these 'thick' connections are pursued and made.

Ronan, for example, an American in his late fifties, runs a small project for young people with impaired hearing. Alongside this, he facilitates contacts between visitors in a Cambodian provincial town and local communities, schools, or groups of potential beneficiaries. In this role, he is sometimes asked by local friends, both Cambodian and foreign, to take hotel guests or personal visitors to projects or communities that he considers worthwhile recipients of donations. He reflects that it is the 'personal connections' that are sometimes made during these trips which prompt visitors to make financial contributions, often towards the end of their stay, as they feel they caught a glimpse of the 'real Cambodia', as Ronan says, as opposed to what they consider a façade presented to tourists. Making these kinds of connections begins, and sometimes ends, with a single donation. Occasionally, though, they set in a motion a train of events, where acts of helping and establishing relationships are closely interlinked.

Such emphasis on experiential immersion surfaced in participants' accounts, as reflected in descriptions such as the enjoyment they derived from 'seeing the smiles on the kids' faces'. This was frequently cited as a key reward when visiting communities or interacting with those they were supporting. This desire for face-to-face contact for a sense of reward and evidence of one's impact was also mentioned by those involved in educational activities. Sawa, for example, was a retired teacher from Japan who had set up a small art school. Together with an assistant, she ran workshops and weekly classes for young people on the outskirts of a provincial town. As she explained to me, she had made a conscious decision not to 'grow' her project, even though that would have been possible, as it would have meant that she would have had less time available to in direct interaction with her students, which was what really mattered to her. Such sentiments are well documented in other human service professions such as in teaching or health care, and in this respect are not unique to citizen aid. They do, however, illustrate the centrality of immediate interaction for those engaged in private aid activities. Citizen aid relations cannot, of course, be considered by default less mediated and more holistic or authentic than other forms of development. Rather, they are mediated to a different extent and in different ways. For example, much of citizen aid is facilitated by local and foreign brokers or facilitators.[33] What matters to supporters is that they often know these brokers personally, and thus feel that the information related through them provides them with a more trustworthy connection than if they received letters from a sponsored child, sent via a large NGO. With regard to relationships being 'direct', then, it is important to recognise that citizen aid also depends to some degree on forms of mediation.

It also becomes clear that the 'personal connection' is understood by supporters as an idiom for personal knowledge and trust. Time and again, those involved in citizen aid projects reiterate how for themselves and their supporters, the sense of 'knowing where the money is going' matters hugely. George, for example, runs a Christian-oriented project for children affected by HIV/AIDS in the capital, Phnom Penh. Talking about how they recruit both donations and volunteers, he explains that after people have visited them, 'they've been touched, they can tell a story about kids and HIV to the people at home – and they tell the others where the money is going to'. While their personal knowledge of the project makes them credible witnesses in the eyes of others, their own lives have been 'touched' by these visits, too – they can 'tell a story' to widen the fundraising circle, but they have also become part of the story themselves.

An example of how this works is provided by Kevin, a UK national in his sixties, who took early retirement after becoming disillusioned with his job in the UK. Having relocated to Cambodia, in due course he became friendly with some families living in the residential area near the Angkor temple complex. He subsequently decided to try fundraising specifically to allow one of the families' children to attend school. To this end, he regularly organises pub quiz evenings in a pub in his home town, with the proceeds directed towards this family. They are often successful, and his friends are inclined to participate because

> with my mates in the UK, they know me personally, it's a personal connection. They know that I know the places that I am fundraising for. Of course you have to have a certain amount of trust, of faith. They know me, and this is for Mai – you know the person it goes to. It makes it more real. It's going to be for Mai's education. I know the pub people all personally, and I take photos and bring them back to them. They are always only one step away from what is happening, and where it goes to.

This, he explains, constitutes the key difference compared to large organisations, which are unable to provide that level of assurance regarding where and how the money is spent, and who exactly it is supporting. A similar effect was identified by Samantha, who runs a small food security project. A 'personal connection' for her exemplifies accountability not just to one's supporters, but to the community her project is serving:

> in my project, I know these kids ... I know what they need, and that they deserve it. You need a business mindset; but it's the personal connection that matters. You don't want to have a disconnect; you come in with these awards ... but these awards begin with the community, and the big organisations, they've lost sight of it.

Rin, for example, a Cambodian graduate in his late twenties, had been working on a small, privately funded project as the 'second in command', as he put it, to the Australian founder for several years. As he explained, why we have foreigners: because of the social connections, the funding connections. When it comes to funding, your need a combination of Cambodians and foreigners. It's not easy for me to look after the donor. They need trust. We need Ben [the Australian founder] to help us with that.

However, Rin found that he, like others, 'need[s] to go to the communities as well. For motivation, but also so I know what has happened there. So I can be a better storyteller for them, so I know the story to tell to the donors'. As in the case of Borey described above, Rin became a mediator between the people receiving support and the private donors to whom he related the stories of what is happening at the ground level. This put him in a position of responsibility, and not least power, as it was in his hands to increase the level of trust and sense of accountability that the project aspires to provide. This is often cited by donors as a reason that draws them to private aid, rather than to formal organisations. For development practice more broadly, it is noteworthy that it was not the well-established monitoring and evaluation practices of large aid agencies but the small-scale, individual relationships enabled by private aid that functioned as a basis of trust and loyalty for supporters.

Connections across similarity and difference

An immersive presence, 'thick' relationships and personal knowledge of founders and beneficiaries can all be part of what it means to 'make a connection'. In order to understand how this matters to citizen aid and development more broadly, I now turn to connections in the sense of establishing personal relationships, the aspect that emerges most prominently in debates in development research. How central this is for citizen aid practitioners emerges in an exchange I had with James, from New Zealand, who set up a community development project in a Cambodian village. When I asked him why had done so here rather than in his native country, he responded emphatically, 'because it's so fulfilling here! It is about making a connection with the people'. His answer pointed to the desirability of relating to people who were very different from himself. Erica Bornstein finds similar experiences among charity volunteers in India, and describes how seeking out and 'empathising with persons or contexts radically different from one's own becomes desirable'.[34] A question, raised at the beginning, then becomes how the making of connections has the capacity to overcome those differences. Bornstein argues that these efforts remain ambiguous. She concludes that 'volunteering has both the potential to enhance distinctions between groups and to surpass them.[35] This leaves out of sight, however, who is in a position to 'reach out' to begin with. In the case of the community project, the initial step had been taken by the village leader, who had put out a vision for his community, and a plea for support on the internet – where it had been picked up by James, who had been both searching Cambodia-related sites for information and scouting, by his own account, for possibilities for intervention. One might read this as another instance of how power imbalances are visible but do not entirely favour the privileged visitors from outside: after all, James was looking for something which the village leader was able to offer him – that is, an opportunity for intervention.

One argument animating this paper was that the desires to 'support' and to 'connect' with others are closely related, and may therefore indeed constitute two sides of the same coin. This may hold to the extent that wanting to 'make a connection' can be a motivation for 'making a contribution', as much as the other way round, as in James's case. The previous sections have aimed to differentiate what participants mean when they speak of such 'connection'. Further, I suggest that a vital component of 'making a connection' is, in a more literal sense, to establish a meaningful, personal relationship with someone who is very different from oneself – but a relationship that nevertheless offers similarities, shared experiences and perhaps mutual recognition. It emerges that such relationships can be highly valued, despite or perhaps because of their possible tensions and the challenges they offer. Among many citizen aid practitioners, there is clearly a desire for connection across national, ethnic, or cultural difference – indeed, this difference may be part of what makes it appealing in the first place. Citizen aid constitutes a prime example of the significance of such personal connections in development, partly because they are actively encouraged (rather than frowned on), and because the search for connection is at the heart of what animates citizen aid activities in the first place.

In many citizen aid activities, a moment of 'connection' becomes a starting point, and a motivation for donors to become involved in more comprehensive forms of assistance. One such example were Al and Donna, a retired couple from Australia, who used to run their own farm, and whose grown-up children had left home. According to their own account, at this stage they were actively looking to 'do something'. As Donna searched the internet, initially for volunteering opportunities, she came across a YouTube clip about a small village school in Cambodia. A school teacher who had posted the video was hoping to raise funds by inviting people to become involved. In Donna's words, 'when I saw this, I was hooked. It was the kids – definitely the kids'. On the strength of this sentiment, they travelled to Cambodia, and after an abortive stint of volunteering at an NGO, they visited the school and decided to get involved, and 'that was it'. It turned out to be the start of an ongoing engagement, first fundraising for the school, then a wider approach including health and livelihood support, as well as a greater role – in collaboration with village residents – in planning, financing, and delivering assistance.

The 'spark' of spontaneous connection is often the beginning of a longer term relationship, where assistance is provided in the context of more personal relationships. Significantly, these are sometimes couched in kinship terms. Ailish, for example, a retired woman from Ireland, 'adopted' a Cambodian young man as her godson, including the obligations of support that this entailed. As her friend Joan explains:

> It's just about human relations – something clicks. My friend Ailish first came here nine years ago – she met a tuktuk driver, sponsored him to go to Ireland, and to buy land here. She's at the moment volunteering with another organisation, near where he is based in Kampong Chang. She made her own connection. There is some spark, and then it takes off from there.

As in Ailish's case, people may engage with organisations to find volunteering placements. Finding the personal relations that they may be looking for can, however, be done informally, and independently: Ailish had 'made her own connection'. This cannot be fully explored here, but it is worth noting that drawing on kinship terminology for shaping and understanding social relations – such as 'adopting' a godson – can accommodate existing socio-economic inequalities, as well as justify (or even call for) ongoing support between a foreign older woman and a younger Cambodian man. Similar practices involving kinship idioms are evident in Bornstein's account of philanthropic activities in urban India.[36]

In cases such as those presented here, the desire for development and the search for connection can be difficult or impossible to disentangle. In others, the wish for continued involvement – with people, a project, a place – is more clearly in the foreground. Ongoing assistance can be a means of maintaining those relations, and can provide a rationale to return. This was the situation for Anette, a retired teacher in her sixties from Denmark, whom I met in Stephane's music school. Stephane's project combined a for-profit school, offering tuition for guitar and piano, with a non-profit section. The latter consisted of two educational projects in deprived areas, where children from the surrounding neighbourhoods took classes in English, information technology (IT), and life skills. Several years ago, Anette had spent time as a volunteer there, and had got to know Stephane, his team, and some of the children well. Following on from this, Anette kept returning, first twice, and now once a year. This time, she and her daughter had come for a two-week visit. When I asked about her ongoing support for Stephane's project, she explained that 'it's all because of having that personal connection'. While some of her time was spent sightseeing with her daughter, they were both keen to visit the classrooms, participate in lessons and wander through the area, greeting people and chatting with those that they recognised from previous visits.

While the 'connection' that Anette was referring to did not always relate to particular young people, but to the team and the project more broadly, in other cases more fine-grained aspects of the relationships became evident. Al, for example, found it important that many residents in the village where they supported the school were rice farmers. He recounted how he and his wife were once invited to sit with some of the villagers under a tree while they were having a break from working the fields. He was particularly touched by how one older woman, knowing Al had been a farmer too, examined his palms to see whether they showed signs of hard work. 'Then she said that "we're similar". That's what makes it so fulfilling', Al explained, 'that we share the experience. We know what it's like to farm, we can talk about crops, we're coming from the same place'. As they went out to the villages, they were looking at some fields, and got talking to the farmers. As they took a break from rice planting, the local people asked them if they wanted to share their breakfast. Al enthusiastically recounted that 'they've never sat down with a couple of white people before and had food with them. So we sat down under the tree together ... it's great to make that connection'.

Al felt that the group of local rice farmers experienced the same enthusiasm of meeting someone very different, yet familiar, that he and his wife did. Significantly, motives and interests that local Cambodians may have to seek a connection or a personal relationship with foreigners tend to be much less explored in literatures of development or voluntourism, or indeed in the emerging debates on citizen aid, although I have indicated some of them above.

As Schwittay[37] points out, while the search for connection may or may not be reciprocal, motivations and opportunities to establish and maintain these relationships are bound to be asymmetrical. While there is some work on social relations among local aid workers,[38] less is known regarding to what extent the desire for connection may be one-sided, reciprocal, or imbalanced. Heron argues that, in her case, some local NGO workers intentionally 'assert boundaries in response to our insistence on relations'.[39] Heron's material, however, was gathered in the context of formalised development, among established NGOs. In contrast, among those involved in citizen aid, the valuing of relationships may take on a different significance.

In some cases, Cambodian founders of citizen aid projects appreciate not just the potential funding streams for their project that are opened up by making connections with foreigners, but also what might be described as cultural or indeed cosmopolitan capital. In the premises of some citizen aid projects, for example, evidence of their transnational connections was pinned to concrete walls, such as images of shared meals and volunteer visits; ornamental, symbolic cheques that had been presented; and drawings and cards that had been sent from afar. Rather than putting up barriers to foreigners' insistence on contact, a more complex picture emerges where such contacts may be purposefully sought, managed and put to service for a particular project, as well as benefitting local founders or facilitators of citizen aid in more personal capacities.

Further, it would be inaccurate to present these relationships solely in terms of their functionality for the purposes of citizen aid projects. In the context of such initiatives, relationships emerge which extend beyond this, and which are experienced as friendships across cultural and linguistic differences. One example was Sophea, a Cambodian who had been working for several years with a café supporting a small NGO, which regularly received foreign volunteers. One year, Sophea struck up a particular friendship with a Dutch young woman, also called Sophia, a coincidence which both remarked upon. Sophea recounted how over the course of the year, they had lots of fun together, learnt from each other, ran the café and improved the project. They got on so well that after Sophia had returned to the Netherlands, she invited Sophea for a visit during the European winter months. While talking with me, more than 5 years later, Sophea pulled out a photo she had taken during that visit, of Sophia's parents' front lawn, covered in snow, with both of them throwing snowballs. Sophea spoke of their friendship with warmth, even though Sophia had not been back to Cambodia since, and had gone on to pursue her university studies; they kept in sporadic contact. Clearly, differences between them, but also apparently incidental similarities such as their shared name, made their relationship a rewarding experience. Perhaps necessarily, it turned out to be temporary, and marked by asymmetries, such as Sophea's limited ability to travel and choice of livelihoods, contrasted with the educational opportunities and outlook available to Sophia.

Conclusion

This paper took as its starting point the observation that relationships matter for development, as recognised in some of the relevant literature. Taking the case of citizen aid as an example, it argued that while the desire to help has been foregrounded in development studies, an equally important role is played by the desire to connect – that is, to establish meaningful personal relations with the people who are being supported. Based on ethnographic research among small-scale aid initiatives in Cambodia, it emerges that the shorthand of 'making a connection' includes physical presence, face-to-face contact with people, and direct experience of aid activities and their tangible efficacy. The examples also demonstrate that 'thick' person-to-person connections are being sought, furnished with first-hand knowledge of the projects. Personal knowledge here stands for trust and accountability towards both donors and local communities. Finally, a key aspect for choosing to provide support, as well as where to direct it, is the creation of personal relationships between those involved. Perceived differences perhaps offer as much incentive as constructed similarities, such as shared past experiences. A complex picture thus emerges, which supports the argument that rather than the desire to help being a primary incentive, the desire to connect may matter just as much. The latter having been rather backgrounded until now, it leads us to nuance our notions of what development is about.

Such understandings must be tempered by the recognition that the search for and the ability to make 'connections' are embedded in wider structural inequalities. On a hopeful note, Barford suggests that making such connectivity and relationality between people more visible[40] might eventually contribute to reducing those inequalities. On the evidence of the material presented here, the workings of power in the making of connections are more complicated. It emerges that those foreigners who are in search of a 'connection' depend on finding an opportunity for intervention. This may be offered to them by local residents who are also looking to make such a 'connection', who have identified a need in their community and are seeking ways to address it. This may be not primarily a need for sharing experiences with a stranger, though that can be part of it, but a need for a more substantive, material form of assistance. Further, the role of some Cambodians in citizen aid activities can be powerful, insofar as they are able to invite donations from visitors and their transnational networks, and direct donations towards causes of their choice. Making connections with foreign visitors affords them a privileged position vis-à-vis their own social contexts. Whether these different forms of connectivity indeed contribute to the reduction of power imbalances, or their redistribution, is a matter for further debate.

What are some of the implications that the search for connection may have for development theory and practice? At the least, it implies that the impulse of philanthropy[41] has been unduly foregrounded, and perhaps limited our understanding of the reasons why individuals become involved in supporting others. In addition, an equivalent 'anthropological impulse' comes into view – that is, the desire to establish connections with others who are in some ways very different from oneself. Rather than pure exotic attraction to a needy other – a distant stranger, as it were – the material here suggests that this is inextricably twinned with a desire to find commonalities and sameness. As Heron suggests, the difference of the other both justifies intervention and creates attraction. At the same time, identifying similarities between oneself and others provides a rationale for where to intervene – for example, supporting someone whom one knows personally, and feels in some ways close or connected to. The tension between similarity and difference, making these relationships challenging as well as desirable, is inherent in making such connections in a development context. Arguably, such tensions complicate and question the well-rehearsed notion of a 'distant stranger' being the object of individual charity donations. On the face of evidence from citizen aid, the wish for familiarity and closeness is a central element in motivating and directing assistance to others. This holds for overseas donors, for visiting supporters, and for both foreign and Cambodian founders and facilitators. It is less clear, and needs exploring, how such connections matter for the people and communities who are being supported. As a way of differentiating existing notions of what drives individual development activities, it is a useful first step.

Disclosure statement

No potential conflict of interest was reported by the author.

Funding

The project was funded by a Leverhulme Research Grant (RF 2013-535) whose assistance is gratefully acknowledged.

Acknowledgements

This paper benefited greatly from discussions at the workshop on 'Citizen Aid and Everyday Humanitarianism' at the University of Sussex, in April 2018. Many thanks to all participants, and for the very helpful comments of two anonymous reviewers.

Notes

1. Pedwell, "Affective (Self-)Transformations," conclusion.
2. Raghuram, Madge, and Noxolo, "Rethinking Responsibility and Care," 5.
3. Ibid., 5.
4. Barford, "Emotional Responses to World Inequality," conclusion.
5. Eyben, *Relationships for Aid*; Chen, *Understanding Development Impact*; Schech, Skelton, and Mundkur, *Building Relationships and Negotiating Difference*.
6. Eyben, *Relationships for Aid*, 2.
7. Ibid., 43.
8. Eyben, "Sociality of International Aid."
9. Girgis, "Capacity-building Paradox."
10. Mawdsley, Porter, and Townsend, "Trust, Accountability and Face-to-Face Interaction."
11. Bornstein, *Spirit of Development*, 170.
12. Bornstein, *Disquieting Gifts*.
13. Heron, *Desire for Development*.
14. Malkki, *Need to Help*.
15. Ibid., 149.
16. Ibid., 134.
17. Heron, *Desire for Development*.
18. Ibid., 55.
19. Ibid., 88.
20. Ibid., 123.
21. Cooper and Stoler, *Tensions of Empire*.
22. Heron, *Desire for Development*, 89.
23. Ibid.
24. The project was funded by a Leverhulme Grant (RF 2013-535) whose assistance is gratefully acknowledged.
25. Kinsbergen and Schulpen, *Anatomy of the Private Initiative*; Schulpen and Huyse, "Citizen Initiatives for Global Solidarity"; Develtere and De Bruyn, "Emergence of a Fourth Pillar; Kinsbergen and Schulpen, "From Tourist to Development Worker"; Haaland and Wallevik, "Citizens as Actors in the Development Field."
26. Though see eg McLachlan and Binns, "Exploring Host Perspectives."
27. Irvine, Chambers, and Eyben, *Learning from Poor People's Experience*.
28. Schwittay, *New Media and International Development*.

29. Kuon, "Pursuit of Authenticity in Tourist Experiences."
30. Schwittay, "Digital Mediations of Everyday Humanitarianism."
31. Bornstein, *Spirit of Development*.
32. Schwittay, *New Media and International Development*.
33. Fechter, "Brokering Transnational Flows of Care," McKay and Perez, "Citizen Aid, Social Media and Brokerage."
34. Bornstein, *Disquieting Gifts*, 121.
35. Ibid., 122.
36. Ibid.
37. Schwittay, "Digital Mediations of Everyday Humanitarianism."
38. Yarrow, *Development beyond Politics*; Goetz, *Women Development Workers*; Heaton Shrestha, "They Can't Mix Like We Can."
39. Heron, *Desire for Development*, 85.
40. Barford, "Emotional Responses to World Inequality."
41. Bornstein, *Disquieting Gifts*.

ORCID

Anne-Meike Fechter http://orcid.org/0000-0002-9654-156X

Bibliography

Barford, Anna. "Emotional Responses to World Inequality." *Emotion, Space and Society* 22 (2017): 25–35. doi:10.1016/j.emospa.2016.10.006.
Bornstein, Erica. *Disquieting Gifts: Humanitarianism in New Delhi*. Stanford: Stanford University Press, 2012.
Bornstein, Erica. *The Spirit of Development: Protestant NGOs, Morality and Economics in Zimbabwe*. Stanford: Stanford University Press, 2003.
Chen, J. "Understanding Development Impact in International Development Volunteering: A Relational Approach." *The Geographical Journal* 184, no. 2 (2018): 138–147. doi:10.1111/geoj.12208.
Cooper, Frederick, and Ann Laura Stoler. *Tensions of Empire: Colonial Cultures in a Bourgeois World*. University of California Press, 1997.
Develtere, Patrick, and Tom De Bruyn. "The Emergence of a Fourth Pillar in Development Aid." *Development in Practice* 19, no. 7 (2009): 912–922. doi:10.1080/09614520903122378.
Eyben, Rosalind. *Relationships for Aid*. London: Earthscan. 2006.
Eyben, Rosalind. "The Sociality of International Aid and Policy Convergence." In *Adventures in Aidland: The Anthropology of Professionals in International Development*, edited by D. Mosse, 230–266. Oxford, New York: Berghahn, 2011.
Fechter, Anne-Meike. "Brokering Transnational Flows of Care: The Case of Citizen Aid." *Ethnos* (2019). doi:10.1080/00141844.2018.1543339.
Fechter, Anne-Meike. *The Personal and the Professional in Aid Work*. London: Routledge, 2011.
Girgis, Mona. "The Capacity-Building Paradox: Using Friendship to Build Capacity in the South." *Development in Practice* 17, no. 3 (2007): 353–366.
Goetz, Anne-Marie. *Women Development Workers: Implementing Rural Credit Programs in Bangladesh*. Dhaka: Dhaka University Press, 2001.
Haaland, Hanne, and Hege Wallevik. "Citizens as Actors in the Development Field: The Case of an Accidental Aid-Agent's Activities in Aid-Land." *Forum for Development Studies* 44, no. 2 (2017): 203–222. doi:10.1080/08039410.2017.1305444.
Heaton Shrestha, Celayne. "'They Can't Mix Like We Can': Bracketing Differences and the Professionalization of NGOs in Nepal." In *Development Brokers and Translators: The Ethnography of Aid and Agencies*, edited by Lewis, David and Mosse, David, 195–216. Sterling, VA: Kumarian Press, 2006.
Heron, Barbara. *Desire for Development: Whiteness, Gender, and the Helping Imperative*. Waterloo: Wilfried Laurier Press, 2007.

Irvine, Renwick, Robert Chambers, and Rosalind Eyben. *Learning from Poor People's Experience: Immersions*. Lessons for Change in Policy and Organisations 13, Brighton: Institute of Development Studies, 2004.

Kinsbergen, Sara, and Lau Schulpen. *The Anatomy of the Private Initiative*. Radboud University Nijmegen, 2010.

Kinsbergen, Sara, and Lau Schulpen. "From Tourist to Development Worker. Private Development Initiatives in The Netherlands." *Mondes en Développement* 161, no. 1 (2013): 49–62. doi:10.3917/med.161.0049.

Kuon, Vannsy. "The Pursuit of Authenticity in Tourist Experiences: The Case of Siem Reap-Angkor." Unpublished master's thesis, Lincoln University, 2011. https://researcharchive.lincoln.ac.nz/bitstream/handle/10182/4306/kuon_mtm.pdf?sequence=5&isAllowed=y

Malkki, Liisa H. *The Need to Help: The Domestic Arts of International Humanitarianism*. Durham: Duke University Press, 2015

Mawdsley, Emma, Gina Porter, and Janet Townsend. "Trust, Accountability and Face-to-Face Interaction in North–South NGO Relations." *Development in Practice* 15, no. 1 (2005): 77–82.

McKay, Deirdre, and Padmapani Perez. "Citizen Aid, Social Media, and Brokerage after Disaster." *Third World Quarterly* (2019). doi:10.1080/01436597.2019.1634470

McLachlan, Sam, and Tony Binns. "Exploring Host Perspectives towards Younger International Development Volunteers." *Development in Practice* 29, no. 1 (2019): 65–79.

Pedwell, Carolyn. "Affective (Self-)Transformations: Empathy, Neoliberalism and International Development." *Feminist Theory* 13, no. 2 (2012): 163–179.

Raghuram, Parvati, Clare Madge, and Pat Noxolo. "Rethinking Responsibility and Care for a Postcolonial World." *Geoforum* 40, no. 1 (2009): 5–13. doi:10.1016/j.geoforum.2008.07.007.

Schech, S., T. Skelton, and A. Mundkur. "Building Relationships and Negotiating Difference in International Development Volunteerism." *The Geographical Journal* 184, no. 2 (2018): 148–157. doi:10.1111/geoj.12199.

Schulpen, Lau, and Huib Huyse. "Citizen Initiatives for Global Solidarity. The New Face of European Solidarity." *Forum for Development Studies* 44, no. 2 (2017): 163–169. doi:10.1080/08039410.2017.1306956.

Schwittay, Anke. "Digital Mediations of Everyday Humanitarianism: The Case of Kiva.org." *Third World Quarterly* (2019). doi:10.1080/01436597.2019.1625267

Schwittay, Anke. *New Media and International Development: Representation and Affect in Microfinance*. London: Routledge, 2015.

Yarrow, Thomas. *Development beyond Politics: Aid, Activism and NGOs in Ghana*. London: Palgrave Macmillan, 2011.

Don't reinvent the wheel: possibilities for and limits to building capacity of grassroots international NGOs

Susan Appe and Allison Schnable

ABSTRACT
How can support organisations build the capacity of volunteer-driven non-governmental organisations (NGOs)? Citizen aid for relief and development has expanded rapidly in the twenty-first century, and the number of American aid organisations operating in the Global South has grown to nearly 10,000. These grassroots international NGOs – GINGOs – are small-budget, volunteer-driven organisations typically launched by Americans without professional experience in international development or nonprofit management. These groups prize the expressive and voluntaristic dimensions of development work, yet face challenges of amateurism, material scarcity, fragmentation, paternalism and restricted focus. We investigate whether support organisations, whose primary goals are to build the capacity of organisations and strengthen the organisational field, offer solutions to GINGOs' inherent weaknesses. We draw on 15 semi-structured interviews with a stratified selection of support organisations, including associations tailored towards international development and towards nonprofit work at large. We find that support organisations offer resources to help GINGOs in managerial and administrative domains. Fewer support organisations help GINGOs build technical development skills, and fewer still push GINGOs to critically reflect on their role in development. We find that peer learning and online platforms could help engage GINGOs volunteers in networking spaces, even as their geographic dispersal in the US encourages their fragmentation and isolation.

Introduction

Citizen aid for relief and development has expanded rapidly in the twenty-first century, as cheap travel and electronic communication have become increasingly available. Thousands of citizens in the Global North have established associations to do volunteer-based relief and development projects. The number of such organisations based in the United States and operating in the Global South has grown to nearly 10,000.[1] These groups typically emerge from tourism (or, less often, family ties) to the South by Americans with no training or professional experience in development. The leaders draw on small donations and volunteer labour to make development a 'personal project'.[2] But these groups often lack managerial competence, technical development skills and an understanding of the political and social contexts of their work. How can support organisations help groups overcome these weaknesses?

We refer to these volunteer-driven groups as grassroots international non-governmental organisations, or GINGOs.[3] These groups operate in Asia, Africa and Latin America, but are most common in Haiti and Mexico (the less-developed countries geographically closest to the US) and in India, Kenya and Peru. The most typical sectors of activity are education (most often school-building or funding scholarships), medical clinics, small business and water.[4] These groups are broadly similar in structure and purpose to citizen aid initiatives based in other countries, such as private development initiatives based in the Netherlands,[5] as well as citizen initiatives based in Norway[6] and Germany.[7] Like the Dutch private development initiatives examined by Kinsbergen,[8] GINGOs are apt to focus on Korten's[9] 'first-generation' development strategies – direct provision of goods and services.[10] While many GINGOs use discourse of 'empowerment' or 'sustainability', in practice their citizen aid is designed around ongoing subsidies and volunteer labour from the US.[11]

GINGOs have the potential to contribute as small-scale development actors thanks to their distinctive strengths. For example, though their budgets are small, relying on donations from everyday citizens grants GINGOs considerable autonomy. They are not subject to the demands of funding cycles or the fickle tastes of donor agencies. They avoid the pressure common in the aid world to carry out projects where results can be tidily measured and the projects taken to scale. As Kinsbergen shows of Dutch initiatives, such organisations can remain in one community over a decade or more on a project of a limited scope, such as supporting a school.[12] Other groups are able to create durable relationships between emigrants and their new home communities and their communities of origin.[13] Some citizen aid groups create small-scale but sustainable partnerships with local institutions such as religious congregations, cooperatives or government ministries.[14]

Yet as we describe below, many of these groups require some capacity building to address the weaknesses built into their approach to aid. Unlike in the Netherlands, volunteer-run development organisations in the US have not been the target of financial support or capacity building from the national development agency or from large NGOs.[15] This is a population of organisations that is young (with the majority founded since 2000) and highly dispersed. Previously, 20% of American organisations working in international development were found in New York City and Washington, DC, but since 1990 this proportion has decreased to about 11%.[16] GINGOs are based in every state and in one-third of all US counties. Such dispersal makes it difficult for GINGOs to identify peer organisations and to see themselves as part of an organisational field.[17]

The most likely candidates to work with US-based GINGOs are *support organisations*: associations with state, regional or national scope whose primary goals are to build the capacity of nonprofit and nongovernmental organisations and strengthen the organisational field. We focus our analysis on support organisations in the US as the majority of GINGO leaders spend only weeks or months a year at their programme sites; thus, most of the organisational management and planning is based in the US. We find, after interviews with 15 support organisations, that these groups are not yet effectively serving GINGOs, but that they have the potential to do so, especially in managerial and administrative domains. They are less suited to building technical development skills or providing spaces for reflection about the field of development. Online platforms and peer learning will be especially important to reach the dispersed population of these groups while allowing them to maintain their voluntary and expressive ethos that makes them distinctive actors in the development field.

Background

Characteristics and critiques of GINGOs

While they are distinct in terms of their funding structure, time horizons and incentives, GINGOs have important similarities and are subject to some of the same critiques as international volunteering and voluntourism programmes. One of these is the importance of emotion in driving Global Northerners' involvement in citizen aid. Interviews with volunteers have shown that feelings of a 'warm glow'[18] and the 'intimacy'[19] within the international volunteering experience motivate some, while others are driven by the 'fun factor' of hands-on international projects.[20] Volunteers for GINGOs resemble the voluntourists studied by Mostafanezhad, who notes the 'centrality of sentimentality' to international volunteering.[21] GINGO volunteers cherish the ideal of personal relationships with individuals in the Global South. But volunteers' emotional attachment to those they aim to help is not necessarily equivalent to solidarity. Haaland and Wallevik[22] are wary of conflating solidarity, or a sense of shared fate, with the personalised charity of citizen initiatives, while Mostafanezhad critiques the sentimentality of these personal encounters for veiling broader power relations.[23]

The primacy of these emotional experiences also creates practical barriers to GINGOs being effective development actors. Americans start these organisations out of an urge to aid particular communities and to 'do it themselves'. Many volunteers prefer to carry out service tasks first hand (eg working in medical clinics, building houses) when local staff might more cheaply or knowledgeably do the work. GINGOs are often reluctant to develop relationships with other aid agencies. In fact, GINGO founders and volunteers often purposefully frame their work in contrast to larger, professionalised, international NGOs working in development aid.[24] They do not seek to professionalise their own organisations, lest their work become tied up in NGO 'red tape' instead of direct relationships with aid beneficiaries. One leader of a GINGO explained: 'We may have been reinventing the wheel – but it was *our* wheel!'[25] Another GINGO founder likewise uses the wheel analogy: 'I don't want to *re*invent the wheel, but there's so much need out there, what I want to do is more, I want to personally connect with people'.[26] In other words, GINGO volunteers prioritise the emotional and relational components of their work at the price of learning development work and organisational management through trial and error. This desire for personal connection and organisational independence might produce a strong sense of commitment by GINGO founders and supporters. But it also risks development approaches that are inefficient in the delivery of aid, or at worst donor-driven, unsustainable and potentially exploitative.

While citizen aid takes some non-organisational forms, we categorise American GINGOs as a subset of the broader field of nonprofit organisations. These groups are bound by the same legal regulations as other US-based nonprofits, and in previous work we found that GINGO leaders informally draw on lessons learned from their involvement in domestically-oriented nonprofit groups.[27] Theorists of the nonprofit sector have distinguished between instrumental and expressive rationales for nonprofit organisations.[28] While an instrumental assessment of the nonprofit sector values the maximally efficient delivery of services, an expressive perspective sees distinct value in the way that volunteers can experience fellowship or satisfaction even if efficiency is sacrificed. From this perspective the nonprofit sector is unique not just because of the variety of services it can offer, but because the delivery of the services offers emotional and moral possibilities unavailable through the state or market.[29] As we have described, expressive rationales drive volunteers' involvement in GINGOs, but GINGOs risk prioritising volunteers' emotional experience over effective aid provision.

Potential sources of building capacity for GINGOs

We focus on support organisations, which serve both international development organisations and nonprofits at large in the United States, as potential facilitators of capacity building. Support organisations are 'value-based agencies whose primary task is to provide services and resources that strengthen the capacities of their constituents to accomplish their missions'.[30] Additional terms used to describe support organisations for nonprofit organisations include umbrella organisations, infrastructure organisations, networks, federations, confederations, coalitions and consortiums. Support organisations exist to serve the sector, often focusing on professional development, research, advocacy and education.[31] We draw on Brown and Kalegaonkar's work on support organisations that aim to address challenges in the nonprofit sector.[32] Brown and Kalegaonkar outline the following internal sector issues: *amateurism, material scarcity, fragmentation, paternalism* and *restricted focus*.[33]

We argue that these challenges, while applicable to nonprofit organisations more generally, are especially acute for GINGOs. As noted above, GINGO founders might be equipped with emotion and passion, but many have little, if any, experience in leading a development organisation. We have found that many GINGO founders are active community members, for example as volunteers in churches and local organisations or as small business owners. While they have some experience in volunteering and managing organisations, many have little experience specific to development work, which aligns with the first internal sector issue outlined by Brown and Kalegaonkar[34]: *amateurism*. This trait is pronounced in the case of GINGOs as much of the work is volunteer-based, which speaks to the organisation's grassroots vision but might also hinder effective achievement of an organisation's mission and objectives. Additionally, GINGOs operate on small budgets based on individual donations, aligning with what Brown and Kalegaonkar call the sector's issue with *material scarcity*.[35] GINGOs tend to have a limited understanding about fund development and often default to unsuccessful bids for grants in lieu of other revenue streams. *Fragmentation* likewise presents particular challenges for GINGOs, as – perhaps in part due to the geographic dispersal mentioned earlier – they have been found to work in isolation. Conceivably by design as they seek personal connection and organisational independence, they are often not linked into larger networks or collaboration opportunities, which can limit effectiveness; this also makes them prone to reproducing failed projects of the past.

Furthermore, GINGOs exemplify the tendency of nonprofit organisations to have what Brown and Kalegaonkar call *restricted focus*. Indeed, many GINGOs focus on a specific programmatic area and/or location, and while this can be considered a positive attribute, it can also inhibit GINGOs' ability to provide effective services because they are selective and fail to see the 'larger picture'.[36] *Paternalism* is the final issue internal to the nonprofit sector identified by Brown and Kalegaonkar. As with many NGOs working in development, paternalism is often unintentional but is a challenge as Northern volunteers in GINGOs control the resources provided to Southern recipient communities, and thus can control the priorities of the communities and risk omitting local knowledge, capacity and responsibility.

Research approach

Because the field of US support organisations is diverse and because we expected that these groups would vary in their understanding of and interactions with GINGOs, we carried out semi-structured interviews with a stratified selection of support organisations. We first generated a population of support organisations that work with NGOs and nonprofit organisations in the US. These groups all are 'associations of associations', although some accept individual members.

The population of support organisations can be divided into four categories, based on their geographic focus and the generalised versus development-specific focus of their membership, all of which were represented in our study (see Table 1). State-level international development support organisations are member-based associations and networks of NGOs working in international development. The geographic scope of membership and participation is within a US state. National-level international development support organisations are member-based associations and networks of NGOs working in international development. Their geographic scope is not necessarily defined. National-level nonprofit support organisations are member-based associations and networks that are national in scope and serve nonprofit organisations across fields of activity (in addition to international development, health, human services, arts, etc.). State-level nonprofit support organisations are member-based associations and networks for nonprofit organisations at the state level.

We employed several strategies to compile the list of support organisations that might serve GINGOs. Some organisations were known to us through previous fieldwork or were suggested by colleagues. We broadened the scope by reading through a sample of 60 websites randomly selected from a database of websites of GINGOs, complied in 2014. Potential support organisations were identified through links and mentions in the website text. We then used a snowball selection method, following web links and 'suggested organisations' on Facebook pages to identify other potential support organisations, until we reached saturation and no additional organisations could be identified. Finally, we identified and selected the state-level nonprofit support organisations through the National Council of Nonprofits' 'Find Your State Association' map.[37]

The interviews were conducted over the phone or by Skype and lasted an average of 50 minutes. The interviews included general questions about the support organisation, membership and participation structure, benefits to the members and other stakeholders it serves, and specific questions about serving GINGOs. Our analysis is also informed by a checklist filled out during the interview by all participants, which listed services provided to their members and whether they are available to GINGOs. Interviews were transcribed and all transcriptions were analysed through a preliminary paper-and-pencil analysis with open coding to identify support organisations' functions and relationships to GINGOs. With a second close reading of the interview transcriptions, we sorted the data into themes and engaged in memo writing[38] to describe support organisations, their capacity building services and their interactions with GINGOs.

Table 1. Interview participants.

Organisation type	Organisation name	Position	Location
State-level international development support organisation	Posner Center for International Development	Program Director	Denver, CO
State-level international development support organisation	Minnesota International NGO Network (MINN)	Board President	Minneapolis, MN
State-level international development support organisation	Global Washington	Executive Director	Seattle, WA
State-level international development support organisation	Global PDX	Coordinator	Portland, OR
State-level international development support organisation	Boston Network for International Development	Executive Director	Boston, MA
National-level international development support organisation	Inter Action	Chief Executive Officer	Washington, DC
National-level international development support organisation	International Network for Education in Emergencies (INEE)	Coordinator for Standards and Practice	Washington, DC
National-level international development support organisation	Society for International Development – Washington Chapter	Chief Executive Officer	Washington, DC
National-level international development support organisation	Accord	Co-chair of Research Association	Washington, DC
National-level nonprofit support organisation	BoardSource	Director of Education	Washington, DC
National-level nonprofit support organisation	Independent Sector	Director of Policy Development and Analysis	Washington, DC
State-level nonprofit support organisation	New York Council of Nonprofits, Inc. (NYCON)	Vice President, Strategic Communications and Stakeholder Engagement	Albany, NY
State-level nonprofit support organisation	Colorado Nonprofits	Statewide Membership Coordinator	Denver, Colorado
State-level nonprofit support organisation	Forefront	Director of Education	Chicago, IL
State-level nonprofit support organisation	California Association of Nonprofits	Chief Executive Officer	San Francisco, CA

The findings of our research follow. First we outline the relationship between support organisations and their members. Second, we summarise the kinds of support currently provided by support organisations to their membership.

Findings: support organisations rarely serve GINGOs

Do support organisations have GINGOs among their members, and do they recognise these organisations' distinct needs? For the most part, no. Only one support organisation among those interviewed had a substantial membership base of GINGOs: the Posner Center for International Development (see Box 1). Most support organisations identified ad hoc ways in which they encountered GINGOs, but confirmed that their interactions with these groups were limited. State-level associations for international development were most likely to serve GINGOs, but did not observe GINGOs consistently using their services and programming. The development-focused support organisations identified GINGOs as a growing constituency and as having been discussed programmatically, but concluded that GINGOs are difficult to target. For example, InterAction's CEO explained,

> **Box 1.** The Posner Center for International Development.
>
> The Posner Center for International Development represents a distinct model among support organisations: a membership organisation of roughly 60 development NGOs, anchored in a co-working space in Denver, Colorado. Member organisations range in budget from less than $25,000 annually to $25 million. Posner's Program Director estimates that half of their members are GINGOs.
>
> Posner provides an office space that is leased by GINGOs, a handful of midsize NGOs, and two large NGOs, Engineers Without Borders – USA and iDE. The office space plays a crucial role in allowing member NGOs to build capacity through intense networking and peer learning. Members have regional working groups, thematic working groups (including a monitoring and evaluation club), and a monthly meeting for executive directors. The centre does capacity building through programmes offered on site – both brown-bag 'development dialogues' and day-long 'toolbox' sessions on technical or management topics. Posner also plays a visible convening role in Colorado by hosting speakers and other events related to international development.
>
> According to the Program Director, Posner's strengths in working with GINGOs come from physical co-presence and the opportunity for GINGOs to learn both from peers and from more established organisations. She explained,
>
> > I think a lot of them are looking … to belong to a certain degree. People who are working out of their houses or I think for a lot of them they get colleagues by coming here. They might be two in the US or one in the US and then there're 18 in Uganda but the day to day can be lonely.
>
> The sharing of space allows GINGO leaders to informally ask for help from more experienced development workers. In turn, GINGO leaders – often young and interested in building social bonds – 'form the heart of the community' that makes the space more appealing to established NGOs and builds the overall visibility of the Posner Center.

> We have discussed grassroots international NGOs. Our challenge has been is, given their limited resources, what can they afford? […] But there's been a sort of lamenting that there hasn't been [contact], we haven't created the space yet for this community to engage.[39]

Support organisations described GINGOs as difficult to serve. The Executive Director of Global Washington, which has worked for 10 years with many types of organisations with a connection to Washington state and doing global work, explained: 'It's kind of a place I think where international NGOs fall through the cracks because they're not being served by some of the other backbone organisations around the nation'.[40] Another executive from a support organisation admits: 'How to get some of the diversity of representation from maybe some of these more grassroots-level ones has been a question for us'.[41]

Often, support organisations lumped GINGOs with other small organisations and recognised that these smaller groups were under-served. Independent Sector laments: '[G]enerally we feel like we don't have enough small community-based organisations, or organisations that have limited staff as a part of our membership or participation. That's an area where we feel like we need to grow'.[42] The state-level nonprofit associations were more likely to offer resources around fund development, basic organisational management and governance that are useful to smaller and start-up nonprofits. Independent Sector's Director of Policy Development and Analysis explains:

> People would say, 'I have a passion, I have a grand idea. I'm starting a nonprofit, I'd like for you to give me funding'. The first thing I try to do is have a conversation about the value of

collaboration and partnerships with existing organisations, before they fully launch into their new venture. I almost always failed, because everybody thinks they can do it better.[43]

Support organisations serving nonprofits tend to get inquiries from smaller, start-up nonprofits who have a working board in charge of day-to-day operations and who need help with governance and systems building.[44]

While national-level support organisations welcome small organisations as members, most report that these groups do not see the value in membership. Independent Sector explained,

> It's usually the larger organisations engaging with us more frequently. I think in part because they have the capacity to think about issues on a more regular basis, than maybe the organisations that are local and on the ground and sort of like, 'I got too much to worry about'.[45]

However, many support organisations offer membership on a sliding scale based on operating budget as a way to attract smaller organisations, and some have started to offer individual memberships. Global PDX found that once it offered an individual-level membership, that organisations of GINGO size tended to join as individuals rather than as organisations in order to reduce the cost, which the Coordinator says was expected: 'That's fine. They're still engaged and we're still supporting them'.[46]

Though seeking to make membership affordable, support organisations vary in how they conduct outreach and target their membership, but the majority do not have systematic strategies to target GINGOs. Support organisations called outreach 'organic'.[47] Many of the support organisations observed that while they use different methods to 'make the case of why there's value of engaging' as a member[48] and seem to 'always sort of [be] pitching' membership and participation,[49] they noted it often is conveyed via word of mouth from peer organisations.[50] Others note that even while there is no specific outreach to GINGOs, GINGOs also did not seek them out. A state-level international development organisation reported occasionally seeing GINGOs request assistance, but that these overtures were the exception rather than the rule.

Other ways in which nonprofits are drawn to support organisations are through services and resources such as access to listservs,[51] job postings,[52] bundling services for members (eg group purchasing programmes)[53] and participating in events such as legal audit clinics.[54] Still, in the end, none of these services and resources are segmented according to member type, nor are any targeted to GINGOs, with the exception of the Posner Center (see Box 1).

What do support organisations offer their membership?

If support organisations are not yet targeting GINGOs, do they offer resources that could help these organisations overcome their weaknesses as development actors? We found that support organisations offer a number of resources to address the sector's problems of amateurism, issues about material scarcity and, to some degree, fragmentation – particularly in the area of organisational management. The support organisations we interviewed collectively offer training and compendia of best practices, opportunities for networking, informational resources, and representation vis-à-vis government and other outside bodies.

Training programmes

Capacity building is a central task for support organisations. One vice president of a nonprofit state association explains: '[We seek] to help nonprofits reach their full potential. We're capacity builders at the heart so our goal is to try to bring together as many resources as we can to support nonprofits and all of their diverse needs'.[55] Support organisations often make these training programmes available to the public for a small fee, often with discounts or fee waivers for their members.

In-person workshops and conferences are the traditional techniques for offering training. Since support organisations serve nonprofits working in a variety of fields, such trainings often are centred on governance and management topics. Every nonprofit-oriented support organisation offered training in board and leadership development, financial management, fund development, strategic planning, and monitoring and evaluation. Additionally, support organisations often respond to demands for specific skill sets expressed by membership. The Minnesota International NGO Network's president reported that members identify needs for training that include fundraising, monitoring and evaluation, communication and marketing.[56] Organisations exclusively supporting international development organisations offered training on topics relevant to international work, such as using geographic information systems (GIS) and impact evaluation in low-resource settings. But except for the International Network for Education in Emergencies,[57] which focuses on the education sector, these internationally oriented organisations offered limited training on specific development sectors, likely because their membership did not achieve the critical mass to demand training in any one development area.

Training models often emphasise peer learning. Independent Sector and Forefront, both nonprofit-serving organisations, run cohort-based programmes that bring leaders together for a series of training sessions. Forefront's Director of Education explains:

> We have found that there's a lot of benefits to that experience of moving through the cohort together. There's that networking that happens, there's the community building that happens. There's a lot of cross-pollinating that starts to happen, especially when we're focused.[58]

Here, networking is integrated into trainings for capacity building, as will be further discussed in the following section.

Forefront also has what it calls a 'micro-mentorship program', with a database of peer advisers.[59] Nonprofit leaders submit to Forefront a request for a consultation with a peer advisor. Forefront searches among its members for a match, and the advisor and advisee meet for a two-hour consultation session. Likewise, BoardSource has created an online service called 'community exchange' which promotes peer exchanges for training purposes. The Director of Education explains: 'through our website, [...] members can sign up, ask each other questions, [and] interact with BoardSource on certain issues' in order to further build their capacity.[60]

Networking and peer-building programmes

The examples of Independent Sector, Forefront and BoardSource suggest support organisations' goals of capacity building and network building are closely linked. Virtually all of the organisations we interviewed named 'connecting' or 'networking' their members as a goal. For example, the New York Council of Nonprofits seeks 'to create community',[61] whereas Forefront in Chicago was initially started to serve foundations and wanted 'to build community amongst their grantees and [build] a network'.[62] Other terms that emerged in interviews included 'communities of practice' to create learning opportunities[63] and spaces like conferences as 'opportunities to connect'.[64] Support organisations want to serve as a 'connector',[65] engage in 'facilitating learning',[66] 'creat[e] a community [to] forge relationships'[67] and form 'clubs' and 'affinity groups' among non-profit leaders.[68]

Why networking? The previous section suggests that networks are an important conduit for peer-based capacity building and learning. Some international development support organisations offered thematic networks or working groups on areas such as monitoring and evaluation, water, and gender and inclusive development. The Director from Independent Sector argued that networks are especially important to support organisations because they provide a structure to transmit the knowledge and skills that are especially salient for members. Other support organisations reflected that creating spaces for networking might specifically address challenges created by GINGOs' dispersal and inexperience. For example, Global PDX's Coordinator explained:

> I think people operate in silos, and so again, they think they're the only person doing something. We have a lot of folks around here who have created a 501(c)(3) [nonprofit organisation] because they have a passion for a certain community, or a passion for a certain approach or whatever, but they may not necessarily know what they're doing.[69]

National-level organisations are also keen to use networks for agenda-setting. International Network for Education in Emergencies convenes several smaller networks among its members. Its Working Group on Standards and Practices generated the Minimum Standards on Education in Emergencies that are meant to guide governments and NGOs working in disaster and post-conflict settings.[70] Independent Sector relied on state- and city-level networks to convene nonprofit organisations in a set of town-hall meetings that helped generate a set of sector-wide accountability standards in 2005.[71]

While shared tasks and structured programmes can help NGOs build their networks, the Posner Center's model of shared space provides additional informal opportunities for networking. Posner describes itself as a 'themed center', not just a joint workplace. It seeks to create 'an environment for sharing'.[72] It draws on techniques used by incubators and Silicon Valley firms to bring their members together. The Program Director explains:

> [I]t's about bringing together the community. [...] Programmatically, every Wednesday, we do cookie 30. Every Wednesday at 2:30, we convene for cookies [...] like a popup party of 15 or 20 minutes and then people go back to their desks. That's a conven[ing] thing that we do.[73]

Sharing information

In addition to capacity building and networking, most of the support organisations provide informational resources to both members and other stakeholders. Two organisations have member-only Facebook pages, where members can share information and post questions.[74] Other organisations described sharing information through member-only reports, newsletters and webpages.[75] Additional resources provided might be job boards, access to online knowledge centres or libraries and available pro bono legal services.

Some support organisations have also sought to provide informational resources (and trainings) to organisations outside of nonprofit organisations, such as to industries that might serve their nonprofit members. For example, Independent Sector has provided information and training to lawyers and accountants about issues related to the nonprofit sector. Others have the logic that getting the word out to external stakeholders about their members will help with revenue and fund development, even when they themselves do not fundraise or provide grants for their membership. The Executive Director of Global Washington said,

> The one commonality across all NGOs is they want fundraising. They want more donations. We don't do fundraising for our members. We don't do grant making, but what we've realised is we have an expertise to raise the profile of our members with a donor audience. We've structured our work now around publicity campaigns to really focus in on our members doing work.[76]

In fact, several organisations reported that resources related to funding are especially important to their members.[77] Colorado Nonprofits circulates funding announcements to its members, while Forefront has provided donor databases to its nonprofit members since the 1970s, when such databases were printed hard-copy lists gathered in binders. However, most support organisations do not themselves offer funding resources. An exception is that the Posner Center has experimented with a small grant programme of $3,000 to $20,000 to encourage collaboration among its members.

All of the support organisations we interviewed have moved to offering resource exchange programmes via online platforms. This includes using webinars, podcasts and LinkedIn spaces, for example.[78] The Boston Network for International Development provides a large amount of open-sourced information across three categories to achieve its objective to be an online network hub with a database of organisations that is fairly updated and robust, a calendar of events, and a database of job openings for organisations, both full-time, paid professional jobs and different volunteer opportunities in international development.[79] These methods of offering resources online and allowing organisations to connect across distance may be well suited to geographically dispersed GINGOs.

Discussion

GINGOs are small-scale development actors with expressive and voluntaristic characteristics. We contend that in order to be effective development actors, they must overcome a number of weaknesses. Having identified support organisations as the bodies best positioned to work with geographically dispersed GINGOs, we turned to the question of whether and how these support organisations can help GINGOs overcome these weaknesses. We found that at present, support organisations do not regularly serve GINGOs. Often, support organisations have diverse membership bases and offer a wide range of services. Services related to trainings for capacity building and opportunities for networking did not have strict boundaries; rather, many capacity-building opportunities were linked to networking and vice versa. Informational resources are similarly linked to other services and are not only one-directional (ie from support organisations to membership); exchanges among peers for learning are increasingly encouraged. Furthermore, various online platforms are being explored to better build capacity and serve the NGO and nonprofit sector.

While we find that support organisations often do not target membership types or segment their services for organisations like GINGOs, the services they provide might mediate some of the challenges that GINGOs face. We contend that of the challenges which Brown and Kalegaonkar outline, support organisations are best positioned to address *amateurism, material scarcity* and (to some extent) *fragmentation* among GINGOs. We found that support organisations are less able to address issues of *paternalism* and *restricted focus* (see Table 2).[80]

The issues related to *amateurism*, particularly weak organisational management and, more commonly, limited experience in development aid work, can further be addressed through training and capacity building. GINGOs are often willing to reinvent the wheel, as long as it is their 'own' wheel. However, these volunteer-run organisations also are similar to other types of small nonprofits in that they tend to need management skills such as financial management, board governance and systems building. Furthermore, while many GINGO volunteers have limited experience in managing a nonprofit organisation, they likely have little expertise in international development. Technical skills related to international development, such as latrine construction or bore well design, represent knowledge that GINGOs might well need but which is in limited supply from support organisations. In fact, support organisations are not the best suited to resolve these *types* of amateurism. Even support organisations that serve NGOs in international development note that they mostly provide their membership with organisational management capacity building such as fundraising, monitoring and evaluation, communication and marketing. The Posner Center might provide the best model for serving needs related to amateurism: it intentionally brings together GINGOs and larger NGOs in ways that allow for informal and peer learning. The co-working model used by Posner relies on larger, more experienced development NGOs to bear a significant financial burden to maintain the space, so while promising, this model is difficult to replicate.

Material scarcity is a reality for GINGOs given their lean budgets. While (again, besides Posner) support organisations did not often provide financial resources, more access to learning and informational resources about fund development might be an area where support organisations can better serve GINGOs. Like many new nonprofits, GINGOs often begin to explore grant funding after an initial phase of individual fundraising. Support organisations might be able to help GINGOs understand that fund development entails more than grant writing, and identify more realistic funding models. Based on our research, grants are likely not a viable or sustainable revenue source for organisations like GINGOs. This provides an example of when support organisations might be able to in part help GINGOs recognise and understand their identity within the broader organisational field of nonprofits and NGOs. GINGOs in practice are expressive, volunteer-based organisations, and as such we contend

Table 2. Potential of support organisations for building the capacity of grassroots international non-governmental organisations (GINGOs).

GINGO weakness[1]	Potential of support organisations to address it
Amateurism	*Mixed*: Support organisations' services can be high for managerial and administrative areas, but lower for technical development skills.
Material scarcity	*Moderate*: Support organisations can direct GINGOs to realistic funding models and sound financial management practices.
Fragmentation	*Moderate*: Support organisations offer good opportunities for convening. Peer and online models are useful here. Mechanisms for improving coordination in aid-receiving countries are needed.
Paternalism	*Low*: State and national-level international development support organisations are more likely to address this issue, but differences among professionalised NGOs and GINGOs require different interventions.
Restricted focus	*Low*: GINGOs are unlikely to overcome this without major increases in budget and staffing.

[1]Drawing on weaknesses internal to the nonprofit sector as discussed by Brown and Kalegaonkar, "Support Organizations and the Evolution of the NGO Sector."

that they are not best suited to write or, if awarded, to manage grants. Support organisations might also address material scarcity through peer learning, as managing finances in international contexts provides particular challenges, especially for those accustomed to Global North practices of banking and purchasing. GINGOs can learn a good deal from peers about the realities of financial management in the field of development.

While support organisations provide good networking opportunities, we question whether or not GINGOs would engage in networking to access expertise and experience given their *fragmentation*. However, potential solutions to these realities are peer-to-peer learning models promoted by support organisations and online opportunities. Peer learning and online platforms such as webinars, livestream training, and perhaps more flexible online forums and exchanges among peers could help engage GINGO volunteers in networking spaces, even if their geographic dispersal in the US encourages their fragmentation and isolation.

Finally, the selected support organisations are not poised to fully address all of GINGOs' weaknesses. GINGOs design projects around the interests of their volunteers and donors; yet, arguably, larger NGOs do the same. More specific to the GINGO model, these challenges are a result of searching for emotional connection with others in the Global South. Therefore, there is a risk that GINGO leaders can neglect how their own efforts relate to broader power relations and the structural constraints on development. The personalised approach to development aid by GINGOs further propels the challenge of *paternalism*. GINGO volunteers in the Global North are making decisions within uncertain environments; at best, they might not know the context where they are working well enough to make effective decisions, and at worst, may implicitly or explicitly disregard the local knowledge and capacity of their Global South recipient communities when making decisions.

Given these consequences, how might support organisations provide spaces that allow GINGOs to critically reflect on their role as development actors? Conversations among NGOs about their failures and about the inherent contradictions of development work are difficult, even for organisations committed to critical reflection. When these conversations are facilitated by support organisations, they happen in smaller settings, usually among peers of professionalised organisations. Support organisations face a challenge in convening GINGOs; since the latter are are motivated by expressive rationales they likely require different interventions in order to reflect on the contradictions and shortcomings of their work. Finally, the issue of *restricted focus* is inherent in the GINGO model; thus, we would argue that, considering GINGOs are in the 'first generation' of development strategies as mentioned, 'solving' this issue is not a priority for support organisations.

Conclusion

We found that there is limited interaction between support organisations and GINGOs. However, our research suggests that there are practices and resources provided by support organisations that might serve GINGOs in addressing their inherent weaknesses in aid provision. Support organisations' services can help GINGOs in operational and management functions, though we find fewer opportunities that address GINGOs' technical skills in the development field. And we suspect that very few support organisations have taken on any leadership in facilitating GINGOs to critically reflect on their functions and approaches in the larger development arena. The means by which support organisations could serve GINGOs, through peer learning and online opportunities in particular, would allow for building capacity and provide potential spaces of reflection about political and social contexts where GINGOs are serving, even while maintaining GINGOs' expressive and voluntaristic characteristics, keeping them distinct from other types of development actors.

We note the limitations of our exploratory study. First, we sought to understand what GINGOs might need in order to be effective development actors. Further empirical research on the operations and development outcomes of GINGOs and other citizen aid groups will allow us to refine our recommendations. Next steps should include the collection of further survey and interview data from GINGO leaders and leaders of other types of citizen aid groups. We encourage, using similar data-collection instruments, more robust comparative research on GINGOs in the US and citizen aid groups in other contexts. Second, our analysis focused on the possibilities for building GINGOs' capacity 'at home'. This research does not capture any relationships or networks in the distant places where GINGOs are operating. We assume these are less common given that GINGO leaders spend only weeks or months each year at their project sites, leaving limited time for on-site networking and learning. However, some GINGOs have noted possibilities of on-site learning; for example, one leader stated, 'It's just easier to brainstorm with people [in Kenya] than back here [in Buffalo, New York]'.[81] The extent of networking and shared or peer learning on the ground in the Global South by GINGOs and its link to building capacity deserves further research attention.

We contend that the field of development needs to explore further opportunities that build the capacity of citizen aid through GINGOs and similar groups. As we observe, GINGOs and citizen aid more broadly are often defined by expressive and voluntaristic characteristics rather than instrumental action. Nevertheless, whatever their size and however great their passion, development actors owe their partners more than reinventing the wheel.

Disclosure statement

No potential conflict of interest was reported by the authors.

Acknowledgements

The authors thank The RGK Center for Philanthropy and Community Service at the University of Texas at Austin for the RGK-ARNOVA President's Award in 2017, which provided seed funding for this research. The authors would also like to thank the anonymous reviewers for their helpful and actionable comments that produced an improved final version of the paper. In addition, they thank the Guest Editors, professors Anne-Meike Fechter and Anke Schwittay, for their leadership in organising this special issue and their support during the review process.

Notes

1. Schnable, "New American Relief and Development Organizations."
2. For a larger discussion on the intersection of the personal and the professional in aid work, see Fechter, "The Personal and the Professional"; and Chambers, "Responsible Well-Being."
3. We dub these groups 'grassroots international NGOs' to acknowledge their similarity in purpose and sources of public legitimacy to international NGOs (INGOs). The adjective 'grassroots' signifies these organisations' small scale and do-it-yourself flavour, and emphasises that they typically work directly with recipients rather than through a long aid chain.
4. Schnable, "Projects, People, and Purposes."
5. Kinsbergen, "Behind the Pictures."
6. Haaland and Wallevik, "Citizens as Actors."
7. Berman, "Contemporary German MONGOs in Diani, Kenya." This present article is part of larger research projects by both authors on US-based GINGOs. See other articles in this issue for studies of citizen aid groups based outside the US, and see Fletcher and Schwittay's introductory essay for an overview of the theoretical and practical questions raised by citizen aid.
8. Kinsbergen, "Behind the Pictures"; Schulpen and Kinsbergen, "50+ and Sexy?"
9. Korten, *Getting to the 21st Century*.
10. Schnable, "Projects, People, and Purposes."
11. Schnable, "Do-It-Yourself Aid."
12. Kinsbergen, this issue.
13. Appe and Telch, "Grassroots International NGOs."
14. Schnable, "Do-It-Yourself Aid."
15. Kinsbergen, "Behind the Pictures."
16. Schnable, "New American Relief and Development Organizations."
17. While research on capacity building for small nonprofit organisations is sparse, Kapucu, Healy, and Arslan provide one of the few empirical studies. They studied capacity building by a university to a defined group of small nonprofits – food banks – which are members of a regional food bank network in Central Florida. Therefore, distinct from GINGOs, these small nonprofits were defined as a network through membership and are also defined by a confined geographical area. Kapucu and colleagues found that funding was the main motivator for small nonprofit organisations to participate in capacity building. See Kapucu, Healy, and Arslan, "Survival of the Fittest."
18. Fylkesnes, "Motivation behind Norwegian Citizen Initiatives."
19. Conran, "They Really Love Me!"
20. Kinsbergen, "Behind the Pictures."
21. Mostafanezhad, "Getting in Touch."
22. Haaland and Wallevik, "Citizens as Actors."
23. Mostafanezhad, "Getting in Touch."
24. Appe and Telch, "Grassroots International NGOs."
25. Schnable, "Do-It-Yourself Aid."
26. Appe and Telch, "Grassroots International NGOs."
27. Schnable, "Do-It-Yourself Aid."
28. Frumkin, *On Being Nonprofit*.
29. Brown and Korten, *Understanding Voluntary Organizations*.

30. Brown and Kalegaonkar, "Support Organizations and the Evolution of the NGO Sector." There are other actors that might build the capacity of GINGOs: universities, chambers of commerce, foundations, research institutes, trade or professional organisations. To date we have seen little evidence for this in our interviews and fieldwork with GINGOs. Given our findings here, online networks and platforms independent of support organisations deserve further attention.
31. Abramson and McCarthy, "Infrastructure Organizations."
32. Brown and Kalegaonkar, "Support Organizations and the Evolution of the NGO Sector."
33. Ibid., 235.
34. Ibid.
35. Ibid.
36. Ibid., 235.
37. See https://www.councilofnonprofits.org/find-your-state-association
38. Miles and Huberman, *Qualitative Data Analysis*.
39. Authors' interview with Chief Executive Officer, Interaction, February 22, 2018.
40. Authors' interview with Executive Director, Global Washington, May 11, 2018.
41. Authors' interview with Coordinator for Standards and Practice, INEE, March 29, 2018.
42. Authors' interview with Director of Policy Development and Analysis, Independent Sector, March 6, 2018.
43. Ibid.
44. Authors' interview with Director of Education, BoardSource, March 19, 2018.
45. Authors' interview with Independent Sector.
46. Authors' interview with Coordinator, Global PDX, May 3, 2018.
47. Authors' interview with VP, Strategic Communications & Stakeholder Engagement, New York Council of Nonprofits, Inc., February 23, 2018.
48. Authors' interview with Interaction.
49. Authors' interview with Coordinator, Global PDX, May 3, 2018.
50. Authors' interviews with Statewide Membership Coordinator, Colorado Nonprofits Association, March 2, 2018; Posner Center, February 27, 2018; Coordinator, Accord, April 3, 2018; Independent Sector, Global PDX.
51. Authors' interviews with CEO, SID-W; personal communication, August 24, 2018; Colorado Nonprofits; Minnesota International NGO Network.
52. Authors' interviews with Executive Director, Boston Network for International Development, June 27, 2018; Minnesota International NGO Network.
53. Authors' interviews with CEO, CalNonprofits, August 7, 2018; New York Council of Nonprofits.
54. Authors' interview with Colorado Nonprofits.
55. Authors' interview with New York Council of Nonprofits.
56. Authors' interview with Minnesota International NGO Network.
57. Authors' interview with INEE.
58. Authors' interview with Director of Education, Forefront, March 15, 2018.
59. Authors' interview with Forefront.
60. Authors' interview with BoardSource.
61. Authors' interview with New York Council of Nonprofits.
62. Authors' interview with Forefront.
63. Authors' interview with Interaction.
64. Authors' interview with BoardSource.
65. Authors' interview with Global PDX.
66. Authors' interview with INEE.
67. Authors' interview with Accord.
68. Authors' interviews with Posner; Independent Sector.
69. Authors' interview with Global PDX.
70. Authors' interview with INEE.
71. Authors' interview with Independent Sector.
72. Authors' interview with Posner Center.
73. Ibid.

74. Authors' interviews with New York Council of Nonprofits Inc.; Minnesota International NGO Network.
75. Authors' interview with Minnesota International NGO Network.
76. Authors' interview with Global Washington.
77. Authors' interviews with Colorado Nonprofits; Posner; Forefront.
78. Authors' interview with Accord.
79. Authors' interview with Boston Network for International Development.
80. Brown and Kalegaonkar, "Support Organizations and the Evolution of the NGO Sector."
81. Authors' interview with GINGO founder, 25 July 2017.

Bibliography

Abramson, A., and R. McCarthy. "Infrastructure Organizations." In *The State of Nonprofit America* edited by L. Salamon, 423–458. Washington, DC: Brookings Institution, 2002.

Appe, S., and F. Telch. "Grassroots International NGOs: Using Comparative Interpretive Policy Analysis to Understand Meanings in Private Development Aid." *Journal for Comparative Policy Analysis: Research and Practice* (2019). doi:10.1080/13876988.2019.1582885.

Berman, N. "Contemporary German MONGOs in Diani, Kenya." In *German Philanthropy in Transatlantic Perspective*, edited by G.R. Witkowski and A Bauerkamper, 227–243. Berlin: Springer, 2016.

Brown, L. D., and A. Kalegaonkar. "Support Organizations and the Evolution of the NGO Sector." *Nonprofit and Voluntary Sector Quarterly* 31, no. 2 (2002): 231–258. doi:10.1177/0899764002312004.

Brown, L. D., and D. C. Korten. *Understanding Voluntary Organizations: Guidelines for Donors*. Policy, Planning and Research Working Papers no. WPS 258. Washington, DC: World Bank, 1989.

Chambers, R. "Responsible Well-Being – a Personal Agenda for Development." *World Development* 25 no. 11 (1997): 1743–1754. doi:10.1016/S0305-750X(97)10001-8.

Conran, M. "They Really Love Me! Intimacy in Volunteer Tourism." *Annals of Tourism Research* 38, no. 4 (2011): 1454–1473. doi:10.1016/j.annals.2011.03.014.

Fechter, A. "The Personal and the Professional: Aid Workers' Relationships and Values in the Development Process." *Third World Quarterly* 33 no. 8 (2012): 1387–1404. doi:10.1080/01436597.2012.698104.

Frumkin, P. *On Being Nonprofit: A Conceptual and Policy Primer*. Cambridge, MA: Harvard University Press, 2005.

Fylkesnes, J. "Motivation behind Norwegian Citizen Initiatives in the Gambia: A Case Study." Paper presented at Citizen Aid and Grassroots Humanitarianism: Development Futures?, University of Sussex, April 19, 2018.

Haaland, H., and H. Wallevik. "Citizens as Actors in the Development Field: The Case of an Accidental Aid-Agent's Activities in Aid-Land." *Forum for Development Studies* 44, no. 2 (2017): 203–222. doi:10.1080/08039410.2017.1305444.

Kapucu, N., B. F. Healy, and T. Arslan. "Survival of the Fittest: Capacity Building for Small Nonprofit Organizations." *Evaluation and Program Planning* 34, no. 3 (2011): 236–245. doi:10.1016/j.evalprogplan.2011.03.005.

Kinsbergen, S. "Behind the Pictures: Understanding Private Development Initiatives." PhD diss., Radboud University, The Netherlands, 2014.

Korten, D. C. *Getting to the 21st Century: Voluntary Action and the Global Agenda*. Sterling, VA: Kumarian Press, 1990.

Miles, M. B., and A. M. Huberman. *Qualitative Data Analysis: An Expanded Sourcebook*. Thousand Oaks, CA: Sage, 1994.

Mostafanezhad, M. "Getting in Touch with Your Inner Angelina: Celebrity Humanitarianism and the Cultural Politics of Gendered Generosity in Volunteer Tourism." *Third World Quarterly* 34, no. 3 (2013): 485–489. doi:10.1080/01436597.2013.785343.

Schnable, A. "Do-it-Yourself Aid: The Emergence of American Grassroots Development Organizations." PhD diss., Princeton University, 2015.

Schnable, A. "New American Relief and Development Organizations: Voluntarizing Global Aid." *Social Problems* 62, no. 2 (2015): 309–329. doi:10.1093/socpro/spv005.

Schnable, A. "The Projects, People, and Purposes of American Grassroots International NGOs: Evidence from a National Sample." Paper presented at the European Association of Development Institutes (EADI) Conference, Bergen, Norway, August 21, 2017.

Schulpen, L. and Kinsbergen, S. "50+ and Sexy? Ten Years of Research on Dutch Private Development Initiatives." Paper presented at the ISTR International Conference, Stockholm, June 28, 2016.

The legitimacy of Dutch do-it-yourself initiatives in Kwale County, Kenya

Sara Kinsbergen

ABSTRACT
Established development organisations face a long-standing legitimacy crisis for not living up to the expectations once set. Meanwhile, thousands of small-scale, voluntary development organisations – referred to as Private Development Initiatives (PDIs) – have joined the field of international development. In this article, I examine the legitimacy of their acts from a local government perspective based on an analysis of four dimensions of legitimacy: regulatory, pragmatic, normative and cognitive legitimacy. The study took place in May 2017 in the Kenyan coastal county of Kwale. A range of government officials were interviewed on how they perceive the interventions of international development organisations in general, and Dutch PDIs in particular, and on their cooperation with these development actors. The study shows that, although many of these PDIs operate in areas that fall under the responsibility of the local government, most of them have a rather limited cooperation with the local government, putting their legitimacy in the eyes of local government officials at stake.

Introduction

This study is based in Kwale County, the most southern coastal county of Kenya, an area of 8270 km² and about 650,000 inhabitants.[1] With the beautiful white, sandy beaches of Diani, Kwale County is one of the top destinations for tourist visiting Kenya.[2] Diani Beach has been awarded 'Africa's leading beach destination' for the past five years. As a result, the hospitality sector is the number one provider of paid jobs.[3] Despite the benefits the county derives from being a popular tourist destination, of the 47 counties in Kenya, Kwale County is one of the five most deprived counties in terms of people living below the poverty line and inequality.[4] Kwale County can count on the support of a very large and diverse group of both national and international development actors in battling poverty, inequality and exclusion. From large-scale bilateral players such as United States Agency for International Development (USAID) and Danish International Development Agency (DANIDA) to small-scale do-it-yourself type of organisations, all of these are active in the county. The composition of the field of development actors there forms a perfect reflection of the changing aid architecture and hence allows for studying a new set of research questions this raises.

Kwale County provides an appropriate case study as it demonstrates that the once relatively uncomplicated reality of (inter)governmental agencies and NGOs as main actors in development is challenged by an ever-growing number of a more diverse group of actors entering the field, each with their own motives and modus operandi. This challenges the notion of international development as a community of actors with a shared language, values or standards, and working methods, as described by Develtere.[5] Besides, new actors contest the existing monopoly of traditional development actors and increasingly turn the development community into an arena characterised by competition for funding, legitimacy and even recipients.[6] This amalgam of actors brings along a new range of research questions. From the perception of the Global North, where many, but certainly not all, of these new actors originate from, these include questions about the distinctive character and role of these actors, the type of synergies and innovation, if any, resulting from this and donors' responses to competitive funding requests from both established and new actors.[7]

From the perception of the aid receiving countries, questions on *relating to* and *governing of* this new aid architecture are very prominent. Studies on proliferation and fragmentation of the field of international development cooperation clearly show that the transaction costs resulting from the increasing number of donor agencies lead to serious, negative consequences for receiving countries. Overlap, duplication and high administration costs involved with managing different working methods, requirements and expectations of different (type of) donors are only some of the consequences.[8]

In this current research, the response of receiving countries towards this diversifying field is central. Specifically, in an exploratory manner, this article focuses on the perceptions of local government authorities in Kwale County with regard to one particular alternative development actor: small-scale, voluntary development organisations, referred to as Private Development Initiatives (PDIs). I focus here in particular on Dutch PDIs operating in the area, building on previous research.[9] This study aims to get a clear understanding of how local government authorities perceive the work of these organisations, and if, how and why they interact with them. The findings will be analysed from a legitimacy perspective. Starting from an understanding of legitimacy as a 'generalized perception [...] that the actions of an entity are desirable, proper or appropriate within a socially constructed system of norms, values, beliefs and definitions',[10] this study aims to broaden our understanding of the construct of PDI legitimacy through the eyes of local government officials.[11] Accordingly, in this analysis, the county government forms the legitimising audience.[12] I use the models of Lister[13] and, partly, Ossewaarde et al.[14] because both stress and incorporate the importance of perspective in their models. In a more or less similar manner, they distinguish between four different dimensions or sources of legitimacy: regulatory, pragmatic, normative and cognitive. Regulatory legitimacy refers to the conformity with regulatory institutions, rules and laws.[15] Pragmatic legitimacy questions if an organisation conforms to the demands of the legitimising audience; it thus rests on the self-interest of an organisation's audience.[16] Normative legitimacy deals with congruence between the values pursued by an organisation and wider 'societal' values; it is based on a collective account of responsibility for the fate of victims.[17] Ossewaarde et al.[18] conclude that mission statements of an international aid agency create a normative source of legitimacy. A final source of legitimacy – cognitive – is based on cognition, referring to 'mental models' of the stakeholders and the agency. It is not just

'Do we agree with the vision of this agency?' (normative legitimacy), but also 'Is this agency "one of us"'?[19] The question addressed here is what characteristics or behaviours the county government considers when assessing the legitimacy of PDIs.[20]

The background section will first provide a more in-depth understanding of the changing aid architecture with particular attention to PDIs as alternative development actors. This is followed by an introduction to Kwale County in general, and its development situation and development organisations' scenery in particular. Third, the research approach is introduced after which the findings of the study are presented, discussed and concluded.

Research context

In the past decade, the world of international development has undergone rapid changes, instigated by what is sometimes referred to as the 'triple revolution'.[21] This refers to the emergence of new development goals (global collective action problems such as pandemics, climate change, energy crisis); the rise of new development actors; and the growing number of new development instruments, a trend also referred to as innovative development finance.[22] This study takes as its starting point the second aspect of the revolution: the increase in number and diversity of players in the field of international development. In academia there is a growing attention for the emergence, role and position of new(ly recognised) actors such as emerging state actors (e.g. China) and more unusual suspects such as celebrity humanitarians and private foundations.[23] Conventionally, three aid channels are distinguished. First, there is the bilateral aid channel, referring to government-to-government support. Second, the bilateral aid channel refers to intergovernmental organisations such as the World Bank and the UN. Finally, there is the civilateral channel including civil society organisations, most often grouped under the heading of non-governmental organisations (NGOs). Actors in these three channels are seen as 'traditional donors' in the sense that they find 'their raison d'être in international development co-operation' and they essentially form 'one community [...] with a domain-specific set of values and norms, codes of conduct, and their own discourse and vocabulary'.[24] Interestingly, and indicative of their position in the field of international development, an omnipresent alternative actor in many Northern countries remains largely untouched: the thousands of ordinary individuals who actively engage in the fight against poverty by starting their own small-scale, voluntary development organisation. I refer to these organisations as PDIs.

In recent years, academic interest in this growing group of 'do-it-yourself' type of development organisations is increasing; with each scholar using its own terminology and definition.[25] The common denominator in this range of definitions is the small-scale (in terms of people involved and budget) and the voluntary character of these groups. With regards to the Netherlands, a PDI is defined as (1) a group of people who (2) give support in a direct way (3) to one or more developing countries. Accordingly, PDIs are not only active in the Netherlands and their task is not limited to (financially) supporting other Dutch development organisations. They offer (4) structural support for organisations, communities or groups of people rather than one-off, individual support. Added to this are three characteristics that clearly distinguish PDIs from established (or traditional) development organisations: PDIs (5) do not receive direct funds from the Ministry of Foreign Affairs, (6) are small in scale and (7) voluntary in character.[26] Small-scale is defined as having fewer than

20 regular members,[27] or an annual budget of less than 1 million euro. The voluntary character is defined on the basis of an upper limit of 20% or less of paid members in charge of the running of the organisation.[28] These demarcations are contestable. However, since organisations have to meet all seven criteria mentioned above to be referred to as a PDI, this group of organisations clearly distinguishes itself from more established development organisations or other alternative development actors.[29]

Two surveys among nearly 900 Dutch PDIs[30] show the following picture: run by, on average, four volunteers, Dutch PDIs spend on average 50,000 euro per year on development projects with a geographical concentration on Africa (e.g. Kenya, Ghana, Uganda) and Asia (e.g. Indonesia, India, Nepal). A large majority (94%) of PDIs is managed only by volunteers. Most Dutch PDIs are founded or run by older persons (55 years of age and above) and established mostly by apparent coincidence after a journey or longer stay in a developing country. For the largest part of their budget, PDIs depend on donations of private donors.[31]

Although PDIs are not a new phenomenon per se, the process of globalisation and economic prosperity in strongly individualised Northern societies has resulted in increased tourism and volunteering opportunities. This is confirmed by the two datasets showing that nearly 45% of the PDIs are established as a result of a holiday, volunteer work or internships in a developing country. In addition, this is reflected in the popular project countries of PDIs, with most of them being popular, long-haul holiday destinations.[32] These large-scale macro processes can hence be seen as important push factors for the 'mainstreaming' of the field international development.[33] Development projects and fundraising plans are designed in living rooms, churches or schools, and executed on a voluntary basis by ordinary citizens. Development cooperation is becoming more and more the task 'of all of us', taking place in everyday life.[34] A process also referred to as democratising development/foreign aid.[35]

However small these individual organisations are, studies' estimates on the (increasing) number of PDIs, the number of people involved and their estimated total budget illustrate that establishing and running a PDI is not anecdotal; they are increasingly present and visible.[36] For the Netherlands, a 2014 study showed 4% of the adult population (about half a million) to be actively involved in one (or more) of the several thousands of PDIs.[37] In 2015, Dutch PDIs received contributions of about 47 million euro from Dutch households.[38] In England and Wales, there were around 2300 internationally operating charities with a budget up to £100,000 in 1995. This number rose to over 10,000 in 2014, of which nearly half had a budget of £10,000.[39] A European mapping of PDIs concluded that PDIs 'are common and widespread throughout Europe, but under different labels, in different quantities, and often unknown as a concept or notion of its own'.[40] In the US, this type of 'do-it-yourself' development is increasingly recognised. Schnable[41] has shown there to be more than 11,000 registered American relief and development organisations of which nearly 60% (6600) have an annual budget less than US$25,000 and hence are presumably run exclusively by volunteers or at least 'bear heavy burdens of voluntary labor'.[42]

Roughly, PDI studies so far can be grouped in three categories: PDIs' *being* (mapping, typifying, coming of age), *doings* (interventions, sustainability, impact, accountability) and *relating* (with stakeholders such as beneficiaries, other development actors, back-donors). This current study belongs to the third category of studies and does so by focusing on the relations of PDIs with local (i.e. global south) governments.

PDIs and local government

The majority of PDIs' development interventions take place at a local (versus national or regional) level and can be characterised as 'service delivery' type of activities, with a large number of projects aiming at children and young people in the area of health care and education.[43] Therefore, most PDIs intervene in areas that generally (but not exclusively) belong to government jurisdiction. Considering this, cooperation between PDIs and local government authorities would therefore be expected. However, studies so far have found that many PDIs tend to ignore local government authorities.[44] As concluded by Appe and Telch, most PDIs keep the government 'at arm's length'.[45] In some cases, this is a deliberate act: they do not wish to cooperate with government officials because of their conviction that this involves corruption and unwanted bureaucracy. For others, working with the government is not how their organisation operates; they have not considered this and are not convinced, or even aware, of the possible necessity to do so. A larger group of PDIs maintains a consultative relationship with the local government in the area wherein they operate. They inform civil servants concerned on their presence and plans or request necessary information. In response to the question if they cooperate with the local government, the founder and manager of a Dutch PDI installing solar systems in primary and secondary schools in Western Kenya states:

> No. We do make ourselves known to the government. But we do not cooperate with them. If the government asks us something, we will do it. But we are not part of the local development programmes. That is because we do not trust the government. They like what we do, but we do not participate in their programmes. We only inform them on what we did. (Interview PDI founder 2010).

In existing studies, only a smaller group could be traced that actively cooperates with the government, with some PDIs establishing a Memorandum of Understanding with government authorities resulting in jointly designed, implemented and funded programmes and others actively trying to influence government policy.

Kwale County's current status

The passing of the Kenyan constitution in 2010 was the start of a process of decentralisation, referred to as 'devolution': transferring power and resources to local governments.[46] Considering this new Kenyan government structure, studying the relation between PDIs and local government authorities becomes particularly pertinent. In the new government constituency, a range of government functions previously belonging to the responsibility of the national government, have been devolved to the 47 counties in the country.[47] Among these functions are agriculture, health, transport and pre-primary education, village polytechnics, home craft centres and childcare facilities. After the 2013 general elections, the first county governments came into office. One of the first tasks of county governments was drafting a five-year (2013–2017) County Integrated Development Plan (CIDP). This plan, starting from a participatory assessment of the development state of the county, offers an overall framework for development. It aims to co-ordinate the work of both levels of the government in a coherent plan to improve the quality of life for all the people. The plan and budgeting resulted from an extensive, active consultation of the local population.

Kenyan citizens have the mandate to hold the government accountable and the government is obliged to report, both on short- and long-term results, to its citizens.[48] Kwale County published its first CIDP in 2013 (2013–2017) and second in 2018 (2018–2022).[49]

Both of these CIDPs, and data of the Kenyan Bureau of Statistics, show that Kwale County faces considerable challenges in terms of socio-economic development of its population. Despite the revenues Kwale County receives via tourism, Kwale is still one of the more deprived of the 47 counties of Kenya: 71% of the population of Kwale County lives below the poverty line compared to 45.9% of the Kenyan population. Moreover, in terms of employment, education, water and sanitation, the living conditions of Kwale's inhabitants are worse compared to other counties.[50] In her historical account, Berman explains in great detail how the coastline of Kwale County, in particular the village of Diani, became an important tourism destination, with Germany in particular heavily investing in tourism infrastructure from the early 1960s onwards. Two main reasons can be distilled explaining why this did not result in a more prosperous state of the county and its population. First, as Berman explains, during the 1980s and 1990s 'building boom', (illegal) land transactions were the order of the day in the Diani area, leaving many local villagers, mainly Digo, landless. As a result, the large influx of tourist did not so much result in increased living standards for the local population, but in a more deprived position.[51] Currently, most hotels are owned and/or managed by foreigners or upcountry Kenyans, meaning a large part of the revenue leaves the county.[52] Second, the hospitality sector caters for the largest part of household income stemming from wage earnings. However, wage earnings make up only 8.6% of the average household income.[53] So only a small part of the county's population directly benefits from incomes generated through tourism.

Whereas unequal distribution of revenues stemming from tourism cannot be referred to as the single origin of Kwale County's present-day situation, it is against this background one should understand the current situation of the county, the challenges the county government is confronted with and the (potential) role development actors can take up in Kwale.

Kwale County and the development architecture

Available government resources are inadequate for achieving the goals set in the CIDP but Kwale County is home to a large and very diverse group of international development actors bringing in large amounts of extra resources.[54] An exhaustive overview of players, their budget and areas of intervention is not available. Nevertheless, Table 1 gives a snapshot of the range of development actors which this current study came across. These are actors that are currently working in the county, or have done so in the recent past. This mapping, as is the study, focused on international development agencies. This overview shows that all different types of development actors are present in the county.

What is particularly striking in the mapping of Kwale County's development scenery is the high density of PDIs operating in Kwale County. This is a direct result of Kwale being a popular tourist destination, with many of these tourists starting their own foundation in the aftermath of their visit.[55] In countries located in what is currently referred to or perceived as the Global South, being a tourism hotspot (countries, regions or towns) often coincides

Table 1. Overview of development scenery Kwale County.

Bilateral	Multilateral	Civilateral	Philanteral
DANIDA (Denmark)	World Bank	Plan International	Agha Khan Foundation
USAID (USA)	IOM	Red Cross International	Base Titanium
GIZ (Germany)	UNDP	ACT International	Several hundreds of PDIs from different nationalities (e.g. Belgium, Germany, UK, the Netherlands)
EU (European Development Fund)	Global Environment Facility	WWF	
FORMIN (Finland)		Search for Common Ground	
SIDA (Sweden)		Agha Khan Foundation	

Source: Interviews Kwale 2017, complemented with web-based search.

with a high density of PDI activity. Examples of this are Gambia, Bali (Indonesia), Moshi (Tanzania), Cape Coast (Ghana), Cusco (Peru) and Antigua (Guatemala).[56] Kwale County forms no exception to this rule. In *Germans on the Kenyan Coast*, Berman describes how interwoven the areas of development ('charity' in her account) and tourism are in Kwale County. She describes how 'many tourist [...] feel compelled to improve the living conditions of African Kenyans and engage in humanitarian aid activities'.[57] An expat living in Kwale County and involved in a charity himself explains the large number of visitors getting involved in a PDI:

> they [tourists] spend ten days in an all-in resort. At the end of their stay, they feel the need to go out and visit an orphanage or a school. They buy some pens or candies for the kids as a way to buy off their guilt. (Informal conversation founder PDI)

Establishing and developing relations with this large and diverse group of development actors is clearly work in progress for the government of Kwale. This can be seen from a comparison of the first and second CIDP. In the first CIDP, the section 'resource mobilisation' does not explicitly mention civil society actors as partners bringing in resources that can be deployed in reaching government plans.[58] Interestingly, the second CIDP does mention 'non-state actors' as stakeholders in achieving the county goals. The documents states that 'they [non-state actors] will be encouraged to invest in governance and development sectors of choice especially on *capacity building* of county governance structures and communities they work with'.[59] 'The following roles for non-state actors are being distinguished: play a critical role in *supporting policy formulation processes*, *financing* projects and programmes, providing *civic education* to the citizenry, providing *watchdog roles*, conducting or supporting *surveys and researches* and development as well as supporting *resource mobilization activities*'.[60]

Achieving this type of cooperation requires, first, that the government is aware of the presence and activities of these external development actors, and second, that such awareness can be translated into forms of coordination and alignment between the local government and the different external actors involved in development in the county. It is a challenging endeavour for the fairly young Kwale County government to ensure that this large in number and strongly diverse group of development actors contribute to reaching the CIDP and benefit the population of Kwale County.

Research approach

This exploratory study took place in May 2017 in the southern coastal county of Kwale County, Kenya. This site was selected because of its high concentration of development organisations in general and PDIs in particular.[61] First, I undertook a web-based mapping of Dutch PDIs operating in Kwale, including an overview of the main characteristics of these organisations. This allowed for obtaining a clear understanding of the presence of PDIs in the county. Their intervention areas, both thematic and geographical, the size of the organisations and historical origins were included in the mapping. Second, I carried out interviews with county government officials of different departments. Departments were chosen in accordance to the thematic orientation of PDIs including health and education. Interviewees were selected based on their function and role within the department. All were in positions where cooperation with development organisations would have been part of their role. Nine interviews took place with different ministers, directors and chief officers. By talking to different officials within one department, it aimed to get a comprehensive understanding of the relations between the government and PDIs. In the interviews with government officials, I focused on aspects of awareness, including if government officials were aware of or familiar with the presence of PDIs operating in Kwale County, and their possible cooperation and perceptions, that is, how government officials perceive the activities of PDIs and their relations with the county government. Although the focus of this study is on PDIs, conversations also turned to other, more established, development actors. This resulted in some, although tentative, comparisons of how PDIs relate to the county government and how established development actors do so.[62]

These interviews were complemented with analyses of government policy documents and interviews with three local small NGOs and one large NGO. In addition, this study builds on previous, qualitative and quantitative research on PDIs that included, among others, work done in Kwale County. All names of respondents and ministries have been anonymised to protect confidentiality.

Findings

The web-based mapping of Dutch PDIs operating in Kwale County resulted in an overview of 49 organisation currently operating in the area, as well as those that have been active in the recent past. These organisations were established in the period 1992–2017, and on average they have been working in the county for 11 years. Figure 1 illustrates the increase of Dutch PDIs working in Kwale. A large number ($n=32$) of these organisations intervene in the area of education, with over half also supporting projects with a different thematic orientation (such as health care). Twelve PDIs have a health care focus. A smaller number supports shelters for children and youngsters, income generating activities and water and sanitation projects. The mapping provides information of the 2016 annual budget of 30 of the organisations. Their annual budgets range from 2300 euro to 260,000 euro. The total annual budget of these organisations amounts to 1,669,420 million euro in 2016. This means that together these 30 PDIs spend on average 2.5 euro per inhabitant of Kwale County. This budget equals 12% of the government's budget for health care and education in that same period.[63] All of the PDIs involved in the study operate in areas that fall under responsibility of the county government, and hence cooperation with the county government would be

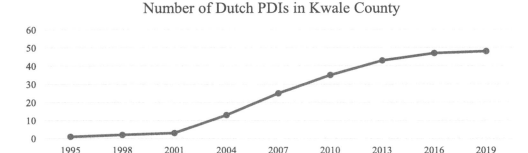

Figure 1. Number of Dutch PDIs in Kwale County. Source: Kinsbergen, PDI Database Kwale County 2017 [Datafile].

expected. For this reason, cooperation between PDIs and the county government is central to the study. For some of the PDIs it accounts that certain aspects of their work belong to the jurisdiction of the national government instead of the county government. However, considering the feasibility of the study, this cooperation is not included in the current study.

Awareness and cooperation

All interviewees were asked to list development actors they were aware of operating in Kwale County. While this resulted in a comprehensive mapping of the more established actors from the bi- and multilateral aid channel and more established NGOs, the number of PDIs mentioned by the interviewees, and in particular Dutch PDIs, did not reflect their actual number. From all the Dutch PDIs included in the mapping, only four of them were mentioned spontaneously. Whereas this might not be surprising considering the large number of small-scale organisations operating in the area, many of the organisations have a long track record and have been bringing in a considerable amount of money over the years. One could expect this to result in a certain level of awareness on the side of the government, or in cooperation between PDIs and the county government.

Interviewees' estimates on the number of development actors deliberately working within the framework of the CIDP range from 30–40%, with the exception of one interviewee who expected 70% are doing so. Government officials felt that many smaller organisations work their way around the local government. One of the interviewees recalled an organisation that had been working for 15 years in the area before coming to the attention of county officials. The method of working of a large majority of the PDIs could be described as taking place 'under the government radar'.

Most bi- and multilateral agencies and part of the established NGOs enter the county through the national government level. The national government in its turn refers these organisations to the county government. PDIs cooperating with the county government approach the government directly or do so via the sub-county level. Experiences from government officials show that the government's room to manoeuvre within the plans of international development agencies varies. The overall experience of government officials is that agencies entering government offices 'have their plan, they come to share' (Interview civil servant I). Informing is, according to most of the interviewees, an important reason for many agencies to make contact with local government offices. Several interviewees stress that often plans are already designed and budgets drafted before they approach the responsible department. In these cases, meeting with government officials appears as a formality they have to go through:

> They come to inform what and where they are planning programmes. They do not really come to ask for approval, they are just informing. (Interview civil servant II)

Although government officials are not of the impression that these agencies are actually asking for permission, some of them come in 'for a signature, to get their funding' (Interview civil servant I). Many institutional donors of these agencies request a formal document including a government signature as a proof of consent by the local government. While the number of PDIs mentioned is small, government officials have experience in cooperating with a number of them. Occasionally, more intensive cooperation takes place between county governments and PDIs. In these accounts, the overall process is as follows: a PDI approaches the government presenting their general plan and preferred working area. In response to this, the government representative brings in the plans of the county government or a specific department. Through discussion both parties look for synergies, draft a joint plan and share responsibilities. Several examples were given by government officials of more established development actors that ceased their activities or changed their plans in response to the new government structure, plans and corresponding roles for development actors:

> Before devolution, the county government had no resources to do so [service delivery]. Now they have. Therefore, some of the NGOs started to revise their strategic plan based on the new constitution. They became more active in the field of governance, capacity building of communities to take up their roles within the new constitution. (Interview civil servant III)

The second CIDP of Kwale County shows that when development actors are being included as (potential) partners in the government planning, it concerns mainly bi-, multi- and civilateral actors. No mention has been made of PDIs neither in the planning nor in the budgeting.[64]

Response of government

The above shows that overall the cooperation between county government and PDIs is limited. The response of government officials towards the seemingly evasive approach of PDIs could be best described as pragmatic: as one informant put it: 'what can we do about it?' (Interview civil servant III). Overall, three lines of reasoning could be distinguished in their responses. First, to a large extent, the government understands the reticence of development actors in general, and PDIs in particular, in cooperating with county government. They are aware of the bureaucratic image of the government and realise this is a reason for many organisations to avoid any form of cooperation or to restrict cooperation to informing responsible authorities on their plans.

Second, several interviewees feel that international agencies in general, and PDIs in particular, need to get used to the new Kenyan government structure. The devolvement of government functions to county level is not yet completely clear to all agencies. Current government structures and officials involved are still relatively new, so finding their way can be challenging. At the same time, they are confident that with time comes understanding and acceptance of the new structure from the side of (international) aid agencies. In addition, there is hope that the new government structure will bring an end to dominant notions of government authorities being corrupt, bureaucratic and thereby a partner to be avoided.

Finally, among the government officials there is awareness of and understanding for the agenda-setting reality of foreign development agencies which limits the room to manoeuvre for county government within the plans. As one of the interviewees mentioned, 'They [the organisations] have their mandate' (Interview civil servant V), determining their thematic orientation and regional focus. Therefore, he understands that at the moment when development agencies enter government offices, agencies' programs and projects are often already determined and not always (directly) support governments policy and plans. Another interviewee pointed to the strong influence of institutional donors who, in their home countries, influence the agenda, plans and budget of agencies. He referred to this as 'the long arm of the donor' (Interview civil servant V), resulting in a preference for programmes and projects that allow for 'quick wins'. He reflected on this by saying, with a shrugging of the shoulders: 'if you cannot beat the system' (Interview civil servant V).

Although there is understanding among government officials for a tendency among PDIs to avoid or limit their cooperation with county government authorities, in discussion it clearly emerged that they are convinced of the need for a closer cooperation. As one of the interviewees stated: 'You cannot just walk in and do what you want' (Interview civil servant VI).

This conviction comes not so much from a legal perspective. At the time of our study, the legal framework of the Public Benefit Organizations (PBO) Act in Kenya was under construction. Therefore, rules of engagement and the assignment of enforcement responsibility still had to be determined. Questions on what are the rules of engagement and what can hence be defined as 'legal' or 'illegal' operations of international aid agencies are open to discussion. Reflecting on the legal framework in the making, the respondents were not keen on drafting a framework with a strong focus on controlling and restricting, with the county government taking up the role of prefect. In addition, with the exception of one interviewee, none of them was in favour of budget support.

The urge of local government officials to enhance cooperation between PDIs and county government was strongly instigated from a development point of view. They aimed for a cooperation with all different stakeholders joining forces to reach the ambitious goals set in the CIDP. They highlighted several important downsides and consequences of non-existent or limited cooperation. Duplication and overlap where mentioned most frequently as negative consequences from a lack of cooperation. Not only did the interviewees consider this to result in inefficient and ineffective use of resources, but also in what they called 'community fatigue', due to the variety of actors operating in the same area, targeting the same people. In order to 'supplement the county [...] it is so good to consult' (Interview civil servant IV). Further, there is a conviction that synergies based on different competences can only come about when cooperation takes place. As one civil servant mentions: 'There are clear areas where NGOs would do better than the government'. He mentions strengthening governance structures, capacity building and accountability. In addition, he states that 'There are clear areas where government is better than NGOs, such as infrastructure'. Therefore, agencies should 'Identify and chose and fill the gaps. Building on the assessment from the government'. Finally, government officials mentioned several other roles they could undertake when cooperating. They could protect international agencies from local actors with suspicious reputation. It would allow them to advise and, where possible, co-finance.

And although not considered as their primary role, it would also allow them to control what type of interventions where supported or implemented, where and by whom. One of the interviewees sums up the importance of cooperation stating that it 'increases the legitimacy, credibility and trust of an organisation'.

Perception

Despite the strong belief of government officials in the importance of more intense cooperation between PDIs and the county government, and the finding that for a large number of PDIs this is limited, overall government officials are broadly positively inclined towards their presence. When reflecting on a potential exodus of PDIs working in Kwale, one interviewee responded: 'this deficit would not be easily filled. We do not pray for that'. This is confirmed by a civil servant from a different department who says 'Investments in [this department] are expensive. If they would leave, it would have a huge negative impact. The government does not have the capacity to take over'. Thus, although many of these PDIs do not directly align their interventions with the CIDP, there is a conviction that 'what they are doing is not irrelevant' (Interview civil servant VI). The needs of the local population are high, as several of the interviews mentioned, resulting in an overall pragmatic approach towards those bypassing government authorities or those approaching governments with plans that do not allow much room for alignment with government policy.

When talking with government officials on their relations with international agencies in general and PDIs in particular, this pragmatic approach is very apparent. Although formally in power, it feels as if the government is 'being governed' in part by the development actors. When questioned how they experience this and how it affects their operations, it becomes clear it frustrates them. Interviews with other, national and international, organisations painted Kwale County government as an ambitious, progressive government, committed to fully take up its role as a new government and determined to bring an end to perceptions of the government as being autocratic, bureaucratic and corrupt. They are concerned by the deprived situation of the county and dedicated to, through the CIDP, improve the living conditions of the population. For this purpose, they feel that strong ties with both national and international development agencies are required. Being confronted with many actors avoiding this cooperation is experienced as a serious challenge to the county government. When discussing this with the government official who was most outspoken on his feelings of frustration, he asked me whether I was a Christian. Without awaiting my response, he followed: 'The Integrated Development Plan [CIDP] is our Bible, when working here, your first priority should be the CIDP' (Interview civil servant II). He stressed the participatory consultation on which the CIDP is based, emphasising that the CIDP is not just a plan from the government, but a plan from the people of Kwale. He summarised his feeling saying: 'people, we survive with them'. This reaction is in line with the pragmatic response described above. A different type of cooperation between the county government and the much-needed development organisations is preferred by government officials. However, their overall feeling is that not much can practically be done to achieve this, and a pathway of enforcement is not considered desirable.

Legitimacy of PDIs

These findings allow for an initial analysis of the legitimacy of PDIs through the eyes of the government of Kwale County. As explained above, the question is what characteristics or behaviours does the county government consider when assessing the legitimacy of PDIs?[65] Following Lister[66] and Ossewaarde et al.,[67] four dimensions are being distinguished: regulatory, pragmatic, normative and cognitive. I will discuss the different sources of legitimacy in turn. The study shows that adherence to rules and regulations by PDIs was of less importance to the civil servants interviewed. Only members of the health department labelled certain interventions by PDIs firmly as, in their terms, 'illegal', such as distributing medicines with no medical professionals being involved. Lister[68] emphasises the dynamic character of legitimacy, with legitimacy of an actor variable over time through changes in the context and in the organisation. Considering that the PBO Act in Kenya is still under construction (at time of writing), the question is if in the near future regulatory legitimacy might gain importance, once the rules and regulations for international aid agencies are set.

All interviewees conclude that, from a normative and pragmatic point of view, PDIs can be considered to be a legitimate player. The demands in Kwale County are huge and diverse. Subsequently, values and missions of PDIs directly respond to the goals of the county government, relating to the normative dimension of legitimacy. In addition, because of the high needs, most interventions of PDIs target one or more areas that are of interest to the county government as well, referring to the pragmatic dimension of legitimacy. However, at the same time respondents underline that bypassing the county government implies the risk that interventions do not align with the priorities set in the CIDP, such as in terms of geographical and thematic focus, and type of interventions, and might even disturb government strategies. It does not allow for creating direct synergies between government plans and those of PDIs. In terms of pragmatic legitimacy, from the county governments' perception, a lot can be gained by starting or intensifying the cooperation between PDIs and government authorities.

The final source of legitimacy – cognitive – brings us to an interesting aspect of the legitimacy of PDIs. It becomes very apparent in this study that many PDIs are unknown to county government authorities. As described above, previous studies found that this is because some PDIs, deliberately or not, avoid the local government.[69] This study shows that lack of or limited cooperation between both is also caused by local government authorities not being aware of or identifying PDIs as part of Kwale's civil society community and thus as serious negotiating partners. This becomes apparent from the stakeholders' meetings held by some of the departments. Although a very small number of PDIs or their local counterparts were invited to and participate in the meetings, the majority are not targeted as potential contributors. Currently, these departmental meetings, also at county level, seem to be largely reserved for established development actors which the county government is familiar with. These are bi- and multilateral aid agencies which offer the county large budgets. For those PDIs and their local counterparts looking for sustainable ways of cooperating with the county government and other stakeholders in Kwale, this was a difficult, somewhat disappointing, experience. One can question if it is feasible and desirable to include the broad spectrum of development agencies in government consultation processes. At the same time, considering that the government budget is not sufficient to address the challenges identified in the CIDP, an open approach towards different types of, often smaller scale, unknown actors might be worth pursuing.

The coincidence of the government's pragmatic response and feelings of frustration brings us to the essence of the power play typical to aid giver–recipient relations. When needs are high and resources are not sufficient, how much room is there for governments to implement a different set of 'rules of engagement'? This might be particularly challenging in relations between PDIs and government officials in areas such as Kwale, were PDIs are not only resourceful as being 'givers of aid' but also as 'tourists'.

Conclusions

The findings show that aligning the plans and budgets of international aid agencies operating in Kwale into its CIDP is a challenging task. The high number and diversity of actors makes this a complex process. This turns out to be especially challenging when it concerns PDIs. Most of these small-scale voluntary development organisations operating in Kwale have limited relations with the county government. Whereas more established development actors are more likely to follow the formal routes, entering the county via the national government, many PDIs start working directly with their local counterparts. Although room for negotiating the plans of bi-, multilateral and established NGOs is limited at times, they make themselves and their plans known to the county government. This allows the government to, at least, take these plans into consideration when designing or implementing their own plans, minimising risks of duplication and overlap.

For PDIs, this working manner it is not self-evident.[70] First, PDIs might not see the added value in cooperating with the local government since many of them have been able to carry out their work without or with only limited cooperation. In addition, discussion with PDIs often show there is the fear that cooperation with the local government requires knowledge, skills and resources they might not possess. For those PDIs that look for cooperation with the county, there is the struggle of being acknowledged as a legitimate actor in the field. PDIs entering government authorities' offices are mostly unknown players to government officials. This is in contrast to, for example, the World Bank and Plan International. When PDIs arrive with small grants and are ignorant of appropriate channels and procedures, they might be considered 'illegitimate' in the eyes of the county government.

In conclusion, there is an interesting tension between the different sources of legitimacy of PDIs. In order for PDIs to gain in terms of pragmatic and normative legitimacy, they would have to invest in close cooperation with the county government and align their interventions consciously with the CIDP of Kwale County. But in order to do so, they would have to be recognised as a serious partner. The mapping from which this study starts can be helpful for the county government in identifying PDIs as an actual actor in Kwale's civil society landscape. Individually, these organisations might be small in size, but as a group they bring in a significant amount of resources to the county. At the same time, individual PDIs and PDIs as a group might want to position themselves and their operation as part of a broader picture and development agenda, acknowledging that in order to implement their individual missions, cooperation with the county government is a beneficial. By doing so, PDIs would gain in terms of cognitive legitimacy. Obviously, all this starts with PDIs operating in Kwale County to make themselves known to the county government. A regulatory framework that requests international aid agencies to register at county level could contribute to this.

In order for synergies to come about, government authorities should acknowledge PDIs as a serious stakeholder that can contribute to achieving the counties goal. PDIs, on the other hand, have to consider themselves as part of a larger community with government cooperation being a requirement.

This raises the question if PDIs are willing to intensify cooperation with the county government. How are their interests being served by staying under the legitimacy radar? Conversely, what do they stand to lose by giving up this position? And how does their 'coming-of-age' affect their interactions with government officials? To broaden our understanding, a follow-up research will take place closely studying the cooperation between PDIs and (local) government authorities in order to understand mechanism inhibiting, stimulating or facilitating cooperation.

Disclosure statement

No potential conflict of interest was reported by the author.

Acknowledgment

I thank Manouk Overkamp for her great support as my research assistant during fieldwork.

Funding

Funding has been provided by Wilde Ganzen Foundation.

Notes

1. Kwale County Integrated Development Plan 2018–2022, 14.
2. Worldtravelawards https://www.worldtravelawards.com/
3. County Government of Kwale, *First County Integrated Development Plan 2013*.
4. Kenya National Bureau of Statistics and Society for International Development, *Exploring Kenya's Inequality*, VI.
5. Develtere, *How Do We Help?* 78.
6. Ibid., 12, 39.
7. Kinsbergen and Tolsma, "Explaining Monetary Donations," 1572.
8. Schulpen et al., "Worse than Expected?" 322.
9. Kinsbergen and Plaisier, *Is Small Beautiful?*; Kinsbergen et al., "Understanding the Sustainability."
10. Suchman, "Managing Legitimacy," 574.
11. In order to get a comprehensive understanding of the legitimacy of PDIs, perspectives of other stakeholders, such as beneficiaries and other type of development agencies, are of great value

as well. However, in this current study, the perception of government officials is central to the analysis. As will be explained below, most interventions of PDIs belong to government jurisdiction. Therefore, studying PDI–government relations is of great importance and, so far, received little academic attention.

12. Lister, "NGO Legitimacy Technical Issue," 179.
13. Ibid., 180–1.
14. Ossewaarde et al., "Dynamics of NGO Legitimacy," 43–5.
15. See note 12 above.
16. See note 12 above.
17. Ossewaarde et al., "Dynamics of NGO Legitimacy," 44; Lister, "NGO Legitimacy Technical Issue," 179.
18. Lister, "NGO Legitimacy Technical Issue," 45.
19. Ibid., 182.
20. Ibid., 179.
21. Severino and Ray, "The End of ODA," 1.
22. Ibid., 8.
23. Schulpen et al., "Worse than Expected?" 323–6; Richey and Ponte, "New Actors and Alliances," 5–7; Dreher and Fuchs, "Rogue Aid?"
24. Develtere and De Bruyn, "Emergence of a Fourth Pillar," 913.
25. A selection of publications on PDIs: Develtere and De Bruyn, "Emergence of a Fourth Pillar"; Kinsbergen, *Behind the Pictures*; Schnable, "New American Relief and Development Organizations"; Fechter, "Brokering Transnational Flows of Care"; Appe and Telch, "Grassroot International NGOs"; Clifford, "International Charitable Connections."
26. Kinsbergen, *Behind the Pictures*, 57.
27. 'Member' refers to both paid and non-paid core members.
28. The demarcation of 'small-scale' and 'voluntary' is based on a comparison of organisations within the CIDIN PDI Database meeting up to criteria 1–5 with NGOs in the Netherlands (IS Academie NGO Database). Since organisations have to meet all seven criteria to be included in the study, the database includes organisations that are clearly distinguishable from more established development organisations. For example: those (rare) cases with a budget (close to) 1 million euro had to meet the voluntary criteria as well in order to be included.
29. This definition was formulated in the first large-scale academic study on PDIs and is applied since then in new studies. Dutch organisations involved in the support of PDIs make use of this definition, sometimes in a slightly adapted way. Kinsbergen, *Behind the Pictures*, 57.
30. CIDIN-PDI Database 2008–2009; Kinsbergen PDI Database 2017.
31. Kinsbergen and Schulpen, "Taking Stock of PIs," 166–7; Kinsbergen, *Unfold Private Development Initiatives*.
32. Kinsbergen, *Unfold Private Development Initiatives*.
33. Develtere, *How Do We Help?* 40; Kinsbergen, *Unfold Private Development Initiatives*, 39–43.
34. Develtere, *How Do We Help?* 183.
35. Desai and Kharas, "Democratizing Foreign Aid," 1112.
36. Plaisier and Schulpen, *Mondiaal Burger Daar en Hier*, 12; Mevis, *Een Snapshot Van de Vierde Pijler*, 1–3; Bekkers et al., *Geven in Nederland 2017*; Clifford, "International Charitable Connections," 458–60; Schnable, "New American Relief and Development Organizations," 313–14.
37. Plaisier and Schulpen, *Mondiaal Burger Daar en Hier*, 12.
38. Bekkers et al., *Geven in Nederland 2017*.
39. Clifford, "International Charitable Connections," 460–1.
40. Pollet et al., *The Accidental Aid Worker*, 36.
41. Schnable, "New American Relief and Development Organizations," 313–14.
42. Ibid.
43. De Bruyn, "New Development Philanthropists?" 41; Kinsbergen et al., "Understanding the Sustainability," 230–1; Kinsbergen PDI Database 2017; Schnable, "The Era of Do-It-Yourself Aid," 5.
44. Kinsbergen, *Behind the Pictures*, 137; Schulpen, *Development in "Africa for Beginners,"* 43–4.
45. Appe and Telch, "Grassroots International NGOs," 12.

46. See Murunga et al., *Kenya, The Struggle*, for a detailed reflection on and discussion of Kenya's new constitutional order.
47. Khaunya et al., "Devolved Governance in Kenya," 27–8.
48. Council of Governors, *County Integrated Development Plans*.
49. County Government of Kwale, *First County Integrated Development Plan 2013*; Kwale County Integrated Development Plan 2018–2022.
50. Kenya National Bureau of Statistics and Society for International Development, *Exploring Kenya's Inequality*, VI.
51. Berman, *Germans on the Kenyan Coast*, 55.
52. Ibid., 183–5, Table 2.
53. Kwale County Integrated Development Plan 2018–2022, 19.
54. Kwale County Budget 2018–2019 shows that 64% of the annual expenditures of the government are covered by contributions of the national government and own revenues; 25% is covered through support of multiple bi- and multilateral development actors. County Government of Kwale, *Annual Development Plan FY 2018–2019*.
55. Berman, "Contemporary German MONGOs," 320–32.
56. Although there is a concentration of PDIs working in tourism destinations, a large number of PDIs also work outside these areas, in countries, regions or villages not (often) frequented by tourists.
57. Berman, *Germans on the Kenyan Coast,* 12.
58. County Government of Kwale, *First County Integrated Development Plan 2013*, 66–76.
59. Kwale County Integrated Development Plan 2018–2022, 212.
60. Ibid. Italics inserted by present author.
61. Berman, "Contemporary German MONGOs," 320–34.
62. Since the term 'Private Development Initiative' is not familiar to the interviewees and since there are not always clear distinctions between different type of development agencies, I distinguished especially between smaller scale organisations and larger scale organisations.
63. Own calculations based on Kinsbergen, PDI Database Kwale County 2019 [Datafile] and County Government of Kwale County Treasury, *Annual Development Plan 2016–2017*.
64. Kwale County Integrated Development Plan 2018–2022, 212, 217; County Government of Kwale, *Annual Development Plan FY 2017–2018*.
65. Lister, "NGO Legitimacy Technical Issue," 179.
66. Ibid.
67. Ossewaarde et al., "Dynamics of NGO Legitimacy," 43–5.
68. Lister, "NGO Legitimacy Technical Issue," 187.
69. Berman, "Contemporary German MONGOs," 235–6; Kinsbergen, *Behind the Pictures,*137; Schulpen, *Development in "Africa for Beginners,"* 43–4; Appe and Telch, "Grassroots International NGOs," 12.
70. Ibid.

Bibliography

Appe, Susan, and Fabian Telch. "Grassroots International NGOs: Using Comparative Interpretive Policy Analysis to Understand Meanings in Private Development Aid." *Journal of Comparative Policy Analysis* (2019). doi:10.1080/13876988.2019.1582885.

Bekkers, René, Theo Schuyt and Barbara Gouwenberg, eds. *Geven in Nederland 2017*. Amsterdam: Walburgpers, 2017.

Berman, Nina. "Contemporary German MONGOs in Diani, Kenya: Two Approaches to Humanitarian Aid." In *German Philanthropy in Transatlantic Perspective. Perceptions, Exchanges and Transfers since the Early Twentieth Century*, edited by Gregory R. Witkowski and Arnd Bauerkämper, 227–243. Cham: Springer, 2016.

Berman, Nina. *Germans on the Kenyan Coast. Land, Charity and Romance*. Bloomington and Indianapolis: Indiana University Press, 2017.

CIDIN-PDI Database 2008–2009 [Datafile].

Clifford, David. "International Charitable Connections: The Growth in Number, and the Countries of Operation, of English and Welsh Charities Working Overseas." *Journal of Social Policy* 45, no. 3 (2016): 453–486. doi:10.1017/S0047279416000076.
Council of Governors. *County Integrated Development Plans*. http://cog.go.ke/about-us/20-the-council-of-governors/484-county-integrated-development-plans.
County Government of Kwale County Treasury. *Annual Development Plan 2016-2017*.
County Government of Kwale County Treasury. *Annual Development Plan FY 2018-2019*.
County Government of Kwale. *First County Integrated Development Plan 2013*.
De Bruyn, Tom. "New Development Philanthropists? The Effects and Characteristics of the (Flemish) Fourth Pillar of Development Cooperation." *Mondes en Développement* 161, no. 1 (2013): 33–47. doi:10.3917/med.161.0033.
Desai, Raj M, and Homi Kharas. "Democratizing Foreign Aid: online Philanthropy and International Development Assistance." *International Law and Politics* 42, no. 4 (2010): 1111–1142.
Develtere, Patrick, and Tom De Bruyn. "The Emergence of a Fourth Pillar in Development Aid." *Development in Practice* 19, no. 7 (2009): 912–922. doi:10.1080/09614520903122378.
Develtere, Patrick. *How Do We Help? the Free Market in Development Aid*. Leuven: University Press, 2012.
Dreher, Axel and Andreas Fuchs. "Rogue Aid? The Determinants of China's Aid Allocation." CESifo Working Paper Series No. 3581, 2011.
Fechter, Anne-Meike. "Brokering Transnational Flows of Care: The Case of Citizen Aid." *Ethnos* (2019). doi:10.1080/00141844.2018.1543339.
Kenya National Bureau of Statistics and Society for International Development. *Exploring Kenya's Inequality. Pulling apart or pooling together?* 2013.
Khaunya, Mukabi Fredrick, Barasa Peter Wawire, and Viola Chepng'eno. "Devolved Governance in Kenya; Is It a False Start in Democratic Decentralization for Development?" *International Journal of Economics, Finance and Management* 4, no.1 (2015): 27–37.
Kinsbergen, Sara. PDI Database 2017 [Datafile].
Kinsbergen, Sara. PDI Database Kwale County 2019 [Datafile].
Kinsbergen, Sara and Lau Schulpen. 2011. "Taking Stock of PIs: The what, why, and how of private initiatives in development." In *The Netherlands Yearbook on International Cooperation*, edited by Paul Hoebink, 161–186. Assen: Van Gorcum.
Kinsbergen, Sara, and Christine Plaisier. *Is Small Beautiful? a Sustainability Study of Development Interventions co-Financed by the Wild Geese Foundation*. Radboud University, 2015.
Kinsbergen, Sara, and Jochem Tolsma. "Explaining Monetary Donations to International Development Organisations: A Factorial Survey Approach." *Social Science Research* 42, no. 6 (2013): 1571–1586. doi:10.1016/j.ssresearch.2013.06.011.
Kinsbergen, Sara, Lau Schulpen, and Ruerd Ruben. "Understanding the Sustainability of Private Development Initiatives: What Kind of Difference Do They Make?" *Forum for Development Studies* 44, no. 2 (2017): 223–248.
Kinsbergen, Sara. *Behind the Pictures. Understanding Private Development Initiatives*. Nijmegen: Radboud University, 2014.
Kinsbergen, Sara. *Unfold Private Development Initiatives*. Nijmegen: Radboud University, 2017.
Kwale County Economic Planning Division. *Kwale County Annual Development Plan FY 2017/2018*.
Kwale County Integrated Development Plan 2018-2022. *Continuing Kwale's Transformation Together*, 2018.
Lister, Sarah. "NGO Legitimacy Technical Issue or Social Construct?" *Critique of Anthropology* 23, no. 2 (2003): 175–192. doi:10.1177/0308275X03023002004.
Mevis, Jacques. *Een Snapshot Van de Vierde Pijler in Vlaanderen*. Brussels: Vierde Pijlersteunpunt, 2016.
Murunga, Godwin, Duncan Okello, and Anders Sjögren. *Kenya, The Struggle for a New Constitutional Order*. Zed Books: London, 2014.
Ossewaarde, Ringo, André Nijhof, and Liesbet Heyse. "Dynamics of NGO Legitimacy: How Organising Betrays Core Missions of INGOs." *Public Administration and Development* 28, no. 1 (2008): 42–53. doi:10.1002/pad.472.

Plaisier, Christine, and Lau Schulpen. *Mondiaal Burger Daar en Hier*. Amsterdam: NCDO, 2014.

Pollet, Ignace, Rik Habraken, Lau Schulpen, and Huib Huyse. *The Accidental Aid Worker: A Mapping of Citizen Initiatives for Global Solidarity in Europe*. Leuven & Nijmegen: HIVA-KU Leuven/Radboud University, 2014.

Richey, Lisa Ann, and Stefano Ponte. "New Actors and Alliances in Development." *Third World Quarterly* 35, no. 1 (2014): 1–21. doi:10.1080/01436597.2014.868979.

Schnable, Allison. "New American Relief and Development Organizations: Voluntarizing Global Aid." *Social Problems* 62, no. 2 (2015): 309–329. doi:10.1093/socpro/spv005.

Schnable, Allison. "The Era of Do-It-Yourself Aid: Possibilities and Perils." *Bridge/Work* 3. no. 1 (2016): Article 2.

Schulpen, Lau, Bart Loman, and Sara Kinsbergen. "Worse than Expected? A Comparative Analysis of Donor Proliferation and Aid Fragmentation." *Public Administration and Development* 3, no. 5 (2011): 321–339. doi:10.1002/pad.619.

Schulpen, Lau. *Development in the 'Africa for Beginners'. Dutch Private Development Initiatives in Ghana and Malawi*. Nijmegen: Radboud University, CIDIN, 2007.

Severino, Jean-Michel and Olivier Ray. "The End of ODA: Death and Rebirth of a Global Public Policy." Centre for Global Development - Working Paper 167, 2009.

Suchman, Mark C. "Managing Legitimacy: Strategic and Institutional Approaches." *The Academy of Management Review* 20, no. 3 (1995): 571–610. doi:10.2307/258788.

Beyond crisis management? The role of Citizen Initiatives for Global Solidarity in humanitarian aid: the case of Lesvos

Hanne Haaland and Hege Wallevik

ABSTRACT
In recent years, what has been called citizen initiatives for global solidarity (CIGS) have grown considerably in numbers across Europe and beyond. Lately, CIGS have also received attention as they are responding to humanitarian crisis across the world. In Europe during 2015, citizens were heavily involved in catering for incoming refugees, putting up loosely organised voluntary-based initiatives. CIGS popped up in places such as Lesvos, which is the focus of our research. Humanitarian CIGS are quick in their response to needs on the ground, are quickly governed by rules and regulations as well as overall ideas about crisis management, and come to work either with or in opposition to other actors. We examine two examples of CIGS positioned at the margins of the humanitarian aid machinery in Lesvos. Through a lens of power and resistance, we discuss how they resisted paradigmatic ideas of crisis management and instead called for a different interpretation of how to think about and do crisis management.

Introduction and background

The year 2015 was historic in Europe in terms of the arrival of refugees to the continent, which particularly impacted parts of Central and Eastern Europe. The UN Refugee Agency (UNHCR) reported that 1,000,573 people reached Europe across the Mediterranean, mainly arriving in Greece and Italy, and another 34,000 crossed from Turkey into Bulgaria and Greece by land.[1] The number of people displaced by conflict and war coming to Western and Central Europe was the highest since the Balkan crisis of the 1990s. People living in some of the small Greek islands, such as Lesvos, Chios, Kos and Samos, felt the intensity of the situation with thousands of refugees arriving every day during the most intense periods of 2015. The islands are well-known tourist destinations in Europe, and the people are highly dependent on tourism as their main source of income. The many refugees arrived in a period where Greece as a nation and an economy was experiencing many challenges. The country continued to struggle with recovering from the financial crisis of 2008, unemployment was generally high and in 2015 capital controls were imposed on the country's banking system.

The influx of refugees added tension to an already strained situation as the tourist industry experienced a severe decline in the number of arrivals resulting from the negative portrayal of the situation in the islands.[2] However, whereas the traditional tourist segment was reduced, a new group arrived: the many ordinary citizens coming to help, often from other European countries.[3] They had learned about the situation not only through conventional media but also through social media.

Social media has become increasingly important in the mobilisation of collective action by ordinary citizens, also in the context of the refugee crisis in Europe. Images from the refugees' arrival situation were displayed in conventional media and social media, which mobilised a flow of resources to established non-govermental organisations (NGOs) and aid initiatives, but also led to the establishment of new citizen initiatives and the mobilisation of people and voluntary labour. Chouliaraki[4] refers to what she calls 'light tough activisms', where one part of our daily multitasking is to provide a daily donation or sign a petition. However, in the context of the refugee crisis some people took this activism further, going to Greece to help and be involved on the ground. This new type of engagement has contributed to the growth of voluntary action aimed at helping,[5] and to a steady stream of volunteers going to the Greek islands, either to start their own citizen initiatives for global solidarity (CIGS) or to work with others whom they have discovered online through their social media activities.[6] Many of them arrived before the UNHCR declared an emergency and the EU decided to allocate resources. As such, new technologies have facilitated a new type of civil society communication and engagement, creating an opening for the participation of many more actors in the production and mediation of humanitarian crisis through their own cultural imagination, rather than only observing them through mainstream media.[7] These volunteers became part of the first humanitarian crew in Lesvos, where locals, volunteers and tourists worked side by side to manage the crisis. When UNHCR arrived, it was both welcomed and criticised in Lesvos, as some saw the humanitarian actors as transforming their island into a Third World country, imposing neo-colonial attitudes[8] instead of building upon the initiatives already in place.

Many of the initiatives that emerged as a response to the influx of refugees to Greek islands had no pre-existing experiences working with refugee or crisis management. Rather, their establishment was the result of a response to a first emotional encounter between individuals (for instance, between voluntary worker and refugee) and thereby resembled other private initiatives emerging as part of the diversification of actors within the field of development cooperation.[9] This group of actors has received increasing scholarly attention over the last decade and is called by many names, all referring to small-scale development organisations set up by private persons in the Global North aiming at improving the living standards of people in the Global South.[10] In this paper, we use the term 'citizen initiatives for global solidarity', a term coined at the First European Conference on Citizen Initiatives for Global Solidarity, hosted in Brussels in 2014. Through a focus on people working in CIGS, we explore how the initiatives emerged on the island of Lesvos. As such we go beyond a development context and explore the work of CIGS in humanitarian aid, particularly how they challenge the so-called humanitarian aid machinery.

Situating CIGS in the contexts of development work and humanitarian crisis

In the past decade, the world of international development has undergone rapid changes, not only through the introduction and shift of development goals (from the Millennium Development Goals to the Sustainable Development Goals) but also through the emergence of new actors in development and humanitarian work.[11] In academia, growing attention has been paid to the emergence, role and position of new bilateral agencies and NGOs[12] and of more unusual actors such as celebrity humanitarians[13] and private foundations.[14] Interestingly, an ever-present alternative actor in many Northern countries has remained largely unstudied: the many ordinary citizens who actively engage in the fight against poverty by starting their own small-scale, voluntary development organisations. As already outlined in the introduction of this article, CIGS refer to efforts and projects set up and run by one or more individuals in the Global North aimed at improving the living standards of people in the Global South.[15] Yet, as the case of Lesvos illustrates, this definition has certain shortcomings, as initiatives are also run in the Global North, to help people from the Global South. Moreover, CIGS are also increasingly engaged as active contributors to secure welfare in the Global North.[16] CIGS can range from being loosely organised and run in an ad-hoc manner on a part-time basis to more structured initiatives with a permanent setup, run on a full-time basis.

Even though the focus on the new individual actors has been limited, a body of literature and studies from a development context has been emerging. The first studies of what Dutch researchers have called private development initiatives (PDIs) emerged from 2005 onwards, in the Netherlands and in Belgium/Flanders. This literature discussed the rise, characteristics and position of PDIs in the field of international development.[17] Research from Belgium refers to the involvement of organisations, institutions and private initiatives as the 'fourth pillar' in development cooperation.[18] In the United States, these initiatives have been described as grassroots international organisations,[19] and in Britain, they are discussed as citizen aid.[20] Ethnographic studies exploring the complex motivations of aid workers[21] and ideas about the neediness of benefactors[22] have provided important insights into the motivations of people engaged in helping, and as such also establishing or supporting CIGS. These and later studies show the need to acknowledge citizens in development and increasingly also in humanitarian work,[23] where growing attention has been paid to the role of volunteers and individuals as humanitarian actors.[24] In discussions of the involvement of individuals as well as small formal and informal groups catering for refugees, terms like makeshift humanitarians[25] and grassroots humanitarians[26] are applied. An insight which emerges from both the field of development work and humanitarian crisis is the need to acknowledge the work of citizens, not only as recipients, donors or supporters but as actively involved aid workers starting their own aid initiatives to meet needs in various contexts.[27] Such an acknowledgement supports the United Nations (UN)'s recognition of volunteer groups as important stakeholders for achieving the 2030 Agenda for Sustainable Development.[28]

Studies on CIGS have also questioned their development efforts and impacts in the Global South. Whilst the studies are positive regarding the achieved, direct results of CIGS interventions, and value the unique nature of these organisations and their comparative advantages such as low overhead costs, voluntary spirit and great enthusiasm,[29] critical concerns have also been raised. Central to them is how CIGS projects are mainly microscopic in nature, based on specific activities and focused on the immediate needs of specific target groups without tackling the structural causes of poverty.[30] Such projects often pay insufficient attention to a thorough context analysis[31] and often have limited knowledge about other actors or agencies active in the same region. Our own research shows that CIGS have relatively little interaction with local institutions and often display limited reflexivity in terms of own power and impacts into the local community beyond the specific projects they engage.[32] CIGS are also critiqued for the lack of building on or linking to local government or other civil society actors.[33] Combining these critiques leads many to question the sustainability of CIGS interventions.[34]

CIGS' activities and way of funding seem to be closely linked with philanthropic behaviour. The growth of such 'vertical solidarity'[35] must be understood in a larger context of global philanthropy and increasing remittances. Global philanthropy, including Brand Aid and celebrity aid,[36] reflects ideas about increasing global solidarity,[37] where some also argue for the need to recognise ideas about global citizenship[38] with common responsibilities and where citizens of the North have a great responsibility for sharing their wealth. Ideas about solidarity have also been highlighted in the literature on voluntary action and humanitarian aid.[39]

It is within this body of literature that we position our work on CIGS in a humanitarian context. Our starting point is that these actors are important contributors towards meeting needs and should be acknowledged for their efforts. During 2015 we observed an increase in ordinary citizens' responses to the refugee crisis in Greece, and we started to explore CIGS in Lesvos, one of the Greek islands that received thousands of refugees. Over a short period of time, people came to the Greek islands from all over the world to help and work, which resulted in the emergence of many CIGS. Some of them have since dissolved and many volunteers (including those combining voluntary work and tourism) have come and left again. However, some CIGS have evolved since their start in 2015 and are still operating among the actors catering for local needs of refugees stuck on the island. Whilst some of the initiatives are mainly concerned with responding to immediate needs, others focus on long-term needs such as education and skills, as the crisis has been prolonged. Many of the CIGS now work together with the local Lesvos government which runs the refugee camp of Kara Tepe and the Greek ministry of migration which runs the larger refugee camp of Moria. These CIGS have become service providers in and around the camps and as such are part of the crisis establishment, referred to as the local crisis management team. In this team the local government, NGOs, UNHCR and selected CIGS contribute.[40] Yet there are other CIGS operating in parallel, often openly criticising the work and the politics of the humanitarian aid machinery and thus the local crisis management efforts.

In our previous work, we have found that the new aid actors evolve as a response to an increased bureaucratisation of development work, and that their efforts reflect resistance to the conventional aid architecture.[41] In this article, we will further explore aspects of such resistance through the work of two CIGS working in Lesvos that have positioned themselves at the margins of the work of the local crisis management team. As we will reveal through our cases, CIGS operating at the margins are nevertheless able to shape and influence crisis management through their resistance, and the cases thus reveal and acknowledge the power embedded in resistance.[42] Moreover, it implies an acknowledgement of agency – that is, that social actors possess knowledgeability and capability which they use in responding and reacting to structures and events.[43] Against this theoretical backdrop, we will now proceed with a few notes on our data and fieldwork before we present our ethnography.

Exploring CIGS in Lesvos: notes on our field research

This article is based on data collected during the period 2015–2019. During 2015 we followed several emerging CIGS through newspapers and social media, focusing on their presentations of how and why they responded to the influx of refugees on the island of Lesvos. We saw a clear link between the engagement in Greece and Northern initiatives operating in the Global South.[44] We paid close attention to the initiatives that were quickly organised into smaller organisations described in the literature review above. An initial mapping of CIGS in Norway conducted by one of our master's students in 2016 showed 350 initiatives appearing in local newspaper articles in Norway from 2000 to 2016. From this sample, we saw a clear tendency that from 2015 onwards, initiatives were increasingly concerned with refugees. Many initiatives are run by people who wanted to help on the island of Lesvos, especially during the peak of the crisis in 2015.

In 2016 we went to Lesvos to interview people involved in the establishment of CIGS, and have since visited the island four times for short periods of fieldwork. During our first visit, we were particularly concerned with getting to know the context. We travelled along the route refugees had walked in 2015 on their way from the shores into Mytilini. We talked to people who had in some way or another been involved in helping. This included our taxi driver, who had been an employee at one of the ad-hoc refugee camps in the northern part of the island. He had also worked as a driver for one of the larger NGOs for some months and became a gate opener to many of the Greek residents we got to talk to during our stays. We conducted 15 in-depth interviews with people from different CIGS working in Lesvos before, during and after the peak of refugee arrivals in 2015, as well as with representatives of local government, UNHCR and humanitarian agencies and established NGOs. Moreover, we visited Pikpa, Kara Tepe and Moria, three of the refugee camps on the island, which allowed us to talk to refugees and observe the work done by CIGS within and around the camps. We had numerous informal talks with local people while staying in different towns in Lesvos during fieldwork. In May 2017 and April 2019, we participated in the 'Mini Lesvos dialogues' – meetings set up to enable actors involved in the crisis to meet and discuss experiences gained and how to meet challenges ahead. Here we were also able to interview relevant informants after the dialogues. The many visits and the fact that we have been able to have discussions with the same people over time have enabled us to explore CIGS longitudinally from various angles. In the following, we present and discuss two particular CIGS.

The emergence of CIGS in Lesvos

> It came about because I saw that clothes were thrown away. Blankets and all these materials were being thrown away. Didn't make any sense to me. And so the moment I saw it, I started. It was a simple thing I saw, that I needed to do something about.[45]

A typical CIGS starts in this way. A person responds to what she perceives as a need in some way or another. Often, an emotional event triggers action. This was the case with Kathrin and her initiative, which has turned into a watchdog CIGS caring for the environment. Kathrin lives in Lesvos and was asked by a Facebook friend overseas to go to the shores of the island to take pictures for a crowdfunding campaign for refugees. Coming to the shore, she described the situation as chaotic; people everywhere, volunteers to rescue refugees who were rushing ashore. She put away her camera and immediately started helping. After a few days, she noticed the amount of wet and dirty clothes and worn life jackets that piled up along the seaside, ready to be thrown away. She also noticed how blankets, used to warm refugees at their arrival, were only used once and then thrown away. She reacted to this and asked why no one collected them. She got no clear answers and started to collect clothes and blankets, and eventually also life jackets so that they could be recycled. Rather than sending pictures to her friend she argued for a crowdfunding campaign to set up an initiative to wash the clothes, sheets and blankets tossed away as garbage rather than being washed and recirculated into the system. Her idea of washing and reusing received a lot of support – friends and people in her network collected money for her to continue her work. For Kathrin, much time and effort went into thinking about how she should position herself to get continued financial support. She established a Facebook profile and found a name for her initiative, which made people notice it as well as provide economic support. She quickly realised she needed more help and took on volunteers to do the work with her, collecting and sorting clothes and blankets before sending them to the laundry. A steady flow of volunteers from abroad came to her initiative to help.

Whilst the large majority of helping hands focused on immediate needs, Kathrin had a different focus – the resources left behind by the many refugees arriving at the shores. Where others saw this as waste, she saw the value in reusing clothes that are culturally appropriate and fit the refugees' needs. As part of her work she has been attending co-ordination meetings for the different actors working with refugees. These meetings are organised by the UNHCR together with the island government and bring together development workers from established NGOs and people working more independently as volunteers or running their own initiatives. The idea is to share information on the work they do, to avoid duplication. However, Kathrin and other informants claim that more happens outside the meetings, through informal chats and via social media, such as WhatsApp. In the meetings and in direct contact with UNHCR, Kathrin advocated for the work of her CIGS as important in handling the long-term environmental impacts of the crisis. Most of the time she was told that her washing services were not needed, as there were plenty of blankets in store. The argument was that since people continue to donate clothes for refugees there is no need for her to wash and redistribute clothes. Even when she argued that large actors ought to have environmental policies in place, she did not get much response. Similarly, her argument for the need for culturally appropriate clothing for refugees was also by and large ignored.

Kathrin's effort is an example of a local, spontaneously emerging initiative which quickly turned into an established CIGS. At the very beginning of her work, she was thinking about registering her CIGS as an NGO, but as a foreigner living in Greece this proved difficult and she continued in a more informal manner. She received funding from international NGOs and private donors. In addition, she had several volunteers helping her in her work and she has been able to extend her services onto the mainland. With time she was increasingly noticed by the more established actors as filling a gap in local crisis management and inspiring other CIGS to focus on the environmental impacts of the refugee crisis. She has also started to redesign the many life jackets that are piling up on the island, linking up with local women who are remaking life jackets into bags for sale and thereby creating local employment. Importantly, the bags are produced as political statements, as reminders of each refugee's difficult journey. She argues for the need to see each refugee as a person with a history. For Kathrin, there is a clear lack of empathy evolving over time, particularly amongst those involved in processing asylum applications: 'this is why we are needed', she says, 'to counter the dehumanising actions refugees are confronted with every day'. She sees CIGS and the many volunteers as necessary to stop the dehumanising of refugees.

Through her work, Kathrin has linked up with other CIGS and their work, as well as locals, volunteers and international funders, and she has now built a large network of helpers. Many of Kathrin's activities are connected to other actors involved in crisis management. To fully understand how her CIGS came about and the impacts it has had on crisis management in Lesvos there is a need to see the activities as part of such relations. Kathrin's continuous focus on recycling in all her meetings with the UNHCR, camp management and other members of the humanitarian establishment has not stopped over the years. Rather, it has intensified, since she claims that it is no longer an immediate crisis, but a prolonged situation without long-term solutions. The UNHCR and the Moria camp management will sometimes ask her for clean blankets, but do not pay for the service. She claims that the local crisis management team sees her as a nuisance, but she says that she will carry on until her work is redundant. The fact that the situation has been prolonged has also influenced Kathrin's activity. Currently, she is supporting the efforts of other CIGS focusing on refugee children deprived of education. Moreover, she uses social media to continuously question and critique the economic dimension of emergency management in Lesvos. She describes herself as an activist, as do the people involved in the second case presented here, The Olive Leaves:

> Yeah, I met him here. In this place here. He came one day, he said: 'I have some people to feed. Make sure you make a better price for me' And, that was it. We were interested to know, to hear this stuff. Because we were activists. Pretty, pretty soon. But I said, 'Whoa whoa, where are these people?' He said, 'In the police department'. I said, 'Take me with you. Let's see what we can do'. And that was it.[46]

This is how The Olive Leaves started, with the encounter described above, a local man entering a shop urging the shopkeeper to help people in need. In its very beginning in the early 2000s, this was a local initiative with mainly local beneficiaries, which also had been helping some of the refugees who had been coming to the island since the early 2000s. The people involved were engaged for different reasons – some for religious reasons, others as social activists wanting to change the larger political and economic system. When the crisis hit Lesvos in 2015, and people came in large numbers, this small initiative was easily able to shift its focus to mainly helping incoming refugees. Volunteers also came in large numbers as the crisis received much attention. One of The Olive Leaves' core members claims that they were able to do good work supporting refugees because of the help of volunteers. Their work was enhanced by cooperating with other locally initiated CIGS working in the same way as The Olive Leaves. Throughout the island, particularly in the harbours in the north where refugees arrived in boats and started their journey, small initiatives popped up. As refugees had to walk on foot from one part of the island to another where they could get on a boat, they passed through the small town where The Olive Leaves is located. Refugees needed a place to stay and dry clothes – not to mention food and water – and sometimes just someone to talk to. Help came through the presence of volunteers and through donations to The Olive Leaves. One of its core members kept describing the situation and their work in a widely read blog, which resulted in funds and gifts from donors. They experienced how gifts can also be challenging – many of the donors had no idea about what was needed. As The Olive Leaves received clothes, shoes, and gifts in addition to funds it became important to try to guide donors in providing useful gifts. This meant that donors at one point were told how there was no need for more teddy bears or clothes and shoes culturally unacceptable to the arriving refugees. These types of gifts increasingly became more of a waste problem than a help. As already mentioned above, this difficulty was also a concern of Kathrin's, reflected in her work – making sure refugees are provided with clothes that are culturally appropriate, working towards meeting the needs of various groups of refugees.

The Olive Leaves has interacted with other initiatives that also position themselves as critical to the efforts of the local crisis management team, being concerned with how locals were pushed aside by foreign, large-scale actors:

> And what's important is: Never, out of ideology. We never accepted government money or European funds. That is something, we were very strict about.
>
> - Why is that?
>
> Because we wished to exert our own principle. Dimitri [the founder] said it was very critical. We also, we still are very critical. And we always believed that NGOs are part of the problem and not the solution to the problem.
>
> - How is that?
>
> NGOs substitute the government. That should not happen. NGOs should be something complementary. And not a substitute. We always see NGOs drawing money from the natives, from the government, from the EU, and doing its jobs. But we believe it's a government's job, it's the citizens' job, to be there. We're substituting. This way, we believe that the very fact of democracy is being undermined. Right now, the money from the EU was given to NGOs. The ministry asked Save the Children for funds, to use for education. That is a degradation. Governments asking NGOs. Who controls the NGOs? Of course, who controls the government? And who trusts the government? It's a big issue.[47]

As we can see from this quote, people working in the CIGS are positioning themselves politically and the work they do has to be seen in relation to what larger, more established actors do. Their frustration is not only with the humanitarian establishment but also with the national government, accused of not assuming responsibility for local affairs. This CIGS has clear ideas of what needs to be done to deal with the refugee crisis, ideas which are very different to how the crisis is managed, not only by the local crisis management team but also at the European level.

This becomes evident through the current work of The Olive Leaves. The main actors involved are ready to help again if the need arises, but the people in The Olive Leaves now work more actively in national and international advocacy networks through blog posts and seminars that urge people to make the overall situation of refugees arriving in Europe more widely known and responded to. One of the central actors involved in the CIGS describes himself as an activist and shows a strong local and international engagement. His critique of 'the establishment', by which he refers to EU politicians and their policies as well as the large NGOs and UN agencies, shapes his activities. In his writings on social media, he accuses these actors of not seeing the larger picture and how the situation in Lesvos is a global problem. He points to how the EU–Turkey deal has left refugees stranded in Lesvos, causing growing xenophobia locally which makes the situation for refugees as well as the Roma population living in Lesvos increasingly difficult. Consequently, the organisation works hard to secure the situation of the islands' most vulnerable people, through supporting education initiatives and basic needs, as well as arguing for continued local solidarity.

Both The Olive Leaves and Kathrin's initiative are promoting alternative perspectives on how to deal with the crisis, critiquing the current regime. Where Kathrin argues for environmental concerns and human dignity, The Olive Leaves argues along the same lines – the need to stop seeing refugees and ethnic minorities as human waste. Both stress how the local is embedded in the international dimension of this crisis, and the need to engage in global responsible actions. In the following section, we analyse the agency and power of these CIGS as forms of resistance.

Power and agency: resistance as a transformative act

As stated above, our previous work reveals how CIGS in a development context evolve partly as a response to the bureaucratisation of aid, where there is limited room for the active involvement of ordinary citizens. Individuals' efforts to start their own initiatives can thus be interpreted as an act of resistance towards the aid machinery. We clearly see similarities between the evolution of the initiatives in a humanitarian context such as in Lesvos and those evolving in a development context. People are triggered by a need to help, often motivated by a first emotional encounter. Where the more established actors are increasingly guided and regulated by the increased universalisation of ideas through institutionalisation and standardisation,[48] the new actors are not restricted in this way. Rather the work of CIGS is guided by a great deal of flexibility and pragmatism, often paying little attention to overall aid policies or national policies in the country they operate in. CIGS emerge as an immediate response to help to alleviate needs, often starting at a very personal level. This has been the case also in Lesvos, where the many CIGS result from a need to act. Yet there are also differences between the development and humanitarian contexts: in the former, CIGS may operate for a long time without becoming subject to national laws, regulations and policies, while CIGS engaged in sea-rescue activities such as some of the ones in Lesvos have become subject to regulations on trafficking and run the risk of criminalisation.

To overcome such challenges, some CIGS chose a strategy in line with what Walker[49] refers to as 'empowerment by similarity'. This implies a mimicking of the practices of more established actors that enables CIGS to continue their work in and near the refugee camps in Lesvos. Becoming more like NGOs allows them to form co-operating agreements and partake in the local crisis management. In such cases, by accepting the paradigmatic modes of attending to crisis, CIGS create a manoeuvring space for themselves, not only in the moment, but also long term. The mimicking allows not only for reproduction of what NGOs do, but also for something new to be constituted. This is a process that Walker refers to as *mimesis*. In his book *Becoming the Other, Being Oneself*,[50] Walker writes about identity and social change, based on ethnographic studies from the Comoros. He describes the act of mimesis as a negotiation of social change, emphasising that people adopt mimesis as a strategy in the meeting between places and cultures. He reveals how people from the Comoros construct their identity in such a way that they can allow themselves to imitate characteristics of the other and at the same time keep what they find to be sympathetic traits with themselves. In Lesvos, we see that CIGS that embrace characteristics of the more established actors at the same time keep some of their own special characteristics. This results in new aid actor identities being created, reflecting practices that allows for both continuity and change. The process is often seen as copying or imitating the other, but Walker argues that we need to go beyond this idea of empowerment by similarity and rather focus on what happens in the process. Using the idea of mimesis allows us to see that even if CIGS in some way copy the practices of established actors, change occur in the process as CIGS also keep some of their own characteristics, which in return influence the established actors. With CIGS working either as co-operating partners or as more independent actors in the humanitarian field, the established aid machinery cannot expect to remain unchanged. As such, this manoeuvring into doing crisis management may be interpreted as an enactment of resistance.

What our two cases illustrate is an even more explicit form of critique and resistance through a positioning at the margins of the local crisis management. Resistance involves an interaction or a relation where one of the involved parts feels a need to react, to respond, to resist what the other part claims, argues or demands,[51] as is the case with our two examples. Kathrin argues against the refusal to acknowledge the environmental dimension of crisis management by the larger actors. By collecting dirty blankets and laundry from both the shore and the camps, she converts waste into resources and claims that she will keep criticising until her work has become redundant. Her critique, however, is not only about a lack of waste management; she also claims that humans are treated as waste in the camps because local and national authorities continue to act as if they are solving an emergency and not dealing with a more permanent situation. The other case reflects a similar critique towards the humanitarian aid machinery, accusing them of taking over the work of governments and citizens, and of dehumanising people through the current way of solving the situation in Lesvos and Greece.

In both cases, the research participants focus on human dignity, not wanting to talk about refugees as a general term, but as people with histories, experiences, identities and, not least, opportunities. The humanitarian system has often been accused of a focus on the biological lives rather than the biographical lives of refugees. As summed up in a discussion by Brun,[52] the difference lies in notions of the future. Where biological life refers to the movement of the living organism, is repetitive and consists of activities that arise out of necessity, biographical life is understood as related to agency – the ability to act and to shape one's own opportunities and future. As Brun pinpoints, to engage with biographical lives entails a potential for change as well as a dimension of hope, which is challenging in humanitarianism, as it challenges ideas of neutrality. Our research informants, however, have no ideas about doing neutral work. Rather, they are actively communicating their resistance to the notion of refugees as a group rather than as individuals.

Scott argues how resistance can be expressed at the individual level; it can be collective, widespread or relatively loosely defined. A wide scale of actions is referred to as resistance, both physical and symbolic.[53] Our ethnography clearly reveals resistance. Both stand-alone CIGS operating outside the local crisis management and those uniting with other actors are expressing through actions their critique of how the crisis is being solved. Keeping in mind the interactional nature of resistance brings us to the importance of power when discussing resistance. As Flyvbjerg[54] reminds us, a privilege of power and an integral part of its rationality is to define what counts as knowledge and thereby what counts as reality to act upon. The greater the power, the greater the freedom in this respect. In community–state interactions, the state often assumes the power of definition. It becomes an expert in a system producing dominant ideas or knowledge. In the case of Lesvos, the CIGS and the humanitarian aid machinery alike have defined the situation as a refugee crisis, but with different power to define what is to be considered acceptable crisis management. Although there are many ways of interpreting the crisis, depending on whose perspective one takes, those actors operating within the establishment, ie the actors partaking in the local crisis team, are more likely to hold decision-making powers. From their standpoint, CIGS unwilling to be cooperating partners are unwanted actors, as they are not contributing in the way defined as necessary in a crisis. Such an interpretation would leave many CIGS operating outside of the aid machinery powerless. But the CIGS presented here have power through their resistance and through advocacy work – speaking in meetings, blogging in social media, continuing with their daily tasks of meeting needs, both among refugees and within the local population. They also resist and challenge through symbolic acts like Kathrin's handbags made from life vests, clearly stating her view on refugees as humans and individuals.

Recognising such symbolic resistance as political behaviour implies a widening of what is considered a political sphere and the power to influence. Thus, even though established actors hold decision-making power, there seems to be space for manoeuvring and for arguing against them, and thus contributing to potentially new understandings of how to deal with the crisis. In line with Rozakou, we see the need to explore changes in the humanitarian world and argue that these CIGS influence the way we think about and act upon the crisis in Lesvos. The CIGS exercise power in a Foucauldian sense,[55] where power is not to be 'had' but comes from everywhere. Moreover, there is no power without resistance, and vice versa. Thus, there is a need to acknowledge the power embedded in their resistance and see these CIGS' resistance as transformative acts.

Concluding remarks: moving into solidary action?

This article illustrates how crisis management as implemented by the crisis management team in Lesvos is not congruent with what the people in the two CIGS do. What is illuminated through our research is the different approach to the crisis they seem to represent. As much as the people within the CIGS respond to immediate needs and partake in dealing with the crisis, the work they carry out assumes more of a watchdog role, also reflecting broader ideas about humanity and solidarity. Rather than engaging in coordinated crisis management work merely as service providers linked to the government and other organisations, they contribute to changing the overall understanding of the crisis and how it is addressed. Through their continuous work questioning the current responses, solutions and approaches, we find that they ultimately aim to reshape power relations within the humanitarian aid sector.

The CIGS explored here call for a different interpretation of how to think about and do crisis management, which also rests upon their ideas about the crisis itself. They argue for an understanding of the crisis as one demanding international rather than only local attention, and long-term solutions rather than ideas about a situation that will pass. For that to materialise there is a need for the international community to take on board ideas about solidarity, social justice, sustainable production and consumption which enable us to think beyond the management of a crisis locally. This implies a move beyond emergency and touches upon larger discourses of global acts of responsibility and solidarity, which needs further exploration. This approach to the crisis aligns well with the Sustainable Development Goals' agenda and the UN's call for ordinary citizens to act to meet that agenda. Considering how some CIGS working in the context of a humanitarian crisis question and challenge dominant power relations as well as perceptions of crisis, we also need to recognise that academic approaches and concepts used in research are an integral part of how we shape our understanding of crisis.[56] As a colleague stated: calling something a refugee crisis is not a descriptive act; rather, it is a discourse that shapes actions at all levels of interaction.[57] Being reflexive and paying attention to the language and concepts used are imperative in research as well as within the practical field of humanitarian aid.

Disclosure statement

No potential conflict of interest was reported by the authors.

Acknowledgements

Thanks to the two anonymous reviewers and to Anke Schwittay, Rebecca Lund and Jørn Cruickshank for reading and providing valuable comments throughout the work discussed in this article.

Notes

1. Clayton, "Over a Million Sea Arrivals Reach Europe 2015."
2. Greek Travel Pages (gtp), editors team. https://news.gtp.gr/2017/01/18/study-refugee-crisis-repercussions-greek-island-tourism/
3. Haaland and Wallevik, Global Solidaritet.
4. Chouliaraki, *Ironic Spectator*.
5. Homane, "Velkommen til Norge."

6. Guribye and Mydland, "Escape to the Island."
7. Pantti, "Grassroots Humanitarianism on YouTube."
8. Rozakou, "Solidarity #Humanitarianism."
9. Schulpen and Huyse, "Editorial: Citizen Initiatives for Global Solidarity"; Haaland and Wallevik, "Citizens as Actors in the Development Field"; Kinsbergen, "Behind the Pictures"; Pollet et al., *Accidental Aid Worker*; Kinsbergen and Schulpen, "From Tourist to Development Worker."
10. Schulpen and Huyse, "Editorial: Citizen Initiatives for Global Solidarity."
11. Severino and Ray, *End of ODA (II)*.
12. Dreher, Nunnenkamp, and Thiele, "Are 'New' Donors Different?"
13. Richey and Ponte, "New Actors and Alliances in Development."
14. Schulpen, Loman, and Kinsbergen, "Worse than Expected."
15. See note 10.
16. Crosby, "Resettled Somali Women in Georgia."
17. Kinsbergen and Schulpen, "From Tourist to Development Worker."
18. Develtere and Bruyn, "Emergence of a Fourth Pillar."
19. Appe and Schnable, "Don't Reinvent the Wheel."
20. Fechter and Schwittay, "Citizen Aid: Grassroots Interventions."
21. Hindman and Fechter, *Inside the Everyday Lives of Development Workers*.
22. Malkki, *Need to Help*.
23. Richey and Choulouraki, "Everyday Humanitarianism: Ethics, Affects and Practices."
24. Ahmad and Smith, *Humanitarian action and Ethics*.
25. Sandri, "'Volunteer Humaniterianism': Volunteers."
26. McGee and Pelham, "Politics at Play."
27. See note 9.
28. https://www.un.org/sustainabledevelopment/sustainable-development-goals/.
29. Kamara and Bakhuisen, *Evaluation of Private Development Initiatives*.
30. Van der Velden, *Citizens' Imagination in Action*.
31. Schulpen, "Development in the 'Africa for Beginners.'"
32. See note 9.
33. Chelladurai, Private Initiatives.
34. Kinsbergen, Schulpen, and Ruben, "Understanding the Sustainability of Private Development Initiatives."
35. Wilkinson-Maposa et al., *Poor Philanthropist*.
36. See note 13.
37. Schuyt, "Philanthrophy in European Welfare States."
38. Pollett and Van Ongevalle, *Drive to Global Citizenship*.
39. Rozakou, "Socialites of Solidarity."
40. Mario Andriotis, personal communication 2016.
41. Haaland and Wallevik, "Citizens as Actors in the Development Field."
42. Scott, *Power*.
43. Long and Og Long, *Battlefields of Knowledge*.
44. See note 3.
45. Interview transcript, 2017.
46. Interview transcript, 2016.
47. Interview transcript, 2016.
48. Brun, "There Is no Future in Humanitarianism."
49. Walker, *Becoming the Other, Being Oneself*.
50. Ibid.
51. See note 42.
52. See note 48.
53. Abu-Lughod, "Romance of Resistance."
54. Flyvbjerg, *Making Social Science Matter*.
55. Foucault, *History of Sexuality*, 93.
56. Høem, "Hva er en krise?"
57. R. Lund, personal communication, 2019.

Bibliography

Abu-Lughod, L. "The Romance of Resistance: Tracing Transformations of Power through Bedouin Women." *American Ethnologist* 17, no. 1 (1990): 41–55. doi:10.1525/ae.1990.17.1.02a00030.

Ahmad, A., and J. Smith. *Humanitarian Action and Ethics*. London: Zed Books, 2018.

Appe, S., and A. Schnable. "Don't Reinvent the Wheel: Possibilities for and Limits to Building Capacity of Grassroots International NGOs." *Third World Quarterly*. 2019. doi:10.1080/01436597.2019.1636226

Brun, C. "There Is No Future in Humanitarianism: Emergency, Temporality and Protracted Displacement." *History and Anthropology* 27, no. 4 (2016): 393–410. doi:10.1080/02757206.2016.1207637.

Chelladurai, S. *Private Initiatives: SBP Projects of Cordaid in India*. Den Haag: Cordaid, 2006.

Chouliaraki, L. *The Ironic Spectator: Solidarity in the Age of Post-Humanitarianism*. Cambridge: Polity Press, 2012.

Clayton, Jonathan. "Over One Million Sea Arrivals Reach Europe in 2015." *UNHCR*, 2015. Accessed March 30, 2017. https://www.unhcr.org/5683d0b56.html

Crosby, D. B. "Resettled Somali Women in Georgia and Changing Gender Roles." *Bildhaan: An International Journal of Somali Studies* 6, no. 1 (2008): art. 9.

Develtere, P., and T. De Bruyn. "The Emergence of a Fourth Pillar in Development Aid." *Development in Practice* 19, no. 7 (2009): 912–922. doi:10.1080/09614520903122378.

Dreher, A., P. Nunnenkamp, and R. Thiele. "Are 'New' Donors Different? Comparing the Allocation of Bilateral Aid between Non-DAC and DAC Donor Countries." *World Development* 39, no. 11 (2011): 1950–1968. doi:10.1016/j.worlddev.2011.07.024.

Fechter, A.-M., and A. Schwittay. "Citizen Aid: Grassroots Interventions in Development and Humanitarianism." *Third World Quarterly*. 2019. doi:10.1080/01436597.2019.1656062

Flyvbjerg, B. *Making Social Science Matter: Why Social Inquiry Fails and How It Can Succeed Again*. Cambridge: Cambridge University Press, 2001.

Foucault, M. *The History of Sexuality: Volume One: An Introduction*. London: Allen Lane, 1979 [1993].

Guribye, E., and T. Mydland. "Escape to the Island: International Volunteer Engagement on Lesvos during the Refugee Crisis." *Journal of Civil Society* 14, no. 4 (2018): 346–363. doi:10.1080/17448689.2018.1518774.

Haaland, H., and H. Wallevik. "Citizens as Actors in the Development Field: The Case of an Accidental Aid-Agent's Activities in Aid-Land." *Forum for Development Studies* 44, no. 2 (2017): 203–222. doi:10.1080/08039410.2017.1305444.

Haaland, H., and H. Wallevik. "Global Solidaritet og Hjemmelaget Humanitær Bistand." Faedrelandsvennen. November 26, 2015, s. 29.

Hindman, H., and A.-M. Fechter. *Inside the Everyday Lives of Development Workers. The Challenges and Future of Aidland*. Sterling: Kumarian Press, 2011.

Høem, I. "Hva er en krise?" *Norsk antropologisk tidsskrift*. November 1, 2017.

Homane, I. "Velkommen til Norge: En studie av Refugees Welcome to Norway og Refugees Welcome to Vest-Agders Kommunikasjon i sosiale medier." MA thesis, University of Agder, Norway, 2016.

Kamara, S., and K. Bakhuisen. *Evaluation of Private Development Initiatives in Ghana*. Den Haag/Utrecht: Cordaid-Impulsis, 2008.

Kinsbergen, S. "Behind the Pictures. Understanding Private Development Initiatives." PhD thesis, University Nijmegen, Amsterdam, 2014.

Kinsbergen, S., and L. Schulpen. "From Tourist to Development Worker: Private Development Initiatives in the Netherlands." *Mondes en Development* 1, no. 161 (2013): 49–62.

Kinsbergen, S., L. Schulpen, and R. Ruben. "Understanding the Sustainability of Private Development Initiatives: What Kind of Difference Do They Make?" *Forum for Development Studies* 44, no. 2 (2017): 223–248. doi:10.1080/08039410.2017.1307270.

Long, N., and A. Og Long. *Battlefields of Knowledge: The Interlocking of Theory and Practice in Social Research and Development*. London: Routledge, 1992.

Malkki, L. *The Need to Help. The Domestic Art of International Humanitarianism*. Durham: Duke University Press, 2015.

McGee, D., and J. Pelham. "Politics at Play: Locating Human Rights, Refugees and Grassroots Humanitarianism in the Calais Jungle." *Leisure Studies* 37, no. 1 (2018): 22–35. doi:10.1080/02614367.2017.1406979.

Pantti, M. "Grassroots Humanitarianism on YouTube: Ordinary Fundraisers, Unlikely Donors, and Global Solidarity." *International Communication Gazette* 77, no. 7 (2015): 622–636. doi:10.1177/1748048515601556.

Pollet, I., R. Habraken, L. Schulpen, and H. Huyse. *The Accidental Aid Worker: A Mapping of Citizen Initiatives for Global Solidarity in Europe*. Leuven: KU Leuven/HIVA and CIDIN, 2014.

Pollett, I., and J. Van Ongevalle, eds. *The Drive to Global Citizenship: Motivating People, Mapping Public Support, Measuring Effects of Global Education*. Antwerp: Garant, 2013.

Rozakou, K. "Socialities of Solidarity: Revising the Gift Taboo in Times of Crisis." *Social Anthropology* 24, no. 2 (2016): 185–199. doi:10.1111/1469-8676.12305.

Rozakou, K. "Solidarity #Humanitarianism. The Blurred Boundaries of Humanitarianism in Greece." *Allegra Lab*, 2016. http://alegralaboratory.net/

Richey, L. A., and L. Chouliaraki. "Everyday Humanitarianism: Ethics, Affects and Practices." *New Political Science* 39, no. 2 (2017): 314–316. doi:10.1080/07393148.2017.1304737.

Richey, L. A., and S. Ponte. "New Actors and Alliances in Development." *Third World Quarterly* 35, no. 1 (2014): 1–21. doi:10.1080/01436597.2014.868979.

Sandri, E. "'Volunteer Humanitarianism': Volunteers and Humanitarian Aid in the Jungle Refugee Camp of Calais." *Journal of Ethnic and Migration Studies* 44, no. 1 (2018): 65–80. doi:10.1080/1369183X.2017.1352467.

Schulpen, L. *Development in the 'Africa for Beginners'. Dutch Private Initiatives in Ghana and Malawi*. Nijmegen: Radboud Universiteit Nijmegen, CIDIN, 2007.

Schulpen, L., and H. Huyse. "Editorial: Citizen Initiatives for Global Solidarity: The New Face of European Solidarity." *Forum for Development Studies* 44, no. 2 (2017): 163–169. doi:10.1080/08039410.2017.1306956.

Schulpen, L., B. Loman, and S. Kinsbergen. "Worse than Expected? A Comparative Analysis of Donor Proliferation and Aid Fragmentation." *Public Administration and Development* 31, no. 5 (2011): 321–339. doi:10.1002/pad.619.

Schuyt, T. "Philanthropy in European Welfare States: A Challenging Promise?" *International Review of Administrative Sciences* 76, no. 4 (2010): 774–789. doi:10.1177/0020852310381218.

Scott, J. *Power*. Cambridge: Polity Press, 2002.

Severino, J. M., and O. Ray. The End of ODA (II): The Birth of Hypercollective Action. Working Paper 218. Washington, DC: Center for Global Development, 2010.

Van der Velden, F. *Citizens' Imagination in Action: External Evaluation. Impulsis Civil Society Initiatives on Education*. Utrecht: Context International Cooperation/Impulsis, 2011.

Walker, I. *Becoming the Other, Being Oneself: Constructing Identities in a Connected World*. Cambridge: Cambridge Scholar Publishing, 2010.

Wilkinson-Maposa, S., A. Fowler, C. Oliver-Evans, and C. Mulenga. *The Poor Philanthropist – How and Why the Poor Help Each Other*. Cape Town: UCT, 2005.

Humanitarianism, civil society and the Rohingya refugee crisis in Bangladesh

David Lewis

ABSTRACT
This paper reflects on responses to Bangladesh's Rohingya refugee crisis in the weeks that followed the increased numbers of Rohingya refugees who arrived from Myanmar after 24 August 2017. Drawing on literature on the local and international dimensions of humanitarianism, and the analytical lens of performance, it explores narratives of helping in relation to the shifting character of Bangladesh's civil society, changing expressions of local and international religious sentiments, and the importance of understanding both formal and informal responses historically in the context of Bangladesh's own experiences as a country born from a crisis in which citizens became refugees fleeing state-sponsored violence.

1. Introduction

On landing at the airport at Cox's Bazar, Bangladesh, in early March 2018, I made my way down the steps from the plane and noticed a small group of well-dressed men standing not far away. They were unfurling a large banner that said 'Humanitarian Relief to Rohinga [sic] Refugees', sponsored by Charity for Life, Sydney, supported by the Tangail and Cox's Bazar Rotary Club, and implemented by Mukhti Cox's Bazar, a small local non-governmental organisation (NGO). They had driven their minivan onto the tarmac to meet two colleagues off the plane from a counterpart Rotary Club association in Sydney and were now posing for a celebratory picture. There followed a series of photographs in front of the banner, which I was also invited to join, perhaps intended as a way of adding to the international flavour of the proceedings, but I declined as I felt I might be getting in their way. But having been asked to become a part of what looked like some kind of performance, and viewed as having something I could bring to what was happening, I began to reflect on what exactly was being performed and why. It appeared to me that I was witnessing a distinctively inclusive and spontaneous form of voluntary action, that was easily stretched across scales and appeared ready to accommodate a wide range of identities.

In 2017, three quarters of a million mainly Muslim Rohingya refugees fled sustained state-sponsored violence in Burma to cross into the Cox's Bazar area of south-eastern

Bangladesh. Makeshift camps were soon set up and the crisis quickly began to receive international media attention.[1] On the ground, there were reports of person-to-person support through which local people began responding, including spontaneous forms of informal helping, volunteering, distribution of packages of clothing and food, and collecting and giving money. While such early responses began as essentially local forms of action, they were soon joined by other help-givers working at national and transnational scales of operation, and over the space of a few months these evolved into a large-scale humanitarian response.

This paper offers a reflection on what happened during those early stages of the response, and considers the ways in which humanitarian actions were performed by various actors as the crisis unfolded. It begins with an account of this early response period in the weeks that followed the increased numbers of Rohingya refugees arriving from Myanmar during late August 2017. Drawing on recent literature on the local and international dimensions of humanitarianism, this narrative is then unpacked in order to explore aspects of citizen aid including the changing nature of Bangladesh's civil society, forms of religious solidarity and charity, and the importance of understanding these responses historically. The discussion draws on local and international press coverage, semi-structured interviews retrospectively conducted with local journalists and humanitarian personnel in March 2018, both in Dhaka and in Cox's Bazar, and the author's longstanding engagement with issues of state and civil society in Bangladesh.

Recognition that humanitarian response takes different forms and operates at different scales is important both in understanding local events and in challenging dominant media and agency representations which tend to give certain forms of response higher visibility than others. Giving attention to forms of small-scale humanitarianism unsettles our more familiar and established narratives of international aid and development to reveal more of the depth, diversity and complexity of humanitarian action. As Redfield and Bornstein have suggested, the concept of humanitarianism is multifaceted: 'a structure of feeling, a cluster of moral principles, a basis for ethical claims and political strategies, and a call for action'.[2] Its diverse manifestations are sometimes expressed as the contrast between large-scale humanitarian action carried out by high-profile NGOs with vast budgets and the less visible acts of helping or giving that are carried out by small groups or individuals seeking to express social concerns and identities. Erica Bornstein also reminds us that everyday forms of person-to-person helping are not only diverse but may also be 'spontaneous, informal, unmediated, and habitual'.[3]

This diversity is partly captured by the general term 'everyday humanitarianism', which has come to be used in various ways in the literature. Some have used it simply to recognise the diversity of humanitarian action within 'myriad forms and practices' from individual to organisational, corporate and state levels.[4] Others have deployed it to contrast 'insider' and 'outsider' forms of helping, or to contrast high-profile, formal humanitarian action with less visible, more spontaneous, smaller scale grassroots responses. Moving beyond these different ideas, and the limitations of formal/informal dualism, at a general level the term helps expand our understanding of the 'aims, technologies, and participants' of humanitarian action, and serves to highlight the sometimes-overlooked experiences of local volunteers as they attempt to navigate different scales of helping and negotiate its associated tensions.[5]

Within less visible worlds of informal voluntary action, other terms such as 'citizen aid', 'grassroots humanitarianism', and 'person-to-person helping' are also used to convey the diversity of such activities. These reinforce the idea that such action needs to be understood on its own terms rather than according to outside categories, and the importance of contextual, structural and historical factors. Such terms are, as the editors of this issue have suggested, somewhat unstable categories that nevertheless offer a useful handle on the diverse forms of citizen helping and may illuminate the wide range of activities and motivations involved in humanitarian action across different settings and scales. As Hilhorst and Jansen have argued, humanitarian space can be understood as an 'arena' in which different actors seek to shape the nature and form of humanitarian action in terms of its 'everyday realities' through a range of different and frequently competing motivations.[6] I argue here that concepts of local helping or everyday humanitarianism also need to be historicised in the Bangladesh case by contextualising them within peoples' own experiences and memories of having themselves once been refugees.

The lens of performance provides a further way of analysing humanitarian response in terms of diversity, process and change over time.[7] For example, James Thompson's analysis of case studies of Kosovo, Darfur and the Asian tsunami highlights how humanitarian performances may be understood as containing certain common characteristics – such as the communication of a narrative of suffering to different audiences, the spotlighting of certain key events within these narratives, and the purposeful contrasting of heroes and victims.[8] These tropes are also ones that feature in the Rohingya case.

The focus in this article is on the early stages of the crisis during the second half of 2017 and on the forms of spontaneous person-to-person helping with which the Rohingya refugees were greeted by many Bangladeshis. These small-scale acts tend to receive less attention than the work of formal agencies such as NGOs and inter-governmental agencies, but they lie at the heart of voluntary action in most societies, and are far from new. At the same time, local citizen responses of this kind cannot be fully understood without reference to the Bangladesh state. The state played an important role not only in coordinating responses to the refugee crisis, but also in *representing* it, in particular through its effort to build representations of the crisis into wider political narratives of national generosity and religious piety. These narratives draw on local and national identities formed within Bangladesh's own history of struggle and crisis, and lend support to the ruling Awami League (AL)'s ongoing efforts to demonstrate to its domestic and international audiences that it has earned the right to be seen as the 'natural' party of government.

2. The 2017 Rohingya crisis and the responses

Although space is not available here to do full justice to the origins of the crisis, some brief background information is required to contextualise the case presented here. The Rohingya are a group of people, predominantly Muslim, who live mainly in Western Burma. Their language, ethnicity and religious identity are regarded by the Myanmar authorities as separate from mainstream Burmese cultural identity. As a result, they have experienced discrimination, persecution and religious oppression for many decades.[9] The historical roots of the problem are complex, going back as far as when the British seized parts of Burma in 1824, from which time the territory of Burma was incorporated as part of British India, and beyond. Today's international border between Bangladesh and Myanmar was simply a boundary between districts during the colonial period, across which the British authorities regularly moved populations in line with labour requirements.[10] Burma's border with India was porous and the boundaries of the coastal region of Arakan (now part of today's Rakhine

State) – the area where most Rohingya live – was not formally demarcated when Burma was separated from British India in 1937. When Burmese independence was obtained in 1948 the large Muslim minority population living in Arakan was excluded from citizenship. A key element of the Myanmar state's continuing refusal to grant citizenship is the assertion that the Rohingya did not form part of the state's pre-1824 population and that they therefore do not therefore qualify as a recognised minority group.[11]

Conflict and instability have led to many waves of Rohingya refugees in recent times seeking refuge in Bangladesh, including in 1978, the early 1990s, 2007 and 2012. Such movements of people have been the result of Burmese government policies and longstanding tensions between Muslims and the majority Buddhist population in Rakhine state, where the Rohingya remain a significant minority, continue to be denied citizenship and are officially viewed as illegal migrants from Bangladesh.[12] In 2012, for example, more than 200 people were killed and 140,000 displaced when Buddhist extremists attacked Rohingya homes and businesses in Rakhine State in retaliation following a reported assault on a local woman.[13] The crisis that began on 25 August 2017 was precipitated by an attack by Rohingya militants on police posts. What followed was a strategy of organised mass violence perpetrated by the Myanmar army and its local collaborators, including the murder of more than 6700 Rohingya in the month that followed, the systematic use of rape as a weapon and the destruction of at least 288 Rohingya villages.[14] This violence prompted the large-scale exodus of people across the border to Bangladesh.

Through highly visible acts of individual and national generosity, first the Bangladeshi people, and then later the government, began to express their solidarity with the Rohingya refugees and initiated various forms of helping. Support started to be offered almost as soon as refugees began arriving in late August. On the Bangladesh side of the border people were immediately moved by the scale of the movement of people to give money, food and shelter in a spontaneous outpouring of person-to-person helping and private giving.[15] Some local businesses started organising meal deliveries, and provided clothes and housing materials to traumatised people struggling to cope. Individuals and groups from around the country also soon began arriving in the small town of Cox's Bazar, some with hired trucks from which they started an *ad hoc* distribution of food and other relief goods.

It was several weeks before the government began to take control of the situation. It was reported to me by one local aid official, who was from a military family, that the emotional responses of members of the local coast and border guards who were on duty at that time were an important factor in drawing attention to the severity of the crisis and driving the response. Some of these guards were so distressed by the condition of the Rohingya people who were arriving, and by their stories of organised violence, killings and rape, that they began sharing their experiences with family and colleagues within the armed forces. Senior military figures reportedly told Prime Minister Sheikh Hasina that they needed the government to act in order to avoid a loss of morale and even discipline among their personnel. This began the process of establishing army control in which land was commandeered and cleared, camp facilities established and governance structures put in place.

Prime Minister Hasina responded by taking on a personal leadership role, although it is not known how far her stance was shared among all members of the cabinet. In a widely quoted declaration, she announced: 'If needed, we will eat a full meal once a day and share the rest with them'.[16] The government agreed to provide food and shelter to the Rohingya, but also made it clear that the new settlements would be only temporary until the refugees – or forcibly displaced citizens of Myanmar, as they were being termed in 2018 – were in a position to return to their homes. Negotiations with the Myanmar government have been ongoing regarding the return of the refugees, but at the time of writing (mid 2019) there are few people who believe that this will happen, given the prevailing conditions in Rakhine state where Rohingya villages remain destroyed.[17]

During the weeks that immediately followed the arrival of the refugees, there were charitable responses from a variety of individuals and groups. These were largely spontaneous and loosely organised, and reports of the generosity of local residents briefly became a global news story. Many of Bangladesh's citizens immediately volunteered and offered help to the Rohingya refugees, including people living in the border region and those coming from other parts of the country. One element of this story is the fact that there was a widespread international perception of Bangladesh as a country more used to receiving aid than giving it,[18] crudely stereotyped as one of the world's poorest and most heavily overpopulated nations.

On 14 September 2017, *Al Jazeera*'s Katie Arnold reported: 'Moved by their suffering, citizens of Bangladesh have rallied together to deliver much-needed assistance to the new arrivals. Most distribute their goods from large trucks that now clog the rural road between Cox's Bazar and Teknaf'.[19] The article highlighted two contrasting modes of spontaneous person-to-person helping – the sharing of resources and space by those with very little, and the charitable distribution of largesse by the better-off – and these can be briefly contrasted. The article includes two briefly sketched portraits of individual 'helpers': one a self-described 'poor farmer' named Abu Hayed from a local village near Teknaf, who was providing shelter on his property to eight Rohingya refugee families; and the other a well-off Dhaka-based middle-class 'digital entrepreneur' named Mehedi Chowdhury, who was reported as having decided to give all his savings to support the refugees. Mr Hayed had given incoming families the use of an 'old cowshed' as a temporary shelter, which offered space for the children to play and access to drinking water, and was providing them with regular food. He explained his actions in terms of simple human support as a citizen expecting his government to take action:

> 'I gave them shelter because I am a human being – it is raining outside, they have nowhere to sleep, they are totally helpless. But I am a poor farmer, with a large family. I am trying to transfer them to a camp, but I am not getting any support', he says, passing a glass of water to one of his tenants.

In contrast, Mr Chowdhury is presented in the report as a successful urban citizen, very much a part of Bangladesh's new dynamic high-growth economy and its growing middle class. For him, the Rohingya crisis provides pause for thought and reflection, and appears to have led him to a moment of questioning and postponement of the materialist dream of this new Bangladesh to make a sacrifice. Rather than buying a new car as he was planning to do, the article explains, Chowdhury had decided instead to use the money to help the Rohingya refugees. He donated around US $9000 in order to buy tents and food parcels and became directly involved in distributing them, hiring trucks and handing out relief goods himself to crowds of refugees. He explains his actions partly in humanist terms, but reports that he is also influenced by a sense of religious solidarity:

> 'They are Muslim, and they are being persecuted because they are Muslim, that strikes a chord with me ... and there is only so many times you can watch videos of someone being beaten or raped on Facebook – I had to come here and help', says the 29-year-old.

This citizen helping effort is portrayed as hugely appreciated by the Rohingya refugees at the roadside, one of whom is quoted as saying 'If it wasn't for the Bangladeshis I don't know how we would survive. There is no space in the camps, and no international organisations have offered us support'.

The first few weeks of the crisis had seen largely uncoordinated 'person-to-person' efforts to meet some of the Rohingya's more immediate needs, but people soon started organising in groups and associations. For example, the national newspaper *Prothom Alo*, as part of its community outreach work, sponsors a network of community groups known as 'bondhu sabha' or friends' clubs. These groups began arranging collections of winter clothes, sanitary towels, biscuits and *lunghis*. Other small community-level associations such as *Shopna Shiri* (Ladder of Dreams) and *Kelagor* (Playroom) collected money and distributed relief materials. A number of small local NGOs that were already working in the area, such as Coast Trust, soon began to undertake fundraising and the distribution of relief goods. At the same time, voluntary action by students from the Cox's Bazar Government College, who became involved in collecting food and relief goods for the refugees, provided another example of the diverse, multiple actors operating across private and public domains. Finally, private sector businesses also became involved, such as the Seagull Hotel where staff prepared and distributed hundreds of free meals each day for refugees, an example of charitable action from the for-profit commercial sector.

Yet there was also a growing sense of unease in the *Al Jazeera* article, as the limitations of such small-scale action were becoming clear. First, certain limits of person-to-person helping became apparent, with the article noting that children could be seen to be fighting over scraps of food in the street. There is also a description of Mr Chowdhury's efforts to throw food parcels from his vehicle outside one of the camps one evening that rapidly escalates out of control, creating a difficult situation in which his truck became surrounded by people engaged in a 'tense and sometimes violent struggle'. When the supplies ran out, people climbed onto the truck to help themselves to whatever was left, leaving Chowdhury reportedly surprised that people could fight over food, and reflecting on his own fear at the sight of such desperation: 'I thought we were going to die'. Brought into closer contact with a section of his own society in ways that he had not previously experienced, he seemed to have become discomfited. Although he is not explicitly critical of the mainstream relief agencies, Mr Chowdhury's prioritisation of the need for immediate and personalised action is reminiscent of Hilhorst and Jansen's category of the 'non-governmental individual' as a form of humanitarian actor whose numbers are growing and whose amateurism and informal helping can sometimes be the focus of criticism by aid professionals.[20]

At the same time as these local efforts were taking place, a more formal response by the Bangladesh government and the international community got underway. For example, the local government's District Commissioner's Office started taking in donations and distributing resources. As Richey and Chouliaraki suggest, tendencies towards formalisation may arise within local humanitarian efforts, and operations become routinised and practices rationalised over time.[21] After the initial month of mainly informal helping, the area around the town of Cox's Bazar quickly became the location for one of the world's largest formal humanitarian response efforts.

This formal response brought together a range of international agencies – with a few local ones – that were soon coordinated by the Government of Bangladesh. The government had already in 2013 put in place a National Strategy on Myanmar Refugees and Undocumented Myanmar Nationals. Under this strategy the government moved during late 2017 to establish a National Task Force, chaired by the Ministry of Foreign Affairs, comprised of 22 ministries and other bodies. This offered strategic oversight of the overall response to the needs of the undocumented Rohingya. The humanitarian agencies were coordinated by the Strategic Executive Group (SEG) located in Dhaka, co-chaired by the Resident Coordinator, the international Organisation for Migration (IOM) and the office of the United Nations High Commissioner for Refugees (UNHCR). The SEG helped the agencies coordinate with national-level government engagement and liaise with the National Task Force.

In broader historical perspective, these administrative arrangements can be seen to rest on two longer term foundations: the history of efforts to manage earlier waves of Myanmar refugee arrivals to the area, and the government's long experience of responding to Bangladesh's own regular humanitarian emergencies, created by its vulnerability to tropical cyclones and large-scale flooding.[22] For example, at the district level, an existing Refugee Relief and Repatriation Commissioner (RRRC), under the Ministry of Disaster Management and Relief, which was established during the early 1990s to look after the 34,000 or so refugees who arrived at that time, had its mandate extended in 2017 to cover operational coordination for the newly increased refugee population. An administrative structure quickly took shape in which the District Commissioner (DC) took responsibility for coordinating operations among the Bangladeshi host communities affected by the crisis, and a Senior Coordinator (SC) was put in place to lead the response on behalf of the humanitarian agencies, liaising with the DC (and with other officials at the sub-district level) and with the RRRC. The SC chaired the Heads of Sub-Office (HoSO) Group that brought together the heads of all the UN agencies and the representatives of the international and national NGO communities, as well as two representatives from the donor community based in Cox's Bazar.

Alongside these government arrangements, many international NGOs also formed a key part of the response, working in a variety of roles. For example, Save the Children Fund (SCF) had been working in the area since 1970, focusing on the needs and rights of children, particularly those unaccompanied and vulnerable to exploitation and trafficking. By early 2018 it had expanded its presence in Cox's Bazar to 1400 staff members and – with a mix of local and international volunteers – distributed tents, cooking and hygiene kits to refugees.[23] Oxfam GB, also present in the area since the 1970s, was active in monitoring responses to ensure that the water, sanitation and hygiene facilities being constructed met international humanitarian standards, and provided clean drinking water, portable toilets and sanitation facilities, and plastic sheets for shelter. Médecins Sans Frontières, active since 1985, had deployed 2000 staff members providing treatment for dehydration, diarrheal diseases and violence-related injuries. Other international NGOs have more recent histories in the area. For example, Action Against Hunger, with a local presence since 2007, deployed around 700 staff members and 1000 volunteers in the delivery of hot meals and water, as well as providing treatment for malnourished children and mental health counselling for the large numbers of people affected by stress and trauma.

Despite the many international NGOs, the largest non-state presence on the ground in 2018 was a Bangladeshi development organisation established in 1972, known as BRAC.[24] One of Bangladesh's leading civil society organisations, BRAC is active throughout the country with its wide range of development programmes.[25] Expanding its relatively small presence in Cox's Bazar, where it had been engaged in community-level work, it moved quickly to deploy 1300 staff, and a further 800 Rohingya refugees were trained as volunteers to undertake health and education activities and measures for the protection of women and girls.[26]

Also active for many years in the overall response efforts are various religious (or 'faith-based') international NGOs such as Islamic Relief and Muslim Aid. The former has worked with the Rohingya since 2008, when it constructed settlements for 10,000 unregistered Rohingya refugees in the Teknaf area. The organisation provided food and shelter to the new arrivals, but along with Muslim Aid was reported as experiencing tension with the authorities after allegations were made that along with some other groups it had distributed materials sympathetic to the Jama'at-i-Islami (JI) political party, which is banned in Bangladesh. This controversy led in October 2017 to restrictions being placed on this organisation's activities, and those of some other religious groups, in the camps.[27] Alongside such organisations there were also less formalised types of transnational religious charity, including *madrasa* support, income-generation skills-training projects and mosque-based initiatives. Also present were diaspora organisations (such as the one encountered by the author in the introduction), through which earlier waves of migrants and refugees may undertake support and advocacy activities with people who are displaced elsewhere in the world.[28]

Individualised citizen response and more formal interventions have continued to operate side by side, though by the end of 2017 the former had become overshadowed by the latter in terms of scale and resources. As the government, the army and the agencies took control of the situation, the humanitarian arena was transformed into a more tightly governed and ordered refugee space.[29] Person-to-person forms of humanitarian action can be understood as a response to the absence or breakdown of order, and as helping to build a transition towards more stable arrangements. Tensions emerged not only within the different levels of the formal response (for example between international and local NGOs, religious and secular agendas, and government and non-state actors) but also with local responses. Informal logics of citizen helping were reported as occasionally coming into conflict with the differently organised world of professional aid and agencies. For example, Chris Lom from the IOM was quoted as being critical of the informal resource-distribution methods used in some small-scale citizen efforts and illustrated by the example of Mr Chowdhury above: 'The only way to do this is to walk through every camp, identify those in need, give them a token and invite them to an orderly distribution centre'.[30]

3. Civil society, continuity and change

Bangladesh's civil society has received considerable attention as one of the contributing factors to the country's achievements in reducing poverty and overcoming the imposition of military government during the 1970s and the 1980s. The role of the student and language movements in the country's struggle for independence has been well documented, as has the growth of the indigenous or national NGO sector that subsequently played a key role in the country's progress with reducing social disadvantage, such as maternal mortality, and improving access to education. By the 1990s it had become common for Bangladesh to be characterised as a vibrant civil society, based on these longstanding traditions of citizen action, resistance and social movements, and on its high-profile set of large-scale development NGOs. These NGOs were not only providing education, health and credit services to poorer citizens but had also begun engaging in forms of 'small p' politics through local community organising and national-level advocacy.[31] Analyses have tended to focus on the developmental and political dimensions of these non-state actors, but less attention has been paid to historical, cultural and performative aspects of the civil society sector, or to its local smaller scale manifestations. The case of the 2017 Rohingya crisis provides a new perspective on these themes and offers insights into the ways that civil society is changing.

Bangladesh has successfully pursued an export-oriented growth strategy over the past two decades. This has aided the expansion of a new middle class, part of which has become associated with a changing religious outlook.[32] The forms of citizen helping that became visible during the Rohingya crisis can be understood as part of middle-class distrust and even rejection of the formalised NGO sector, viewed by some people as over-professionalised and too corporate, or as tainted by political interest and corruption. NGOs have come to be seen as part of an increasingly partisan and compromised civil society. While NGOs were once associated with poverty reduction, social innovation and radical rights-based action, today's version of civil society is less diverse and homogenised by the dominant emphasis on market-based approaches and service delivery. It is more constrained – in the sense of having been captured by party interests and patronage networks – leaving its organisations unable to play progressive roles in strengthening democratic citizen participation.[33]

For a substantial element of this new middle class, the renewal of Islamic identities is providing alternative ways of imagining and performing charity and philanthropy, and is contributing the shaping of a different kind of civil society.[34] As Samia Huq points out, while Bangladesh's founder Sheikh Mujib's earlier nation-building narrative had initially emphasised secularism, this initial period is increasingly remembered as one 'where the issue of religion, especially that of the majority population, was inadequately factored into discussions of national identity'.[35] The 2017 refugee crisis and local responses offer one entry point for gaining insights into the ways that some social groups, and the government itself, are now seeking opportunities for a resettling of this discussion. Within this changing vision, religiously informed public action serves as a counterweight to the perceived corruption of secular public officials, political party activists and civil society leaders, while more personalised forms of direct helping offer an alternative to the image of the domestic and international poverty industry with its cosmopolitan professionals, air-conditioned offices, donor money and expensive 'logo-ed' sports utility vehicles.

The religious and personal dimensions of everyday forms of humanitarian action may be understood as part of efforts to modify or even purify what some citizens have come to regard as a tainted secular vision of civil society, and as a microcosm of the wider secular-religious shifts taking place in Bangladeshi society. The government seeks to maintain its legitimacy and its support base by tracking and reflecting these changing religious sensibilities, both by building coalitions with religious groups and by ensuring that it signals public recognition of religious sentiments. For example, in 2018 the government moved to make the Qawmi Madrasa *hadith* qualification equivalent to a master's degree in Islamic Studies and Arabic. This strategy is also reflected in the government's handling of its humanitarian response to the Rohingya crisis. It is not surprising, then, that religion has a powerful role in today's landscape of compassion and voluntary action. The fact that the Rohingya are predominantly Muslim and have been so visibly the victims of religious persecution is important for understanding both local and international responses to the crisis. This resonates with Erica Bornstein's concept of 'lifestyle evangelism' in which faith can be understood as a key motivator for humanitarian and development work and provides an important 'logic for its expression'.[36]

Bangladesh secured its independence from Pakistan less than five decades ago, and there is a strong sense in which it remains a 'state in the making', in that both its system and its legitimacy remain under construction.[37] The struggle to balance multiple and potentially contradictory strands of secular and religious identities continues, and remains unfinished business. Definitions of national identity based on a majoritarian Muslim national identity have come to dominate over earlier versions of a multicultural Bengali identify that offered equal rights to religious and cultural minorities. Tensions continue, although the urge to understand national identities only through such binaries is also increasingly questioned.[38] While secular Bangladeshi identities may be in retreat, the country nevertheless remains relatively free of religious extremism, and alarmist predictions made during the 2000s that it might become 'the next Afghanistan' did not come to pass.[39]

Public representations of citizen responses in the early weeks of the Rohingya crisis were striking in the ways they seemed to reference and chime with aspects of Bangladesh's own history (Figure 1). The Bangladesh media's coverage of the Rohingya refugees fleeing genocidal violence to arrive at the Bangladesh border revived powerful memories of earlier humanitarian action during the country's own traumatic birth, when 10 million Bengali refugees poured into India following the violent repression by the Pakistan army and its collaborators.[40] The abuse of Rohingya rights, the violence perpetrated by vigilante groups orchestrated by a repressive militarised Burmese state, and the systematic use of rape as a weapon of war were all tropes that served to reawaken memories of this earlier period when Bengalis were themselves subject to severe state-sponsored military violence.

Conditions faced by the Rohingya were articulated in media accounts, and reinforced by people's personal stories, as being analogous to those endured by Bangladeshis during the 1971 crisis. A Bangladeshi aid worker told me that in 1971 when (soon-to-be) Bangladeshis were fleeing the abuses of the Pakistan army in the Chittagong area, some had been protected by Rohingya people across the border in Burma, suggesting an element of reciprocity in the popular Bangladeshi response to the events of 2017. She also drew attention to ideas of selflessness within this contemporary humanitarian discourse to the Rohingya: 'they are poor as we were, and as a citizen I'm proud to do this even if we have to sacrifice some of

Figure 1. Visual continuities: (a) Cox's Bazar, 2017; (b) Salt Lake Camp, Calcutta, 1971.

our standard of living'. I also encountered a more patronising view from some Bangladeshis, that today's Rohingya were poor, uneducated people, with large families and with low levels of inoculation, making them easy to identify with since they were reminiscent of a Bangladeshi population from an earlier age, before it had become developmentally transformed. From this perspective Rohingya were therefore people deserving of both solidarity and charity, and were in a condition that rendered them ready for a 'developmental' or humanitarian response.

An NGO worker and activist who had helped coordinate the international NGO refugee response effort in West Bengal during 1971 drew attention to parallels of representation between the two periods. There are striking similarities in the way photographs of refugees in the local media struck a chord with citizens in both periods, and the juxtaposed image were widely circulated in the Bangladesh press during the crisis.[41] This historical framing resonates with James Thompson's conceptualisation of the performance dimension in humanitarian action, in the sense that we can see those who were once 'victims' are now portrayed as (at least having the potential to take on the role of) 'heroes'.[42] Here also we can see how the working of humanitarian affect and of the power of reciprocity both serve to reinforce the authority of humanitarian action. They also reinforce the need to historicise understandings of local forms of helping and humanitarianism, and the increasingly recognised need to engage with the power of representation in development more widely.[43]

Returning to the idea of a changing NGO and civil society and sector, the crisis offers insights into the ways that Bangladesh may now be moving towards a 'post-NGO' civil society landscape. The main organisations that contributed to its reputation as leading the way in NGO-led 'alternative' development approaches during the 1980s and 1990s have either faded away or morphed into other forms of hybrid private organisation.[44] The large-scale local development NGOs that are still operating tend to be focused on microcredit, business development and services rather than rights-based or social mobilisation work – and can these days be more accurately characterised as private 'non-profit' or 'third sector' service providers. BRAC, one of the last of the original large national NGOs that once dominated the country's civil society sector, now presents itself primarily as a 'social business', rather than as either an 'NGO' or a 'civil society organisation'.

BRAC has itself been changed by the Rohingya crisis. Its roots were in relief and emergency work during the country's early years, but during the 1980s the organisation had largely moved away from the emphasis on short-term relief and reconstruction to concentrate on development work in support of long-term change. For founder Sir Fazle H. Abed, the opportunity to become involved in the Rohingya relief effort during the 2017 crisis was not only a humanitarian priority but also a chance for organisational renewal by returning to BRAC's original mandate.[45] In this way, the impulse of everyday humanitarianism does not necessarily bring a break with the past, but returns to and feeds cyclically upon it. In BRAC's case this reconnection with its earlier purpose has given it a sense of organisational rejuvenation as it has thrown itself into the Rohingya relief effort, mindful of its own origins in the humanitarian crises that followed the country's devastating November 1970 cyclone and the aftermath of its bloody 1971 Liberation War.

Religious narratives animate local and international helping, but they may also play into historical anxieties about the future and the past. For example, certain 'faith-based' NGOs were, as we have seen, accused of serving unwelcome political interests during the early stage of the crisis period. This reinforces the idea that humanitarian action rarely serves to create pure moral or non-political spaces, and highlights its entanglement with politics. In October 2017, it was reported that the government's NGO Affairs Bureau, which screens foreign organisations and controls the flow of international funds to local NGOs, had refused permission for three Islamic NGOs – Muslim Aid, Islamic Relief and the Allama Fazlullah Foundation – to work in Cox's Bazar with the refugees. The authorities investigated rumours that these organisations had been distributing JI materials and propaganda. The press reported that the government had explained that barring the organisations was 'a preventative measure against potential radicalization in the camps'.[46] As Didier Fassin has pointed out in the context of Western humanitarian efforts, here too in Bangladesh, 'rather than becoming separate, humanitarianism and politics are tending to merge'.[47]

An uneasy accommodation exists in contemporary civil society between the AL government and various religious interest groups. As the AL government has sought to consolidate its dominant position in recent elections, it has worked hard not only to maintain support among its traditional secular support base but also to build new political coalitions, including with religious interests. For example, the largely middle-class 2013 Shahbag street protests in Dhaka were a response to concerns that the AL government's International Crimes Tribunal – which had been set up in 2009 to retrospectively secure justice in relation to war crimes committed during 1971 by the Pakistan army and its collaborators – was wavering in its administration of justice 'long delayed'.[48] In 2013 it had wobbled in its determination to follow through on the execution of those convicted of collaborating with the Pakistan authorities in the massacre of Bengali civilians.[49] The protests were an assertion of secularism that quickly became portrayed as anti-religious by interests sympathetic to the JI leaders who were implicated in the trials. A backlash followed, including a counter-protest that was coordinated by the Hefazat-i-islami religious movement based in the country's *madrasas*. Since that time the government has been careful to appease Hefazat, including giving in to demands in 2017 that it remove a newly commissioned statue of a female symbolising justice from outside the country's Supreme Court building.[50]

Local humanitarian responses also need to be positioned within the global political economy of Islamic charity, from acts of small-scale private giving to the larger scale Saudi funding of mosques and *madrasas*. There have been concerns over cases of under-the-radar 'low-profile' private giving from Middle Eastern sources through government channels, particularly in the minds of secular-minded Bangladeshi journalists and civil society activists working in the area. One was keen to explain that he had recently observed a wealthy individual donor from the Middle East covertly visiting the local government office with the offer of a project for skills training that was also connected to funds for *madrasa* development, and that many such overtures were being received and in some cases accepted.

The performance of piety was a visible feature of the local response. In a roadside area near Baluakhali Camp, one local landowner spoke of his generosity in allowing a group of Rohingya families to erect shelters on his land, while at the same time gesturing towards the mosque he was now busy constructing based on his request for donations. Here is perhaps an example of what Margrit Talpalaru has termed 'conspicuous giving',[51] in the form of highly visible acts, which in this context increasingly take religious shape as acts of piety. Disquiet has been voiced in the media about increased numbers of mosques that have been appearing since the crisis began, and the ways in which interest groups from outside may use charity as a vehicle to pursue particular religious agendas.[52] This resonates with Talpalaru's ideas around visibility and representation: that certain types of charitable acts are performed in public space in order to attract public recognition.

Charitable activity is sometimes understood as separate from market processes, but this does not mean it is somehow unconnected to them. This particular landowner also explained that he was now charging these refugee households rent as they went about setting up their small roadside businesses. He was also beginning to profit from the situation and to extend his reputation. Humanitarian action and local helping, and the acts of piety with which these may be associated, may be intimately connected with markets, sometimes creating new forms of mini markets, or new opportunities within existing market processes. Opportunities arise for local business and entrepreneurial activity, with many relief goods such as solar lights and high-energy biscuits highly visible in Cox's Bazar as they were being resold by refugees to local traders in street-side markets. This was reminiscent of the 'fluid' technologies that Scott-Smith observes working with, rather than against, the market in contemporary humanitarianism.[53]

The performance of charity is not the exclusive preserve of donors, NGOs, civil society and organised citizens, but is also part of the work undertaken by government in its efforts to represent, build and sustain its legitimacy. The Bangladesh state can be seen not only in instrumental terms as coordinating the refugee response effort, but also as engaging in another type of performance: that of not only ensuring, but also demonstrating, that it has everything under control among the camps and the refugee population. This performance is part of the ruling party's enactment of its governance role, where it makes considerable effort not only to manage the crisis but also to control representations of its response to the crisis, in order to build political capital locally, nationally and internationally. The most obvious evidence of this are the banners and posters that dot the roadsides around the country. Many observers in the international community have rightly given the government credit for the ways it is handling the crisis, but this recognition sits uneasily with the fact that the AL's own human rights record is under heavy domestic and international scrutiny.[54]

Little of this uncertainty has found its way into the story the government is attempting to tell. Large banners hung across the roads in Cox's Bazar proclaim that 'Hasina is the mother of humanity' and the 'champion for human rights' (Figure 2), but there is disquiet among local people in Cox's Bazar about the effects on the local economy, and increased indifference at the national level about the Rohingya. One concern is the numbers of unoccupied and potentially disaffected young people in the camps, whose direct experience of religious persecution may make them vulnerable to Islamist political groups that may be operating under the cover of humanitarian work. Another is that in the local economy of Cox's Bazar the prices of essential goods have risen, while the cost of labour has fallen dramatically. A day of labouring on a fishing boat that once brought Tk600 for a day's work can now be hired from a Rohingya worker for Tk200.[55] Many Bangladeshis now worry that there is every chance that the country will simply be left to permanently absorb another million people. Meanwhile, the government has reportedly signed on to a potentially dangerous plan to relocate some of the refugees to the silt island of Bhasan Char in the Meghna River estuary, despite protestations from human rights groups.[56] The diverse impulses of small-scale humanitarianism that were observed during the early stages of the crisis have now dissipated, on the one hand overtaken by the formal mainstream international humanitarian machinery, and on the other co-opted by the state's own continuing quest for legitimacy and its need to project a stable representation of its governance role.

Figure 2. The visual politics of humanitarianism. Photo by the author.

4. Conclusion

The crisis that engulfed a small fishing town in the south-east of Bangladesh beginning in late August 2017 generated a varied and complex set of local, national and international humanitarian responses. Following Hilhorst and Jansen, I have analysed humanitarian space as an 'arena' in which a range of actors have shaped humanitarian action through different sets of motivations and everyday realities.[57] In Cox's Bazar, almost immediately, ordinary citizens were moved to offer individualised forms of person-to-person helping, and both informal and formal local organisations soon began improvising relief efforts. NGOs, national and international, some of which were already working in the area, scaled up their work, attracting media coverage and new resources from the international aid system. Once this space was established, the government, with the army, took on an overall coordination role. We have argued further that the analytical lens of performance is useful to frame these forms of helping in relation to themes of history, identity and visibility. If we return to Thompson's framework,[58] we can identify from the case certain key characteristics of humanitarian performance in the form of events (the sudden large-scale movement of 700,000 refugees across the border), constructions of heroism (Hasina as the 'mother of humanity') and narratives of suffering (portrayals of historical continuities between 1971 and the present).

Our focus on citizen helping during the early stages of the crisis also provides insights into two sets of interrelated changes within Bangladesh's civil society. One was an observed gap between the efforts of ordinary citizens who wanted to provide immediate help through a 'do-it-yourself' approach, and the responses of the public authorities, the formal NGOs and the international aid system. In part this followed from a time lag between informal, individualised responses and formal, organisational ones, but it also reflected the growing preference among citizens – in common with that observed elsewhere in the world – for more direct forms of helping alongside, or in place of, formal initiatives and organisations. Local responses to the Rohingya refugees illustrate how more flexible forms of small-scale civic action – as opposed to more formal, externally funded types delivered through professionalised organisations such as NGOs – are becoming increasingly visible within humanitarian and developmental action. The other was that these forms of citizen helping may also reflect growing tendencies among Bangladesh's growing middle classes for more religiously informed modes of helping within a civil society that is de-secularising. A heightened level of religiosity is part of a wider trend in Bangladeshi society in which the tradition of 'secular rationality or religious neutrality' has shifted in recent years to one in which 'religiously informed voices are now part of the plurality of voices'.[59]

Performances of humanitarian action therefore need to be understood against a changing and sometimes contradictory set of wider political and historical factors that impinge upon the 'social script' that informs charity and helping in Bangladesh society.[60] These include the efforts of the Bangladesh government to build and balance alliances with both religious and secular interest groups, and, more widely, the rise in transnational religious giving. Despite these trends, the forms of small-scale citizen action discussed here are not entirely new. They echo earlier patterns, including those that occurred five decades earlier during the country's 1971 War of Liberation. In this sense such activities do not offer a decisive break with the past but can also be understood as cyclical, connected perhaps to 'afterlives of development' that continue to echo within 'the spirit of previous development regimes'.[61] One cannot fully understand Bangladesh's response to the Rohingya crisis without historical reference to the country's own experience as a nation born in the aftermath of civil and ethnic conflict, following horrific violence perpetrated by a hostile military leading to the creation of a large-scale refugee crisis.

Structural processes have influenced forms of local helping, such as the changing ideologies and aspirations of the country's rapidly expanding new middle classes, the shifting international geopolitics of religious charity, and the Bangladesh state's own ongoing efforts to consolidate power within an increasingly authoritarian democracy.[62] In those initial seconds on the tarmac at Cox's Bazar airport, between receiving my spontaneous invitation to briefly become part of one such performance and then deciding instead to go on my way, for a short moment it was as if I was present at one of the interfaces of these changing forces and felt its weight.

Disclosure statement

No potential conflict of interest was reported by the author.

Funding

No formal funding was used in the production of this paper.

Acknowledgements

I am very grateful to Dr Abul Hossain of Green University, Dhaka, with whom I travelled to visit to Cox's Bazar, for our many stimulating conversations. I wish to thank Julian Francis, who discussed with me his experiences responding to the plight of Bengali refugees in 1971 and his impressions from earlier visits to Cox's Bazar, which helped inform parts of this paper. The draft has benefited greatly from comments from Anke Schwittay, Meike Fechter and participants at the Citizen Aid and Grassroots Humanitarianism workshop, 19–20 April 2018, University of Sussex.

Notes

1. Although this coverage dwarfed the scale of earlier reporting, this was not the first time the Rohingya refugees had made the international news, such as in 2012. See Brooten and Verbruggen, "Producing the News."
2. Redfield and Bornstein, "Introduction to the Anthropology of Humanitarianism," 17.
3. Bornstein, *Disquieting Gifts*, 174.
4. Richey and Chouliaraki, "Everyday Humanitarianism," 314; and Bornstein, *Disquieting Gifts*.
5. Thomas et al., *Everyday Humanitarianism*. See also the work of the Southern Responses to Displacement initiative (https://southernresponses.org), which highlights community-level action taking place.
6. Hilhorst and Jansen, "Humanitarian Space as Arena," 1117.
7. Schechner, *Performance Studies: An Introduction*.
8. Thompson, *Humanitarian Performance*.
9. Palmer, "Analysing Cultural Proximity," 96.
10. Ullah, "Rohingya Refugees to Bangladesh," 139.
11. Holliday, "Addressing Myanmar's Citizenship Crisis," 404.
12. See for example van Klinken and Aung, "Contentious Politics of Anti-Muslim Scapegoating," 353.
13. Brooten and Verbruggen, "Producing the News," 440.
14. BBC, "Myanmar Rohingya: What You Need to Know about the Crisis," April 24, 2018. Accessed September 14, 2018. https://www.bbc.co.uk/news/world-asia-41566561. A UN fact-finding mission in 2018 argued that members of the armed forces should face prosecution under international law for genocide, crimes against humanity, and war crimes. See UN News, "Myanmar Military Leaders Must Face Genocide Charges – UN Report," August 27, 2018, https://news.un.org/en/story/2018/08/1017802.
15. There has been a growing appreciation and understanding of what has been termed 'community-led protection' in humanitarian situations. See for example Carstensen, "Understanding and Supporting Community-led Protection."
16. *The Independent*, 'Bangladesh Vows to Support One Million Rohingya Muslims Fleeing Burma: "If Needed, We'll Eat a Full Meal Once a Day and Share the Rest with Them," October 7, 2017. Accessed December 16, 2018. https://www.independent.co.uk/news/world/asia/rohingya-muslims-bangladesh-latest-updates-flee-burma-million-food-shelter-a7987761.html

17. A report by the Australian Strategic Policy Institute based on satellite mapping of Rakhine State found continuing destruction of Rohingya villages and 'no evidence of widespread preparation for Rohingya refugees to return to safe and dignified conditions'. See "Mapping Conditions in Rakhine State," July 24, 2019, https://pageflow.aspi.org.au/rakhine-state/#211793.
18. The country has struggled to escape its labeling during the 1970s by a United States official as an international 'basket case'. See Lewis, *Bangladesh: Politics, Economy and Civil Society*.
19. Arnold, 'A Farmer, a Techie: The Bangladeshis Helping Rohingya," *Al Jazeera*, September 14, 2017. Accessed December 16, 2018. https://www.aljazeera.com/indepth/features/2017/09/farmer-techie-bangladeshis-helping-rohingya-170914084039681.html.
20. Hilhorst and Jansen, "Humanitarian Space as Arena," 1131.
21. Richey and Chouliaraki, "Everyday Humanitarianism."
22. Roy, Hanlon, and Hulme, *Bangladesh Confronts Climate Change*.
23. Volunteering within the formal international NGO sector is another way that everyday humanitarianism has been taking place, but this phenomenon is not the main focus of this article and deserves separate treatment.
24. BRAC originally stood for 'Bangladesh Rural Advancement Committee', but today it stands as an organisational name rather than an acronym.
25. See for example Smillie, *Freedom from Want*.
26. Some use the idea of everyday humanitarianism to understand the experiences of formal volunteers within the NGO sector (see Thomas et al., *Everyday Humanitarianism*), as well as the contrasting forms of voluntary action analysed here as 'informal' types of local helping that took place during the initial moments of the crisis.
27. Harvard Divinity School, "As Rohingya Flee Myanmar, Bangladesh Bans Three Muslim Aid Groups," October 20, 2017. Accessed September 13, 2018. https://rlp.hds.harvard.edu/news/rohingya-flee-myanmar-bangladesh-bans-three-muslim-aid-groups.
28. Olliff, "From Resettled Refugees to Humanitarian Actors," 658.
29. Hilhorst and Jansen, "Humanitarian Space as Arena".
30. Arnold, "A Farmer, a Techie" (see note 19).
31. Lewis, *Bangladesh: Politics, Economy and Civil Society*.
32. See for example H. Z. Rahman, "The Middle Class Is Transforming," *Dhaka Courier*, August 30, 2017.
33. See Tasnim, "Politicized Civil Society in Bangladesh." Civil society today therefore contains contradictory elements of marketisation and politicisation that are both complementary and, perhaps, also potentially contradictory.
34. Wood, *Clashing Values in Bangladesh*.
35. Huq, "Muslim Aspirations in Bangladesh," 249.
36. Bornstein, *Spirit of Development*, 54.
37. Lewis, *Bangladesh: Politics, Economy and Civil Society*.
38. Riaz, *Lived Islam and Islamism in Bangladesh*.
39. Karlekar, *Bangladesh: the Next Afghanistan?*
40. Francis, "Refugees 2017 and 1971."
41. Ibid.
42. Thompson, *Humanitarian Performance*.
43. See Schwittay, *New Media and International Development*; and Lewis, Rodgers, and Woolcock, *Popular Representations of Development*.
44. Lewis, "Representing the Poor, in a Clientelistic Democracy," 1545.
45. Personal communication, Sir F. H. Abed, Dhaka, March 15, 2018.
46. Harvard Divinity School, "As Rohingya Flee Myanmar, Bangladesh Bans" (see note 27).
47. Fassin, *Humanitarian Reason*, 224.
48. Chowdhury, *Paradoxes of the Popular*, 3.
49. See Murshid, "The Shahbag Uprising," 13.
50. "Statue of Woman Removed from Bangladesh's Supreme Court," www.nytimes.com/2017/05/26/world/asia/bangladesh-statue-justice-supreme-court-islam.html
51. Talpalaru, "Blake Mycoskie, Toms, and Life Narratives," 168.

52. Bangladeshi migration to the Gulf states since the 1980s is one factor believed to have contributed to changing religious attitudes in the country.
53. Scott-Smith, "Sticky Technologies," 3.
54. See Human Rights Watch, "Bangladesh: Violent Repression of Opposition," https://www.hrw.org/news/2019/01/17/bangladesh-violent-repression-opposition
55. $1 US is worth around 85 Bangladesh Taka.
56. "Bangladesh Prepares to Move Rohingya to Island at Risk of Floods and Cyclones." *The Guardian*, July 19, 2019.
57. Hilhorst and Jansen, "Humanitarian Space as Arena," 1117.
58. Thompson, *Humanitarian Performance*.
59. Riaz, *Lived Islam and Islamism in Bangladesh*, 9.
60. See Moeschen, *Acts of Conspicuous Compassion*.
61. See Rudnyckyj and Schwittay, "Afterlives of Development," 8.
62. Lewis and Hossain, "Local Political Consolidation in Bangladesh."

ORCID

David Lewis http://orcid.org/0000-0003-0732-9020

Bibliography

Bornstein, E. *Disquieting Gifts: Humanitarianism in New Delhi*. Stanford, CA: Stanford University Press, 2012.

Bornstein, E. *The Spirit of Development: Protestant NGOs, Morality, and Economics in Zimbabwe*. Stanford, CA: Stanford University Press, 2005.

Brooten, L., and Y. Verbruggen. "Producing the News: Reporting on Myanmar's Rohingya Crisis." *Journal of Contemporary Asia* 47, no. 3 (2017): 440–460.

Carstensen, N. "Understanding and Supporting Community-led Protection." *Forced Migration Review* 53, (2016): 4–7.

Chowdhury, N. S. *Paradoxes of the Popular: Crowd Politics in Bangladesh*. Stanford, CA: Stanford University Press, 2019.

Fassin, D. *Humanitarian Reason. A Moral History of the Present*. London: University of California Press, 2012.

Francis, J. "Refugees in 2017 and 1971 – Reflections." *bdnews24.com*, *2017*. Accessed September 13, 2018. https://opinion.bdnews24.com/2017/09/28/reflections-on-refugees-1971-and-2017/

Hilhorst, D., and B. Jansen. "Humanitarian Space as Arena: A Perspective on the Everyday Politics of Aid." *Development and Change* 41, no. 6 (2010): 1117–1139.

Holliday, I. "Addressing Myanmar's Citizenship Crisis." *Journal of Contemporary Asia* 44, no. 3 (2014): 404–421. doi:10.1080/00472336.2013.877957.

Huq, S. "Muslim Aspirations in Bangladesh: Looking Back and Redrawing Boundaries." In *Being Muslim in South Asia: Diversity and Daily Life*, edited by R. Jeffrey and R. Sen, 249–268. Oxford: Oxford University Press, 2014.

Karlekar, H. *Bangladesh: The Next Afghanistan?* New Delhi: Sage, 2005.

Lewis, D. *Bangladesh: Politics, Economy and Civil Society*. Cambridge: Cambridge University Press, 2011.

Lewis, D. "Representing the Poor in a Clientalistic Democracy: The Rise and Fall of Radical NGOs in Bangladesh." *The Journal of Development Studies* 53, no. 10 (2017): 1545–1567. doi:10.1080/00220388.2017.1279732.

Lewis, D., and A. Hossain. "Local Political Consolidation in Bangladesh: Power, Informality and Patronage." *Development and Change* (2019). doi:10.1111/dech.12534

Lewis, D., D. Rodgers, and M. Woolcock, eds. *Popular Representations of Development: Insights from Novels, Films, Television and Social Media*. London: Routledge, 2014.

Moeschen, S. C. *Acts of Conspicuous Compassion: Performance Culture and American Charity Practices*. Ann Arbor: University of Michigan Press, 2013.

Murshid, N. "Shahbag Uprising – War Crimes and Forgiveness in Bangladesh." *Economic and Political Weekly* 48, no. 10 (2013): 13–15.

Olliff, L. "From Resettled Refugees to Humanitarian Actors: Refugee Diaspora Organizations and Everyday Humanitarianism." *New Political Science* 40, no. 4 (2018): 658–674.

Palmer, V. "Analysing Cultural Proximity: Islamic Relief Worldwide and Rohingya Refugees in Bangladesh." *Development in Practice* 21, no. 1 (2011): 96–108. doi:10.1080/09614524.2011.530226.

Redfield, P., and E. Bornstein. "An Introduction to the Anthropology of Humanitarianism." In *Forces of Compassion: Humanitarianism between Ethics and Politics*, edited by P. Redfield and E. Bornstein, 3–30. Santa Fe, NM: School for Advanced Research Press, 2010.

Riaz, A. *Lived Islam and Islamism in Bangladesh*. Dhaka: Prothoma Prokashan, 2018.

Richey, L. A., and L. Chouliaraki. "Everyday Humanitarianism: Ethics, Affects and Practices." *New Political Science* 39, no. 2 (2017): 314–316. doi:10.1080/07393148.2017.1304737.

Roy, M., J. Hanlon, and D. Hulme. *Bangladesh Confronts Climate Change: Keeping Our Heads above Water*. London: Anthem Press, 2016.

Rudnyckyj, R., and A. Schwittay. "Afterlives of Development." *POLAR: Political and Legal Anthropology Review* 37, no. 1 (2014): 3–9. doi:10.1111/plar.12047.

Schechner, R. *Performance Studies: An Introduction*. 2nd ed. London: Routledge, 2006.

Schwittay, A. *New Media and International Development: Representation and Affect in Microfinance*. London: Routledge, 2015.

Scott-Smith, T. "Sticky Technologies: Plumpynut®, Emergency Feeding and the Viscosity of Humanitarian Design." *Social Studies of Science* 48, no. 1 (2018): 3–24. doi:10.1177/0306312717747418.

Smillie, I. *Freedom from Want: The Remarkable Success Story of BRAC, the Global Grassroots Organization That's Winning the Fight against Poverty*. Boulder, CO: Kumarian Books, 2009.

Talpalaru, M. "Blake Mycoskie, Toms, and Life Narratives of Conspicuous Giving." *Biography* 37, no. 1 (2014): 168–190. doi:10.1353/bio.2014.0009.

Tasnim, F. "Politicized Civil Society in Bangladesh: Case Study Analyses." *Cosmopolitan Civil Societies: An Interdisciplinary Journal* 9, no. 1 (2017): 98–123. doi:10.5130/ccs.v9i1.5247.

Thomas, N., M. B. Smith, S. Agerhem, J. Cadesky, B. V. Paz, and B. Fadel. *Theme Paper 1: Everyday Humanitarianism*. Stockholm: Swedish Red Cross (SRC), 2018.

Thompson, J. *Humanitarian Performance: From Disaster Tragedies to Spectacles of War*. Calcutta: Seagull Books, 2014.

Ullah, A. A. "Rohingya Refugees to Bangladesh: Historical Exclusions and Contemporary Marginalization." *Journal of Immigrant & Refugee Studies* 9, no. 2 (2011): 139–161. doi:10.1080/15562948.2011.567149.

Van Klinken, G., and S. M. T. Aung. "The Contentious Politics of Anti-Muslim Scapegoating in Myanmar." *Journal of Contemporary Asia* 47, no. 3 (2017): 353–375. doi:10.1080/00472336.2017.1293133.

Wood, G. *Clashing Values in Bangladesh: NGOs, Secularism and the* Ummah. ESRC Research Group on Wellbeing in Developing Countries, WeD Working Paper 31. University of Bath, 2007.

Citizen aid, social media and brokerage after disaster

Deirdre McKay and Padmapani Perez

ABSTRACT
In a crisis, aid providers deliver humanitarian relief across a hierarchy of organisations where influence and capacity map to their scale of operations. On the front lines of crises, 'citizen aid' is what small, local and informal groups offer to fellow citizens. These citizen aid groups are well-networked in place and tend to work through longstanding personal relationships. In the Philippines, citizen aid groups frequently support their activities by documenting their work with photos of beneficiaries to solicit donations from within the country and around the world across social media platforms. This paper builds on recent debates on brokerage through a case study of citizen aid in the relief effort after Typhoon Haiyan (2013–2017). Using this case-study approach, we demonstrate how social media has produced novel forms of brokerage shaped by circulating images online. This new kind of brokerage involves a layered network of brokers that both shapes citizen aid efforts and creates new channels for localising aid, enhancing the control of citizen groups in the Global South over aid.

Introduction

In a crisis, aid providers deliver humanitarian relief across a hierarchy of organisations where influence and capacity map to their scale of operations.[1] Beyond households and beneath formal non-governmental organisations (NGOs), 'citizen aid' is what local and informal groups offer to fellow citizens on the front lines. Such groups are a key part of civil society. Tied to place, they work through longstanding personal relationships and have remained invisible to scholarship on disaster relief.[2] Increasingly, citizen aid groups document their work with photos of beneficiaries to solicit donations across social media platforms.[3] Scaling up their efforts by utilising social media, these groups can extend their reach to become involved in wider recovery efforts.[4] Such groups then act as brokers of humanitarian assistance. With the imperative to localise aid, citizen aid could potentially become vital in humanitarian emergencies. Grouping all such aid efforts under the rubric of 'civil society' obscures the diversity of citizen aid. Scholars need to differentiate among the actors involved.[5] There are gaps – what Saban calls 'structural holes' – in disaster response.[6] Citizen aid in the Global South innovates to fill these gaps.

This paper maps how we can understand the kinds of initiatives and activities that fill these structural holes in disaster recovery. We learned about social media and citizen aid during our work as practitioners after typhoon Haiyan (Yolanda) hit the Philippines in November 2013.[7] Here, the affordances of social media were key to the recovery effort.[8] Academic studies of social media in this recovery have focussed on donor-sponsored transparency and accountability initiatives clustered around the worst-affected areas in the Eastern Visayas region. Some of these efforts produced information that merely performed accountability and was never taken onboard by large aid donors.[9] From our own observations, we knew of small-scale, local recovery initiatives that also deployed social media, but had yet to be explored in depth. Such initiatives appeared to be small and low-profile, operating in areas which had comparatively less loss of life and damage to key infrastructure. Here, local civil society retained the capacity to act as first responder.

1. Locating citizen aid

The literature on disasters recognises that our characterisation of civil society lacks nuance and is working to differentiate the actors involved. Bankoff and Hilhorst focus on the perceptions of disaster management that distinguish governments from NGOs.[10] Aldrich and Sou focus on households, while acknowledging 'other non-state actors' that are not NGOs.[11] Forrest et al. recognise localisation and the growing role of civil society in disaster response requires differentiation beyond this NGO/household distinction. We need studies that explore the middle ground of smaller, informal initiatives. Our definitions of civil society, such as McIlwaine's 'actors and groups that are non-state, formally or informally constituted … part of the voluntary sector' or Aldrich and Cook's differently-scaled 'networks of trust and reciprocity among citizens' need to be explored empirically to map the emergent ecology of aid groups.[12] Scholarship here recognises that the continuum between households and NGOs must extend through different scales of informal and formal organisation, but we lack systematic investigation of this space beyond explorations of volunteering.

Studies of volunteering offer accounts of citizen participation in informal organisations, but focus on its benefits for volunteers and donors, rather than generating a broad typology of such initiatives.[13] Where volunteering research considers disaster recovery, it tends to privilege Northern mobilities, tracing the movement of 'global citizens' from North to South, rather than focussing on South–South interactions. However, we know volunteers and development actors in the Global South develop different careers and cultivate different kinds of selves when they contribute to humanitarian aid.[14] To understand the South–South dynamics of citizen aid, we approach it through the lens of brokerage. Our approach builds on a long tradition in Development Studies that considers development intermediaries as brokers. This tradition, in turn, extends on studies of brokers in political anthropology.[15] A brokerage focus complements the study of social media post-disaster, expanding our account of 'digital humanitarianism' to show how not only human actors but also technologies, images, platforms and algorithms shape aid delivery.

Our preliminary analysis classified citizen aid actors identified through social media into four categories. First were Philippines-based companies or groups of volunteers who formed new informal aid organisations. These groups geared up to deliver relief, switching from their day-to-day business to do short periods of unpaid work. Often first on the ground in affected areas, they left guiding sailing tours for tourists to deliver aid packages or shifted from running a nursery school to operating a soup kitchen. On social media, their posts amplified their efforts and solicited funds. The second group were material and in-person responders. A global and diverse range of people who had prior connections to affected areas (tourists, out-migrants or through their client or customer base). These people contributed their own labour or donated material resources. The third group was comprised of established NGOs who temporarily switched their focus from their other activities to relief work. The final category of aid workers worked online-only to amplify the work of the first three. These people were private individuals with time, personal networks and social media skills. They created channels for disaster response information on social media platforms and amplified posts to support others. There was, of course, lots of interaction between these categories. Many citizen aid workers operated across two or more of these categories over the duration of the 2013–2017 Haiyan recovery and rehabilitation period.

1.1. Methodology

We began our research by tracking the activities of citizen aid providers across Facebook and Twitter. We located social media posts hashtagged Haiyan and Yolanda 2013 and identified those which solicited cash donations. We selected these groups to review in-depth. Members of these groups had left their day-to-day jobs in business, the academy, the arts or the third sector. Each group had supported their aid activities primarily by raising funds and recruiting additional workers over social media. Their aid initiatives had primarily operated in the least-affected areas of the region hit by Typhoon Haiyan. In these places, local people had immediate capacity to deliver aid and to other aid workers. From each group, we requested a series of interviews with at least two staff. We asked each interviewee to map the group's origins, efforts and post-disaster relief contribution. We also requested site visits for open-ended interviews with aid recipients and local government officials in beneficiary communities.

We initially identified 11 potential groups. We received positive responses to emails from seven. However, three of these seven initiatives had disbanded. Their former members had no way to contact former beneficiaries and lacked capacity to engage our research. Former staff from four initiatives agreed to participate in our iterative interviews and facilitate site visits. Of these four groups, one was a completely voluntary group and their members and beneficiaries had remained in touch. Two groups had spun out from NGOs in other sectors and their members had returned to charity work. The final initiative was attached to a travel business.

Our initial analysis triangulated between online posts and transcripts of interviews. We coded them thematically to identify relationships and circulation of both images and monies. We mapped the movement of photographs and of humanitarian resources, usually cash but also in the form of social capital. All respondents named this form of social capital (in English) as 'trust'. As described by Ong and Combinido, this use of trust described ongoing, personal and dyadic exchange relations founded through reciprocal expressions of compassion and appreciation or gratitude.[16] Our data were clearly ambivalent about this trust: how it was established, performed and sustained, particularly on social media, and the efforts of the business-based citizen aid effort.

Looking for evidence of trust relationships, our initial analysis assessed the online networks of these citizen aid actors. We saw some were 'friends' with beneficiaries and also with staff from larger aid groups and, sometimes, people who donated to their efforts. However, we found no evidence of friend relations between beneficiary community members and aid donors. All transfers of information and money between donors and beneficiaries was brokered by citizen aid actors through social media. Thus, there were no trust relationships between donors and beneficiaries, only with their citizen aid intermediaries. Hence, we decided to apply a brokerage approach in our analysis.

1.2. Brokers and brokerage

Brokers are actors who draw together and facilitate exchanges between disparate systems, peoples and spaces. Brokers act to their own advantage whilst advancing the interests of others and generating value through their actions.[17] Brokers extemporise, challenge existing scripts for behaviour and set up new flows of resources and information in order to shape exchange relationships. Brokers thus prevail in spaces where a weak state cannot impose its own rationality on a recalcitrant local. In development aid, brokers often act within established organisations and channels, but at the edges of their formal processes. In this location, they can set up competing channels for flows of value, information or concern from global or national-level organisations into the local context where they operate. Aid brokers minimise the effects of attempts by higher-level organisations to intervene in local relationships. Instead, these brokers control the local by enlisting clients to whom they have promised services or goods, often reinvigorating inactive obligations from previous exchanges in order to create a constituency for their activities. While in recent studies brokers have focussed largely on cash payments and accumulation of finance capital, there is a long tradition of brokers accumulating – or reshaping and deploying – other forms of capital e.g. social, cultural or educational capital.[18] Brokers sustain trust with their clients by providing access to this capital for them. Our brokerage approach thus extends the focus on social capital in disaster recovery developed by Aldrich, shifting it towards exchanges brokered through social media.[19]

Brokers need their clients to trust that they will deliver some approximation of the service they've promised them, eventually. Aid brokers attract and attempt to control their clients in various ways. They appropriate and redirect resources, limit clients' access to services, create modes of preferential treatment or refuse to enact policy directives, among other expressions of autonomy. Brokers are often resented by clients, but are tolerated because they have connections and resources that may yet be useful to locals. While brokers sometimes deliver on their promises, they are also very obviously operating in ways that put their own interests first, or at least on par with those of their clients.

Brokers' autonomous actions lie outside the existing norms of institutional conduct. This location is the key to brokers' operations. By working in their own interest to subvert the formal processes and regulations of aid governance, aid brokers remain powerful yet vulnerable. They can be accused of corruption and fraud, and forced to respond to claims they have failed to deliver the results promised to both donors and beneficiaries. Brokers' activities often generate frustration and mistrust. Yet, where brokers' actions connect people across two or more complex systems of social relations – e.g. international non-governmental organisations (INGOs) from the Global North and local government officials in the Global South – brokers' activities show how systems of governance and aid delivery really function by revealing where those systems are dysfunctional.[20] Brokers highlight the various ways in which aid does not work or has yet to meet needs for service and information. Brokers thrive where the business-as-usual mode of aid governance is not working. In disaster relief, it is not surprising that aid brokerage roles proliferate, filling structural holes in the disaster response.[21] These structural holes vary in shape and citizen aid is diversifying to fill them. Seeing that our four citizen aid initiatives were very different, we selected one to explore in-depth.

1.3. Case study approach

The last initiative we examined – which we call EcoTrek – had the largest scope and greatest success in terms of monies raised through social media. We sought to understand how their approach distinguished them as a citizen aid initiative, and how their staff thought they established and performed trust. Our analysis follows the extended case method, demonstrating how in-depth analysis of one case study can reveal the possibilities within the wider field of citizen aid and diversify the ways civil society can be understood.[22]

EcoTrek is an ecotourism provider that operates on a remote western island in the Philippines' Southern Tagalog Region. We interviewed three EcoTrek staff members in person and via Skype on three separate occasions each. We also conducted two site visits to EcoTrek beneficiary communities. There, we interviewed two local government officials each and a total of 17 EcoTrek aid recipients. EcoTrek used social media to support recovery and then rehabilitation after Haiyan, both collaborating and competing with NGOs and government. New to both development aid and humanitarian relief and, initially, not well-networked in the development industry, EcoTrek quickly generated significant resource flows, having an international scope for direct fund-raising. While other citizen aid initiatives had more experience, the scale of EcoTrek's fundraising made it prominent in the recovery effort on the outlying islands where it operated. EcoTrek's success in delivering aid relied on expanding their established global social media channel. This allowed them to broker exchanges between disaster-affected villages and (largely) foreign donors. Victor, the company's owner, explained:

> we had … basically a logistics company … we have all these boats … we have all these connections with the villages. It was just perfect. It was just like typhoon, next day: carry on. But we can show it to people.

EcoTrek circulated photographs to raise funds. Their brokerage efforts localised aid in new ways. Describing how their network emerged, we privilege the voices and interpretations of EcoTrek staff and our community interviewees. We seek to establish how they, as organic intellectuals in the Global South, and new to humanitarian relief and development more broadly, understood their citizen aid experience. Offering extensive quotes and 'deep data', we suspend judgment on EcoTrek's claims of efficacy, difference, altruism and trust with donors and beneficiaries. Instead, we focus on the novelty and reach of their aid-delivery model. This citizen aid model is potentially replicable and may give citizen groups in the Global South greater control over disaster relief. Because of this potential, our case study of EcoTrek seeks to set out its strengths and shortcomings in depth.

2. Citizen aid in action: EcoTrek's story

EcoTrek's proprietors and staff began to organise their online response shortly before Typhoon Haiyan entered the Philippine area of responsibility. They posted images and text updates to Facebook. Initially, Philippine staff managed these posts, but this wasn't sustainable during their first response and assessment efforts. Cheryl, a former intern based in Europe, set up a new relief-oriented EcoTrek Facebook page to support staff on the ground. EcoTrek's owners, Teddy and Victor, delegated the task of managing Haiyan-related posts to her. Meanwhile, EcoTrek staff delivered aid to coastal settlements on comparatively remote islands where people depend on fishing as their main source of livelihood. EcoTrek landed their boats in areas without telecommunications and with no means of contacting national relief efforts. This first wave of EcoTrek aid responded to immediate community needs: potable water, food, tarpaulins for temporary shelter and materials needed to rebuild homes.

Cheryl is Filipino, knew the remote islands targeted and was familiar with EcoTrek's operations. She had strong relationships with both Teddy and Victor and some former EcoTrek guests, both Filipino and European. Cheryl explained:

> EcoTrek … managed to take a boat around the islands and figure out the injuries, the losses, the needs … And luckily, in the age of smartphones, they were also able to send pictures … of what the villages actually looked like … And those very quickly went up online.

Cheryl received images and then posted in English. She ensured posts were published quickly and in chronological order: 'so you would see that this group is really putting their money where their mouth is … It was me being the communication link'.

Brokering images, Cheryl selected those she thought would raise funds while not undermining EcoTrek's longer-term interests in encouraging visitors. Cheryl, as a multilingual, globally-mobile member of the Filipino elite, was in a very different role from the digital humanitarian workers who ran the feedback mechanisms offered by larger aid operations in Leyte Province.[23] Within three days, Cheryl's page had over a thousand followers. Most were former EcoTrek guests added from her personal profile and EcoTrek's corporate page. These friends reposted EcoTrek posts to their own timelines. Their friends on Facebook shared them onwards. Cheryl explained: 'even if someone can't donate, their likes, and their shares, and their comments – It helps. I mean, just the way the algorithms of Facebook are made, every like, every share kind of spreads it further and further'. Supporting this, Facebook itself worked as a broker.

Four days after Haiyan, Facebook USA asked Cheryl if they could help. Facebook made a short video featuring Cheryl in Europe helping with the Haiyan response in the Philippines. The video publicised EcoTrek's relief efforts and described how Facebook helped Cheryl start the EcoTrek relief operation page. On reflection, Cheryl considered it 'all marketing' for Facebook. The video nonetheless marketed EcoTrek to a wider group of Facebook users who might then consider donating to the Haiyan relief effort through EcoTrek rather than established INGOs. A Facebook employee shared Cheryl's video on her own profile. This personal 'share', combined with the circulation of Chery's initial posts, generated many donations from Europe. Facebook, however, did not advise on the design of EcoTrek posts.

The images themselves instead had agency as brokers in this process. EcoTrek learned which images were most effective at generating donations by correlating posts with deposits. Teddy forwarded Cheryl selected images received via MMS (mobile messaging service) from EcoTrek staff in the field. Cheryl used Facebook Analytics to see who donated in response to what kinds of posts. Teddy, based in Manila, followed the posts and provided feedback to Cheryl on the amounts of money arriving in EcoTrek's account. Cheryl called it 'learning by doing … You learn along the way how much attention and how many views each post gets'. When Cheryl noted that donors were more likely to give money for tangible packages of goods, she asked EcoTrek staff to organise pictures of the contents of aid packages.

EcoTrek staff took photographs in beneficiary communities intended to demonstrate transparency and accountability to donors. Victor recounted:

> We report every step … taking photos of the shipment … of the sacks … of the tarp … People are asking [online] 'what do you need', and they [in the typhoon-hit areas] are saying 'nails', and people on Facebook see nails, and they say 'okay $500'.

Lacking previous experience of humanitarian relief or development assistance, this was a key insight for EcoTrek. In response, Teddy designed their most successful image, a photo of EcoTrek's relief package:

> I … laid it [all the goods] out on the table … like a viral shot … 65 Euros is enough of donation to get a fisherman's family back on their feet. 65 Euros, that's how much we needed [per donor] … They [the Facebook audience – DM] loved it … it's a manageable sum and … it's the people that actually trust you.

Teddy's point about trust is key. Donors had already had personal contact with EcoTrek's businesses, staff and host communities in the Philippines before they donated. Other donations then came via their personal networks, in a lateral expansion of trust relations:

> The people that donated are people who's been on our trips … They've seen our communities. So, they're actually like oh, like 'Okay, these guys'. And you know, they persuaded others to go and donate and don't go to the big ones [NGOs and INGOs] because, you know, but I think there was a trust there as well that we … tell them 'this is what we're doing' … Trust.

EcoTrek tried to establish trust online with images of aid delivered. Their posts curated images from recipient communities that inevitably concealed other frictions in brokerage relations. These images performed what seemed to be current trust in an attempt to build ongoing trust.

2.1. Images as brokers

On Facebook, for those who saw and 'liked' or 'shared' EcoTrek posts, these images accumulated digital social capital. The images enhanced people's profiles and online reputations as humanitarian and knowledgeable. EcoTrek then sought to convert and channel this value into aid donations while also promoting their core tourism business to potential guests.

EcoTrek needed to protect their tourism business at the same time as eliciting aid. They avoided creating and sharing images that replicated typical visual tropes which other aid-delivering groups were circulating after Haiyan. EcoTrek excluded photos focussed on human suffering, competition and chaos, and mourning.[24] They circulated positive images of recovery that they attributed to both 'culture' and the performance of gratitude by beneficiaries for the aid they had received.[25] Cheryl recalled:

> And at some point, we were like, 'well, it's all so much drama', but when in fact, actually, the point of our page is to alleviate this drama ... We weren't saying, you know, 'Donate your money because these people are in crisis'. We were saying, 'Hey, look at these families smiling about the bag of rice they just got. Let's help another one'.

EcoTrek staff shooting and sharing these images were also brokers for the tourism industry and broader economy on the island. EcoTrek prioritised what they assessed as the longer-term recovery needs of their target communities. They chose to challenge what they saw as dominant representations of post-disaster geographies and affects on social media in order to sustain tourism. All three EcoTrek interviewees – Victor, Teddy and Cheryl – told us this in various phrasings. Teddy explained:

> I posted about the beauty of [the island] and it was more promotional. It's still beautiful. Because people are like ... 'I don't see how I can come on holiday, with total devastation and people ... dying'. [I showed] it's not like that ... Us, we are a tourism business; we need visitors.

EcoTrek's social media thus reflected the business's 'currency' of operation (in Teddy's terms). EcoTrek ran on paying tour customers not 'followers' or virtual acknowledgements or appreciation. Respectful and positive representations of affected communities both generated donations and sustained their business.

Images also brokered EcoTrek's claims to trust and efficacy. Donors could see the aid 'loop' (from donation to delivery and impacts) being closed through EcoTrek posts. Their images may have been staged and curated, set up via unequal exchange or representative of only partial success, but they circulated on social media as evidence of aid delivery. They were intended to extend trust between EcoTrek and their donors over time. EcoTrek deployed images to broker aid in four ways: to act as information in themselves, to trigger action (donations, comments, circulation), to report the outcomes of donations, and to evidence aid delivery and so, by extension, perform accountability. EcoTrek images also brokered new kinds of North–South relationships within the geopolitics of aid.

EcoTrek's autonomy let them develop an ethos around social media images where nationals from 'donor nations' never featured prominently in their posts. Where non-Filipinos appeared at all, it was eyes facing forward, gaze directed away from the camera, carrying boxes of donations under the direction of Filipinos. Some of EcoTrek's European guests out on cruises at the time of the typhoon stayed on to help. A group of tourists stranded on the islands also came to volunteer. Victor wrote to people who had cruises booked after Haiyan and explained that there would be no cancellations; they should come, keep the economy running, and help in the recovery by offloading relief goods from EcoTrek boats. Volunteers from the Global North were labour, not managing operations or posting to Facebook. Volunteers' accounts of transformative experiences were, however, never shared across EcoTrek's social media feed. EcoTrek represented all their efforts as 'South–South' aid, delivered from Filipino to Filipino, supported by donations from the Global North which they controlled.

Their autonomy enabled EcoTrek to flout global expectations for accountability and transparency. EcoTrek often found donors' requests for receipts for donations naïve. Not being a registered charity or NGO, EcoTrek was not required to issue receipts or publish accounts. This made aid efficient and direct, as Teddy explained:

> if you send it to us, you have to trust where it's going. If you want me to track all our bank records, find your surname and find out how much and send you an email to confirm that we got that, that's what creates the 45% administration fee that you're complaining about with Red Cross! If you trust us, then we cut out the admin and that [donation] goes directly to these people.

Images EcoTrek 'reported' on social media served as receipts in themselves, showing how donations were converted to goods and delivered. Victor recounted:

> Be an on the ground partner and use our logistics ... For a fixed period ... two weeks, three weeks. Get people up on their feet. Just short-term ... Our report is the receipt. That's it. So, we don't have to do ... all the administrative work.

All EcoTrek interviewees considered their recovery effort a success. Their social media fund-raising brought them global visibility as a socially-conscious business and bolstered trust in their ongoing local relationships: 'People saw that it was genuine ... it wasn't just a business for ourselves. We did actually ... care'.

3. Analysis: mediating global trust

Clearly EcoTrek's recovery effort would not have been as successful if it had not been brokered by Facebook. Using the platform to work across a number of physical world and online sites gave their aid initiative a global reach. What was different from many other digitally-mediated kinds of aid was that EcoTrek extended trust relations initially built through offline, real-world exchanges. Most of their initial donors had been on one of their cruises. Thus, they relied on reactivating trust relationships online and extending them to elicit further donations. EcoTrek thus cannot be considered a classic digital or online aid broker, or even an entirely 'entrepreneurial broker' which operates primarily to generate profit.[26] Reactivating these relationships and extending this trust, however, necessarily glossed over frictions in the field.

The key points of friction in EcoTrek's story reveal defining characteristics of mediated citizen aid and layered brokerage. What is important is not to distinguish EcoTrek as either a citizen aid operation *or* a broker, but to understand how EcoTrek combined aspects of both functions and identities and what that combination can then tell us about the new space of humanitarian aid. Donors, local government and communities, and the broader aid sector all saw different aspects of EcoTrek. While these aspects seem contradictory, it is the ability to hold together and sustain relationships across these contradictions that made EcoTrek an effective broker. EcoTrek negotiated trust relations across these contradictions in the following three ways.

3.1. By expanding up and out

EcoTrek cascaded local trust relationships up the humanitarian relief hierarchy of organisations towards national NGOs and local government relief efforts. Being first on the ground and establishing a visible online presence very rapidly lent EcoTrek credibility. EcoTrek's high profile online and initial resource base then made it sought after as a formal

– and thus trusted – local partner for smaller Filipino and INGOs, the Catholic church and the Local Government Units in target communities.[27] Several national-level NGOs coursed their relief goods/donations through EcoTrek because they saw – online – that EcoTrek was both working within long-established local relationships and performing accountability.

EcoTrek maintained autonomy, even where activities were delegated to them by other donors. They refused to partner with NGOs that wanted to offload resources and make EcoTrek staff do the groundwork of locating recipients for inappropriate donations. EcoTrek refused to do monitoring of distribution channels and to distribute goods that had political-party logos on them. This meant they refused to support factions within provincial and national politics. EcoTrek could do so because of their citizen aid status. Because delivering development aid or seeking project grants would never be their core business, EcoTrek did not need either future consideration from donors or political favours.

Social media enabled EcoTrek to operate at a global scale within informal knowledge networks. People from other citizen aid initiatives got in touch via Facebook. Teddy received the most useful advice on structuring their recovery effort via an unsolicited Facebook message. A Swedish citizen aid worker in the 2014 post-tsunami recovery in Thailand advised him on handling online enquiries:

> quickly write a little e-mail saying: if you want to help, donate. And give them a bank account. The peek will only come once. It won't come back. So, you got to catch it straight away … you're gonna get a lot of offers for help … But don't accept them, if … people [f***ing] flying over there to paint people's houses and all this b******t … Go give [the funds raised] to the beneficiaries as soon as possible 'cause after that you get bogged down in the politics of it.

3.2. By remaining relatively invisible to government

Avoiding getting bogged down in local aid politics became EcoTrek's strategy. Their activities both competed with and complemented aid distributed by other actors on the ground. Because EcoTrek relied on flows of private monies, they could circumvent the bureaucracy governing large INGOs and government aid. EcoTrek's activities were thus comparatively less visible to local government officials than those of large charities and NGOs like the Red Cross and Oxfam, which had formal collaboration agreements in place. EcoTrek could often get aid in first, before other actors had secured the requisite government approvals and resources, but being invisible also had drawbacks.

In interviews with Local Government officials in recipient communities, we found a notable lack of awareness of citizen aid activities after Haiyan, including those of EcoTrek. In a municipality where EcoTrek had operated, the municipal Disaster Risk Reduction Management plan did not include volunteers or citizen aid groups. Our government interviewees saw no need to include citizen groups because they operate 'just as they can'. Local government offices appeared to have limited or no purview over citizen aid. Instead, local government officials had themselves been aid brokers for national government and national and INGOs. Though elected officials, they had used their own personal networks to channel resources received from national government and international donors to selected community-level beneficiaries after Haiyan.[28] Local government officials thus saw themselves – informally – as competing with citizen aid for donor resources.

Asked specifically about the use of social media to mobilize resources after Haiyan, local government interviewees did not recognise its values. They considered citizen aid as best left to operate independently, and social media as being largely beyond their area of concern. They all described relief efforts led by citizen aid as *'kanya-kanya'* or 'to each his own'. While they knew that 'some people' had come to the Local Government Units (usually Barangay Halls or Municipal Halls) to inform government officials that they were doing their own relief work after Haiyan, they thought this was 'only small'. They were unaware of the scope of the international fund-raising operation or the local activities of EcoTrek. EcoTrek had handled many tens of thousands of dollars of aid donations – likely just as much, if not more, money than had come through Local Government-brokered recovery efforts.

EcoTrek interviewees told us they had avoided local government except where necessary, only making courtesy calls. They had foreseen local government requirements would be obstructive and collaboration difficult. Early on, they encountered a complex local authorisation process required to borrow a government boat (that was not being used at the time) to deliver relief goods. They thought keeping a government boat docked and restricting its use for disaster response was unethical. Reflecting on this, Victor explained that citizen aid ethics were based on personal trust and thus incompatible with the impersonal bureaucratic ethos of local government: 'we're not … choked by any bureaucracy … I think it's a trust thing. It's much more of a "I'll give it to you personally. I don't care what you gonna use it for" … But I know what you do'. This perceived mismatch in ethics meant collaboration with local government was infrequent.

Autonomy, global networks and this lack of local visibility created a particular niche for EcoTrek. Performing accountability online gave evidence of EcoTrek's efficacy, but this did not meet accepted aid-industry standards. This inability to produce key audit and accountability measures then in turn limited the scope of their activities. Funds donated by corporations who required a charitable donation receipt remained inaccessible to them, as did funds flowing from INGOs who required proper accounting reports.

EcoTrek's commitment to flexible informality thus drove them towards even more social media fundraising from private individuals in their international networks. Their online, trust-based and dyadic approach produced a horizontal rather than vertical flow of humanitarian aid. Instead of placing themselves in competition with other national and international fund-raising efforts at the larger-scale donor level, EcoTrek remained smaller-scale. And, since they were not visibly competing with local government aid brokers, EcoTrek were seen as irrelevant to officials' interests. EcoTrek thus carved out a new niche for themselves in the humanitarian ecology.

3.3. By meeting immediate needs

Pre-Haiyan, trust in local government was not high among communities in the typhoon-affected areas.[29] Post-Haiyan, people in our beneficiary interviews did not trust that their local government officials had provided aid when it had become available. Instead, aid beneficiaries contrasted EcoTrek's aid to their experience of aid channelled through local government. They considered government aid to take too long and to be corrupt in its delivery and distribution. Those who had successfully accessed local government aid complained about the layers of bureaucracy surrounding relief goods and funds. Asked how aid delivery could improve, these interviewees answered: '*direkta sa tao ang bigay*' [give directly to the people]. They reported only EcoTrek and the Red Cross – which had a high-profile local presence – had come directly to the grassroots level to deliver aid after Haiyan.

'Giving directly' was not necessarily so direct. Despite their rhetoric, EcoTrek did not keep local government interests entirely at a distance. EcoTrek relied on local elected leaders at the Barangay (village) level to distribute aid. Rather than recruiting municipal officials as brokers, they worked at the next level down with wealthy or prominent local households, school teachers and Barangay Council members. In one instance, they relied on the personal networks of the family of a Barangay Councillor to distribute some of their' second wave' of relief goods. Not surprisingly, this family gave away the goods to people others perceived as their friends, rather than those in most need. However, when compared to similar local government aid channels where aid got stuck in the Municipal Hall and never made it out to the villages, our community interviewees found this arrangement to be more accessible and transparent.

Beneficiaries forgot that EcoTrek's efforts had been shaped by business interests. In their opinion, EcoTrek was a charitable organisation. Our community interviewees discussed EcoTrek as if it were a formally registered NGO, which it was not. They told us that NGOs worked better than the government because they were faster and came directly to the people, then offered EcoTrek as an example. Thus, one effect of EcoTrek's successes as a citizen aid broker was to reinforce mistrust of government efforts. Yet their claim to greater trust and influence in local communities is relative. EcoTrek also struggled, as brokers do, to establish continued trust and create the kinds of programmes that would deliver long term rehabilitation. EcoTrek staff considered the problems they faced arose with competition from other aid donors.

3.3.1. *Transparency, trust and refusal*

EcoTrek's fund-raising success generated a surplus. This let them extend their efforts beyond immediate recovery and move into rehabilitation. EcoTrek commissioned and donated fibreglass fishing boats to fishing families who had lost their boats. These donated boats, however, weren't immediately put to use in fishing. Recipients apparently did not trust the new material. Instead, fibreglass boats were left on shore and some eventually became planters for vegetables. EcoTrek decided to repossess the donated boats. EcoTrek did not have to account to donors higher in the aid hierarchy for this apparent failure in their strategy. Instead, Victor set out the reasons for the boat recall on a social media post, under a photo of a fibreglass boat full of soil and greens. He recounted:

> we pulled [the boats], it's transparent ... if that's a big organization, why would you pull that boat out if they're not using it in the village? That's causing problems in the relationship ... But we just want to make it work 'cause we know that it took us three months to make those boats and how much, like millions, that we spent on those boats. And if you're gonna plant pechay [cabbage] in it: 'NO'! There's much more passion in what we do than – [than just handing things out].

Fishing households eventually decided to try out the boats some months later. EcoTrek loaned out boats for one-third of their cost (PHP 6000), arranging for the debts to be collected by the boat recipients' Barangay Council. Barangay Councils were free to use the funds collected for their own projects, as long as they informed EcoTrek about what they had done with the money. Here, EcoTrek was attempting to work at the local level for long-term development.

EcoTrek considered the problem with offering fishing households replacement boats had been the timing. Victor reflected: 'around December [2013], [the island] was flooded by people giving them things, throwing them money ... already people offering to re-build their house because they have these ideas'. Even as the boat project faltered, EcoTrek continually refused to participate in rehabilitation initiatives they felt were neo-colonial and/or did not fit with the existing livelihoods of affected communities. Their staff were confident in their own expertise and particularly scathing about ill-considered but well-meaning approaches from international donors. Victor explained:

> if they say, 'Oh no, we have a Danish architect'. No. F**k your Danish architect. They don't know. 'We have a very famous Danish architect who's designing sustainable ...' Yeah, but he doesn't f**ng know the island, so, no.

EcoTrek staff resented international donations of flashy housing projects and inappropriate gifts of food. EcoTrek used their surplus funds to set up a charitable foundation attached to their business and hired Filipino development professionals to scope and identify new collaborative projects across their area of operations. They currently greet all their tour clients and new staff with the story of EcoTrek's contribution to the recovery after Typhoon Haiyan and explain how the costs of tours support the projects of this foundation. Teddy explained: 'We think long-term, and it's really "no hand-outs". Don't give anything on a plate but run a company. Now we're in a mix of, is it a foundation? Is it social enterprise?'

Participating in the recovery as a citizen aid group transformed EcoTrek's business from one with a social ethic into a social enterprise that supports local development directly. EcoTrek staff consider this shift to represent an extension of their underlying ethos into new activities. Setting up the foundation – now operating as a registered charity – was the ethical choice for the unanticipated windfall generated by their successful social media strategy.

4. How social media reshapes citizen aid

This case reveals how social media has enabled an expansion of citizen aid initiatives as brokerage activities. Images circulated on social media mediated trust by expanding the scope of aid activities up and out while simultaneously concealing that scope from local authorities and meeting immediate community needs. Social media connected disparate groups, brought together different logics, representations, meanings and materialities, enabling citizen aid groups to act with autonomy as aid brokers.[30] Of course, there is evidence of both exploitation and altruism in these activities, as we would anticipate with brokerage. Brokers are neither entirely motivated by selfless charitable concerns nor true 'disaster capitalists' but operate in the middle ground. While EcoTrek's new charitable foundation gives them additional cachet with potential guests, it nonetheless delivers community programmes at the grassroots level.

The affordances of social media enabled the upward cascade of brokerage relations on which their success relied. EcoTrek's success enabled them to create offline social and political space for themselves. While such citizen aid groups may not initially want formal relationships with government and other donors, the reputation they establish online increasingly opens up the 'invited spaces' where they can form formal partnerships with government and registered NGOs. Citizen aid can then meet with resistance because it refuses to change its mode of operation. Thus, liaison or co-ordination between citizen aid and government units or registered NGOs remains weak and highly problematic. Individual staff, members or volunteers from citizen aid groups do not typically move on to careers in humanitarian or development work. Instead, they return to their previous occupations, though perhaps with a different ethos in their work. Thus, rather than producing a durable and competing set of networks that undermine local government legitimacy or other civil society organisations, citizen aid groups occupy a comparatively complementary space in the aid ecology. They do not so much pose a direct threat to existing hierarchies of aid provision through government channels, but supplement and diversify them, filling some of the structural holes of the post-disaster recovery aid ecology.[31]

The emergence of citizen aid brokers on social media thus represents an important new form of aid brokerage. Social media can be used to make previously incommensurable forms of capital fungible, converting social capital expressed as social media 'shares' and 'likes' into donations, and those donations into trust relationships with donors and beneficiaries. The global reach of social media offers citizen aid an exponential increase in the number of global/external brokers which they may bring under their influence and partial control, enrolling them into their transformation of capitals. Importantly, these brokers are not just human actors – the familiar donors, guests, businesses, government officials and INGOs we anticipate – but images, platforms and algorithms.

These new digital actants are becoming vital in disaster recovery. But digital actants can also operate in ways that their human originators have not foreseen, creating their own brokerage effects. This potential agency in digital technologies means citizen aid is best understood as a layering of interdependent brokerage relations creating a global assemblage of aid brokers. Ironically, this citizen aid assemblage is *least* visible at the scale of municipal and provincial government where most other aid is received and distributed. Globally, however, this brokerage assemblage has potentially powerful effects in its performative impact on the locus of control over resources, representations and narratives in humanitarian aid.[32]

Citizen aid groups deploy social media to control representation of themselves as Southern and local actors – people in touch with on-the-ground realities, engaged with local communities, knowledgeable about their area and mobile. Citizen aid challenges the usual disaster story by portraying a quick recovery on the ground that is attributable to local efforts, expertise and resilience. Performing recovery efforts as South–South aid on social media, citizen aid generates support for aid policy and delivery – albeit comparatively informal and smaller-scale – being transferred to actors in the Global South. Media skills and social media reach are thus key to building and sustaining citizen aid's new position in the aid ecology. Building these skills and constructing this position gives citizen aid brokers both autonomy and increased moral capital. Citizen aid's trust-sustaining efforts thus privilege South–South solidarity and service, enacting a global ethics of compassion, rather than seeking the approval of international donors, other aid actors, local government or potential volunteers through formal bureaucratic channels. Citizen aid groups thus argue that their work is the most authentic way of 'localising' aid.

Conclusion

Where citizen aid brokers fit in the shifting aid ecology is still being negotiated in the push towards localisation.[33] People may potentially come to trust these citizen aid groups more than local government or larger donors, in terms of their local knowledge and their perceived responsiveness and transparency.[34] Yet the outlook remains uncertain. Facebook, which has been key to these new aid initiatives, has been widely discredited for facilitating and profiting from political interference. This complicates the story, because the affordances of this platform have quickly become vital to citizen participation in disaster recovery operations.[35] Citizen aid may thus be curtailed or undermined by social media's problematic entanglements with political manipulation if this platform is not replaced by other, less exploitative, services. Equally, the image-production strategies and ethics citizen aid groups develop and deploy will be something to which social media executives should pay closer attention, lest they lose the trust of beneficiaries and donors alike. We see here how brokerage's necessary-but-ambivalent relationships could potentially be made more transparent through online performances of accountability, but much nonetheless remains concealed behind the screens.

Social media has shifted the dynamic relations of trust between citizen aid groups and communities. Circulating images enabled citizen aid brokers coordinating across multiple sites to assemble global resource packages of materials, skills and knowledge quickly and efficiently. It offered personal, tailored and rapid responses to queries about needs and the routing of material resources. This performance of speed and targeting potentially threatened to subvert the authority and position of other, more traditional, aid brokers, because local trust in brokers was directly related to their perceived responsiveness to immediate recovery needs.[36] All brokers build the trust they enjoy by establishing integrity: delivering what they promised. Citizen aid delivered by performing online accountability to both donors and communities for the funds raised, accompanied by easily-understood and convincing explanations of the group's actions. This practice of making-visible aid delivery was part of an ongoing process of renewing and expanding trust that created citizen aid's 'brand' reputation. This process drew together interpersonal relationships with beneficiary communities and external connections to global donors mediated via a social networking site. The result, in this case, produced more value than could be delivered as 'aid'. However, in the future, communities may come to regard this kind of brokerage as less a kind of 'help' than a new form of profiteering or commercial exploitation.

Finally, there are implications for the wider space of humanitarian aid. If comparatively inexperienced and improvisational citizen aid brokers can use the economic bricolage inherent in online and long-distance fundraising efforts to powerful effects yet are typically left out of discussions on 'local aid' and disaster-preparedness or response plans, then structural holes in aid delivery will become larger. Such vital actors should not be excluded from planning discussions because their contributions are time-limited, informal and unregistered. The same or similar groups will re-organise and re-emerge in response to new disasters, so changes in practice are needed to create invited spaces where these groups can participate. Citizen aid should be engaged in plans for emergency preparedness and in broader discussions about the ethics of mediated disaster recovery efforts.

Disclosure statement

No potential conflict of interest was reported by the authors.

Acknowledgements

The authors thank their respondents at EcoTrek for their generosity, reflection and candour – opening up a novel set of activities undertaken in crisis conditions to academic investigation is a courageous move. We also thank colleagues in the Newton Tech4Dev Network (https://newtontechfordev.com) and

De La Salle University for initial input on the project. We are grateful to the Department of Anthropology at the University of Sussex for hosting the Citizen Aid workshop and colleagues who attended that workshop for their generous comments, the editors of the Citizen Aid special issue for their encouraging insight and, finally, the anonymous reviewers for their collegial critique. The usual caveats apply.

Funding

Research was supported by a British Council Newton Agham Fund Institutional Links Award held by between the University of Leicester, UK, and De La Salle University, Philippines.

Notes

1. Fouksman, "Civil Society"; Mercer and Green, "Making Civil Society Work."
2. Fechter, "Brokering Transnational Flows"; Sanchez et al., "Scars of Good Intentions."
3. Bonacker et al., *Localisation in Development Aid*.
4. Dawes, "H2H."
5. World Humanitarian Summit, *Financing*; Bonacker et al., *Localisation in Development Aid*; Forrest et al., "Civil Society Contributions."
6. Saban, "Entrepreneurial Brokers."
7. Both Perez and McKay reposted citizen aid posts and made cash donations after Haiyan. Perez also donated items and sorting resources collected in Manila in support of citizen aid efforts on the island. She is herself a citizen aid worker, having organised recover efforts after Typhoon Parma in 2009.
8. Atienza et al., *Urban Poverty*; Eadie and Su, "Post-Disaster Social Capital"; Ong and Combinido, "Silenced in the Aid Interface"; Madianou et al., "The Appearance of Accountability."
9. Ong and Combinido, "Silenced in the Aid Interface."
10. Bankoff and Hilhorst, "The Politics of Risk."
11. Aldrich, *Building Resilience*; Sou, "Sustainable Resilience."
12. Aldrich and Crook, "Strong Civil Society," 279; McIlwaine, "Civil Society."
13. Laurie and Baillie Smith, "Unsettling Geographies"; Malkki, *The Need to Help*.
14. Laurie and Baillie Smith, "Unsettling Geographies."
15. Lewis and Mosse, *Development Brokers*, 11–13; Hönke and Müller, "Brokerage, Intermediation, Translation," 335–6; Lindquist, "Brokers and Brokerage."
16. Ong and Combinido, "Silenced in the Aid Interface."
17. Hilhorst, *The Real World of NGOs*.
18. Lindquist, "Brokers and Brokerage"; Shrestha and Yeoh, "Introduction"; Ortiga, "Education as Early Stage Brokerage."
19. Aldrich, *Building Resilience*.
20. Lewis and Mosse, *Development Brokers*, 12.

21. Saban, "Entrepreneurial Brokers."
22. Small, "How Many Cases."
23. Ong and Combinido, *The Filipino Aid Workers*.
24. Ong et al., "Obliged to be Grateful"; Ong and Combinido, "Silenced in the Aid Interface."
25. Ong et al., "Obliged to be Grateful."
26. Saban, "Entrepreneurial Brokers."
27. Cornelio and Kuah-Pearce, "Religious Philanthropy."
28. James, "Mediating Indebtedness."
29. Bankoff and Hilhorst, "The Politics of Risk."
30. Koster and van Leynseele, "Brokers as Assemblers."
31. Saban, "Entrepreneurial Brokers."
32. Jensen, "Epilogue."
33. Bonacker et al., *Localisation in Development Aid*.
34. Ong and Combinido, "Silenced in the Aid Interface."
35. Ong and Cabanes, "Architects of Networked Disinformation"; McKay, "The Virtual Meets Reality."
36. Ong and Combinido, "Silenced in the Aid Interface."

ORCID

Deirde McKay http://orcid.org/0000-0002-9019-2207

Bibliography

Aldrich, D. *Building Resilience: Social Capital in Post-Disaster Recovery*. Chicago: University of Chicago Press, 2012.

Aldrich, D., and K. Crook. "Strong Civil Society as a Double-Edged Sword: Siting Trailers in Post-Katrina New Orleans." *Political Research Quarterly* 61, no. 3 (2008): 379–389. doi:10.1177/1065912907312983.

Atienza, M., P. P. Eadie, and M. Tan-Mullins. *Urban Poverty in the Wake of Environmental Disaster: Rehabilitation, Resilience and Typhoon Haiyan (Yolanda)*. London: Routledge, 2019.

Bankoff, G., and D. Hilhorst. "The Politics of Risk in the Philippines: Comparing State and NGO Perceptions of Disaster Management." *Disasters* 33, no. 4 (2009): 686–704. doi:10.1111/j.1467-7717.2009.01104.x.

Bonacker, T., J. von Heusinger, and K. Zimmer, eds. *Localization in Development Aid: How Global Institutions Enter Local Lifeworlds*. Abingdon: Routledge, 2017.

Cornelio, J. S., and K. E. Kuah-Pearce. "Religious Philanthropy in Asia." *Asian Journal of Social Science* 43 (2015): 349–355. doi:10.1163/15685314-04304002.

Dawes, M. "H2H – A New Formula for Aid?" CDAC Network, 2017. http://bit.ly/2nXubMB

Eadie, P., and Y. Su. "Post-Disaster Social Capital: Trust, Equity, Bayanihan and Typhoon Yolanda." *Disaster Prevention and Management: An International Journal* 27, no. 3 (2018): 334–345. doi:10.1108/DPM-02-2018-0060.

Fechter, A.-M. "Brokering Transnational Flows of Care: The Case of Citizen Aid." [Early View]. *Ethnos* (2019): 1–16. doi:10.1080/00141844.2018.1543339.

Forrest, S., E.-M. Trell, and J. Woltjer. "Civil Society Contributions to Local Level Flood Resilience: Before, during and after the 2015 Boxing Day Floods in the Upper Calder Valley." *Transactions of the Institute of British Geographers* 44, no. 2 (2019): 422–436. doi:10.1111/tran.12279.

Fouksman, E. "Civil Society Knowledge Networks: How International Development Institutions Reshape the Geography of Knowledge." *Third World Quarterly* 38, no. 8 (2017): 1847–1872. doi:10.1080/01436597.2016.1233490.

Hilhorst, D. *The Real World of NGOs: Discourses, Diversity, and Development*. Quezon City: Ateneo de Manila University Press, 2003.

Hönke, J., and M. Müller "Brokerage, Intermediation, Translation." In *The Oxford Handbook of Governance and Limited Statehood*, edited by A. Draude, R. Börzel, and T. Risse, 335–352. Oxford: Oxford University Press, 2018.

James, D. "Mediating Indebtedness in South Africa." *Ethnos* 83, no. 5 (2018): 814–831. doi:10.1080/00141844.2017.1362450.

Jensen, S. "Epilogue: Brokers – Pawns, Disruptors, Assemblers." *Ethnos* 83, no. 5 (2018): 888–891. doi:10.1080/00141844.2017.1362455.

Koster, M., and Y. van Leynseele. "Brokers as Assemblers: Studying Development through the Lens of Brokerage." *Ethnos* 83, no. 5 (2018): 803–813. doi:10.1080/00141844.2017.1362451.

Laurie, N., and M. Baillie Smith. "Unsettling Geographies of Volunteering and Development." *Transactions of the Institute of British Geographers* 43, no. 1 (2018): 95–109. doi:10.1111/tran.12205.

Lindquist, J. "Brokers and Brokerage, Anthropology of." In *International Encyclopaedia of Social and Behaviour Science*, edited by J. D Wright, 2nd ed., 870–874. Amsterdam: Elsevier, 2015.

Lewis, D., and D. Mosse. *Development Brokers and Translators: The Ethnography of Aid and Agencies*. Bloomfield, CT: Kumarian Press, 2006.

Madianou, M., J. C. Ong, L. Longboan, and J. S. Cornelio. "The Appearance of Accountability: Communication Technologies and Power Asymmetries in Humanitarian Aid and Disaster Recovery." *Journal of Communication* 66, no. 6 (2016): 960–981. doi:10.1111/jcom.12258.

Malkki, L. *The Need to Help: The Domestic Arts of International Humanitarianism*. Durham, NC: Duke University Press, 2015.

McIlwaine, C. "Civil Society." In *International Encyclopaedia of Human Geography*, edited by R. Kitchin and N. Thrift, 136–141. Amsterdam: Elsevier, 2009.

McKay, D. "The Virtual Meets Reality: The Policy Implications of E-Diasporas." Australian Strategic Policy Institute, 2017. https://bit.ly/31y4J11

Mercer, C., and M. Green. "Making Civil Society Work." *Geoforum* 45 (2013): 106–115. doi:10.1016/j.geoforum.2012.10.008.

Ong, J. and J. Cabanes. "Architects of Networked Disinformation." Newton Fund Tech4Dev Network, 2017. https://bit.ly/2EhunPD

Ong, J., J. Flores, and P. Combinido. "Obliged to be Grateful: How Local Communities Experienced Humanitarian Actors in the Haiyan Response." Plan International, 2017. https://bit.ly/2KheCdM

Ong, J., and P. Combinido. "Silenced in the Aid Interface: Responsible Brokerage and Its Obstacles in Humanitarian Interventions." *Philippine Sociological Review* 65 (2017): 39–64.

Ong, J., and P. Combinido. *The Filipino Aid Workers of Typhoon Yolanda*. Communication Department Faculty Publication Series 52. Amherst: University of Massachusetts, 2017. https://bit.ly/2WNThQd

Ortiga, Y. "Education as Early Stage Brokerage: Cooling out Aspiring Migrants for the Global Hotel Industry." *Pacific Affairs* 91, no. 4 (2018): 717–738. doi:10.5509/2018914717.

Saban, L. "Entrepreneurial Brokers in Disaster Response Network in Typhoon Haiyan in the Philippines." *Public Management Review* 17, no. 10 (2015): 1496–1517. doi:10.1080/14719037.2014.943271.

Sanchez, M., P. P. Perez, and F. Perez. 2016. "The Scars of Good Intentions: Lessons from post-Parma Volunteer's Relief and Recovery Interventions in Benguet, Philippines." In *Resilience and Sustainability*, edited by A. Flor, A Ciencio, and C. Sta-Maria-Abalos, 171–185. Baguio: University of the Philippines, Baguio.

Shrestha, T., and B. Yeoh. "Introduction: Practices of Brokerage in the Making of Migration Infrastructures in Asia." *Pacific Affairs* 91, no. 4 (2018): 663–672. doi:10.5509/2018914663.

Small, M.-L. "'How Many Cases Do I Need?': On Science and the Logic of Case Selection in Field-Based Research." *Ethnography* 10, no. 1 (2009): 5–38. doi:10.1177/1466138108099586.

Sou, G. "Sustainable Resilience? Disaster Recovery and the Marginalisation of Sociocultural Needs and Concerns. " *Progress in Development Studies* 19, no. 2 (2019): 144–159. doi:10.1177/1464993418824192.

World Humanitarian Summit. "Financing: Investing in Humanity" 2016. http://bit.ly/1NVKEbR

Digital mediations of everyday humanitarianism: the case of Kiva.org

Anke Schwittay

ABSTRACT
The proliferation of Web 2.0 platforms that aim to facilitate social action, often connected to international development or environmental sustainability, has contributed to the ongoing popularisation of development. In this article, I argue that it has resulted in the digitally-enabled constitution of everyday humanitarians, who are everyday people supportive of poverty alleviation. Kiva.org, a US-based online microlending platform that invites everyday humanitarians to make US$25 loans to Kiva entrepreneurs around the world, is a prime site to study these processes. I show how Kiva cultivates supporters through the mediated production of affective investments, which are financial, social and emotional commitments to distant others. This happens through the design of an affective architecture which in turn generates financial and spatial mediations. While these result in microloans and attendant sentiments of affinity, they also lead to financial clicktivism and connections that obscures the asymmetries and riskscapes resulting from Kiva's microlending work.

Bob Harris is a Kiva executive's dream. Since becoming a Kiva lender in January 2009, he and his lending team of 2200 members have made more than 200,000 loans totalling over US$9 million.[1] Bob has travelled the world to visit many of his borrowers and written a book called *The International Bank of Bob*.[2] Playing with the ubiquity of the name Bob for ordinary, middle-class Americans and their depiction in popular media, the book claims that everybody could become a Kiva lender and enjoy it. In one particular scene, Harris describes how every time he sits down in front of his computer to log into his Kiva account, he feels like he is running a mini-foundation. This feeling is echoed by Kiva's long-term president who observed that on Kiva, 'the average person can be like a Bill Gates or a Rockefeller'.[3] Such sentiments have appealed to over 1.6 million lenders since Kiva's founding in 2005, making the organisation a prime site to study the constitution of everyday humanitarians in digital space. As laid out in the introduction to this special edition, this term refers to everyday people supportive of poverty alleviation. This contemporary subject position is created by the fact that 'we are more likely today to have sympathy for, and even do something to alleviate, the suffering of people and animals distant for ourselves – geographically, culturally, in their species being – than were men and women three centuries ago'.[4] As one of the Kiva co-founders expressed it in more pragmatic terms, 'we were interested in engaging average income people to unlock a new type of more connected capital'.[5] This capital comes in the form of small loans to 'Kiva entrepreneurs' all over the world.

Kiva operates in the highly contested space of microfinance. This once highly regarded global poverty alleviation practice, in no small part due to the work of Muhammad Yunus, has come under. A recent collection of essays, called *Seduced and Betrayed* and co-edited by practitioner-cum-ardent critic Milford Bateman, captures the tone of the debate.[6] Its criticisms, often based on in-depth ethnographic research with women, who are still the main targets of microfinance programmes, focus on microfinance's implications in ruinous neoliberal policies, its often detrimental gender dynamics and the exploitative effects of microfinance's commercialisation. In addition, microfinance's contribution to poverty alleviation remains unproven, while it can undermine local economies and social networks.[7] Such studies are absolutely critical in showing the destructive effects of microfinance, especially when pursued as a global, commercialised development intervention. And they raise the question of why it continues to be a popular practice with everyday humanitarians, many of whom regard it as a 'panacea of choice'.[8]

Kiva is often mentioned in writings aiming to answer this question. For some, it is a manifestation of 'millennial development' embraced by young people wanting to make poverty history,[9] while others contribute this persistence to the rise of 'pop development' that is no longer the domain of (economic) experts.[10] There are arguments that Kiva is an example of humanitarianism's theatricality[11] and that continued support results from the organisation's representational practices that engender humanitarian sentiments.[12] This article expands on these critiques by taking serious the materiality of Kiva as a technological platform and argues that we can understand its popularity as a result of processes of mediation to which this materiality gives rise.[13] The organisation has been called a 'matrix of intimate mediations'[14] and on its website these mediations take technological, financial and spatial forms. Anne Vestergaard, drawing on Lilie Chouliaraki's seminal work, posits mediation as constituted by processes of hypermediacy and immediacy. The former looks at how technologies and institutions shape relationship between donors and beneficiaries, while the latter focuses on how connectivity is established through practices of representation that give rise to 'affinity and agency as key devices for overcoming distance'.[15] Affinity is informed by notions of kinship that establish a sense of responsibility towards others, and agency bestows a sense of efficacy that one's actions can positively contribute towards poverty alleviation. Drawing on this conceptualisation, I show how Kiva cultivates everyday humanitarians through the mediated production of affective investments.

Confirming the observation that 'people care if they are invested',[16] affective investments are emotional, social and financial commitments to distant others to alleviate their poverty. While affect itself has engendered numerous debates in a variety of scholarly disciplines,[17] my analysis draws on research that highlights the role of affect in enabling global connections through subject formation. Here, 'affect structures cultural logics of global connection, as affective management techniques shape the situated subjects who enact global networks'.[18] In addition, affect shapes what matters to people, within fields of possibilities that circumscribes its effects. As Larry Grossberg has argued, 'affect is the coloration or passion within which one's investments on, or commitments to, the world are made possible'.[19] Affective investments speak to the entanglements of calculations and emotions in the practices of development supporters, whose commitments are shaped by their heads and their hearts. In the case of Kiva, financial contributions are the most visible manifestation of affective investments, but they are embedded in a moral grammar of sentiments and relationships. It is precisely the articulation of the three different dimensions – financial, social and emotional – that makes affective investments so powerful and enduring and worthy of closer academic analysis. From Kiva's co-founders' Jessica Jackley and Matt Flannery own affective labour as a newly-wed couple pursuing their passions in growing Kiva, and the ongoing popularity of the organisation, especially in the US, to the imaginary connections that are established between Kiva lenders and borrowers via the website, Kiva is suffused with humanitarian affect.

Research on Kiva began informally in 2006, when I was living in the San Francisco Bay Area and heard Flannery and Jackley speak about their fledgling organisation at different events. Formal research took place from 2009 to 2014 and consisted of extensive online research, partly as a participant-observer through my family's Kiva loans, fieldwork with Kiva partners in Mexico and Indonesia, and interviews with Kiva staff, volunteers and lenders. In the remainder of this article, I present brief observations on everyday humanitarian affect, before examining Kiva's technological, financial and spatial mediations.

Everyday humanitarian affect

In *A Theory of Moral Sentiments*, published in 1759, Adam Smith wrote about 'the emotions that direct our attention to the suffering of others and make us want to remedy them'.[20] From the mid-eighteenth century onwards, moral feelings of love, friendship, trust and solidarity were seen an equally important as a rational sense of obligation to incite action to help distant others.[21] This has led Didier Fassin to argue for the crucial importance of a '"humanitarian emotion": the affect by virtue of which human beings feel personally concerned by the situation of others'.[22] Similarly, Lisa Malkki has shown that the 'historical shaping of "international opinion" has much to do with the shaping and circulation of affect'.[23] This humanitarian affect has been cultivated in everyday people over the last 250 years, articulating with religious, politico-economic and social factors to constitute everyday humanitarians. Specifically, Thomas Haskell has identified four preconditions for the historic emergence of humanitarianism, from the existence of ethical maxims to help suffering strangers to the perception of involvement in the causes of this suffering, to the ability to see a way to end it. Most importantly, 'the recipes for intervention available to us must be ones of sufficient ordinariness, familiarity, certainty of effect and ease of operation'.[24] In other words, when these recipes draw on everyday practices, be they the consumption of sugar or online activities, they facilitate the constitution of everyday humanitarians. The practices enabled by these recipes should, by their fit with people's daily activities and experiences, create the confidence that taking action would make a difference. This is coupled with the conscience that not taking action would make people complicit in the perpetuation of suffering. Such confidence, conscience and know-how were, and continue to be, unevenly distributed.

The movement to abolish slavery which began in the late eighteenth century is often identified as one of the earliest humanitarian campaigns. Its followers 'succeeded in arousing sympathy and in awakening moral qualms so powerfully as to mobilize political action'.[25] For everyday people, this included boycotting slave-produced sugar and rum. Another early event that contributed to the formation of everyday humanitarians was the 1755 Lisbon earthquake, whose reporting in newspapers and inexpensive pamphlets focused on the suffering of ordinary people and thereby 'brought into consciousness a global, imagined empathy with the sufferings of distant strangers'.[26] It resulted in empathetic identification that supported emerging notions of a singular, shared humanity, which articulated with changing ideas about causal action at a distance to create the conditions under which sentiments of caring for far-off suffering others could emerge.

These sentiments drew on older religious ideas of brotherly love and the equal worth of all human beings,[27] as well as contemporary texts such as Smith's. The 1776 US *Declaration of Independence* and the French Declaration of the *Rights of Man and of the Citizen* 12 years later also inspired followers of the nascent humanitarian movement,[28] during a time when 'moral sentiments became the driving force for politics' more broadly.[29] In addition, capitalism's growth provided new insights into the causes of human affairs and how these could be made predictable across space and time, and also produced the discipline and technologies to act on these insights.[30] The expansion of international trade brought with it a new sense of interconnectedness, and early achievements of science and technology, wrapped up in modern ideas of progress and improvement, led to new understandings of responsibility and obligations.[31] Secular solutions were also beginning to be applied to fighting poverty and, together with changes in media, advertising and marketing, gave rise to mass humanitarianism.[32]

Since the early twentieth century, nascent humanitarian organisations have been working to 'compel care' among ever more people.[33] Their proliferation has led to the current democratisation of development, whose proponents observe that 'the fight against poverty, which was once almost exclusively restricted to aid officials and learned experts, has become one of the twenty-first century's most popular causes'.[34] The hundreds of thousands of online lenders, together with their fellow volunteers, child sponsors and campaign donors, feel responsibilised to make poverty history and are finding, or creating, the tools to do so. In addition, the involvement of celebrities in humanitarianism has contributed to its emotionalisation.[35] Coupling such celebrity appeal with an invitation to consume, Brand Aid is another way in which everyday humanitarians can gain emotional satisfaction from helping distant others.[36]

It is important to acknowledge the limits of humanitarian affect. According to Luc Boltanski:

> emotions can be discredited as foundations and symptoms of a moral disposition due to their circumstantial character – bound up as they are with a particular situation in which they are tethered to the real or imaginary presence of a particular unfortunate – which does not enable one to construct a moral duty with general validity.[37]

Humanitarian sentiments are often generated by individual stories of suffering that invisibilise structural causes and can depolitise development. As a result, action is often undertaken on an individual level as well. Sentiments can be fleeting and therefore provide unstable ground for action.[38] Indeed, while it is action that will sustain compassion, the translation of humanitarian affect into either charitable or political action is far from guaranteed.[39] When such action does occur, it is characterised by a tension – between compassion giving rise to a politics of inequality that focuses on the poor and a politics of solidarity that sees the other as an equal.[40] In its most extreme, humanitarian sentiments can lead to hatred, racism and chauvinism.[41] Last but not least, examining poverty and its alleviation through an affective lens must not neglect their material conditions, political dynamics and structural causes; instead it can enrich our understanding of how these work in the world, in line with broader attention being paid to the role of emotions in international development.[42]

This (necessarily) brief and general overview of how humanitarian affect participates in the constitution of everyday humanitarians has shown some of the ways in which over the last 300 years, diverse technologies, representations and institutions have played key roles in establishing links that have allowed everyday people to realise how they are connected to distant others and how their actions can hinder or help them. In the remainder of this article, I examine Kiva lenders as such everyday humanitarians and the ways in which their actions are mediated, beginning with the foundations of technological mediation.

Technological mediations

Kiva partakes in what has been called Giving 2.0, in reference to the role that new digital technologies play in philanthropic giving more generally.[43] By forging new connections, first and foremost among everyday humanitarians in the Global North, and, to a smaller extent, between them and their beneficiaries in the Global South, these technologies contribute to the popularisation of development. There are web-based campaigns, crowd-sourcing platforms and online marketplaces that combine the reach of the internet with the stickiness of social media and the aggregation of scalable models.[44] In this section, I examine how Kiva's characterisation as both a platform and an online marketplace shapes interactions on it and ultimately fosters a form of financial clicktivism.

Kiva as platform and marketplace

Kiva enables action at a distance through its 'technology platform'.[45] The term platform, which has been popularised by companies such as a Google and Facebook, 'is drawn from the available cultural vocabulary by stakeholders with specific aims, and carefully massaged so as to have particular resonance for particular audiences inside particular discourses'.[46] In other words, referring to a technology as a platform is a deliberate choice towards the achievement of specific aims. Consolidating the various meanings of the term around four main categories – from architectural (a physically raised stand) to figurative (a basis for action) to political (an ideological position) and finally computational (its most recent meaning) – Gillespie defines a platform as 'an infrastructure that supports the design and use of particular applications'.[47] In the current imaginary, the term implies neutrality and populism and is imbued with libertarian overtones of possibility and opportunity. This fit Kiva's vision of 'a world where all people hold the power to improve their lives' and of Kiva lenders being 'be[ing] part of the solution and mak[ing] a real difference in someone's life'.[48] Instead of poverty, Kiva's focuses on opportunity, improvement and progress.

Platforms have a particular architecture, which in Kiva's case can be described as an affective architecture. In a literal sense, the architecture of a website refers to the initial planning and design of its technical, functional and visual components so that it can best fulfil its purpose and requirements. Kiva's core business is to facilitate loans and its architecture supports that through a number of features that mobilise affective investments among its supporters. These begin with the representational practices so eloquently analysed by Shameem Black who shows how Kiva's photos and micronarratives create humanitarian sentiments via establishing affinity and connectivity.[49] There are also features to make lending on Kiva 'addictive', according to Flannery who notes that 'every time you load our website, it should be different. Every minute, loans are being purchased and repaid, and stories are being told about the borrowers'.[50] Continuous change produces continuous consumption by self-professed Kiva 'addicts' and 'Kivaholics', who get much pleasure from collecting countries and borrowers, from being able to complete a loan just before it is about to expire and from showing of their achievements.[51] This has resulted in Kiva being called 'a consumption playground where the poor are objectified and consumed, rather than empowered ... through the appropriation of borrowers as collectible items, resources for personal amusement and play'.[52] Another element of this gamification is the interaction among lenders via lending teams, which also highlights the competition at work on the website.

Most visibly, microfinance institutions (MFIs) and their borrowers displayed on the website are competing for the attention and investments of lenders, with hundreds of loans seeking to be filled at any given moment. Once again, how borrowers are represented, through the mediation of various Kiva agents, is crucial. However, lenders are also competing through membership in more than 37,000 lending teams. While in earlier instantiations of the website a leaderboard, showing which team had raised the most amount of money and recruited the most numbers of new members was prominently displayed on the home page, this information is now buried in a subpage of the website accessed through a link at the bottom of the homepage.[53] This might have been in response to misgivings from early lenders who were contacted for feedback before the lending teams were instituted. According to one of these lenders, 'the biggest piece of it for them [Kiva staff] was the opportunity for competition; teams of lenders battling one another to see which could make most loans ... I remember being shocked, because I thought the whole thing was about cooperation and working together'.[54] Perhaps the lender should not have been so surprised, as Kiva's co-founders conceived of the organisation as a 'self-regulating lending marketplace' where especially smaller MFIs that might not have access to conventional development financing would be able to compete for loan capital.[55]

Kiva is also an example of the 'online do-good 2.0 platforms' that have proliferated with the easier accessibility of interactive web tools.[56] Bram Büscher has analysed how the architecture of these platforms is both intensifying familiar development dynamics and creating new ones. Most important for this essay is the 'algorithmisation' of development causes, 'as individual online ... engagements are guided, influenced and informed by and through algorithms' that order information according to users' online history.[57] What visitors to the Kiva website see is linked to their other online activities and therefore shaped by their own affinities and preferences. This is reinforced through the increasingly fine-grained categorisation of loans to make it easier for lenders to find just the borrowers they are looking for.

Platforms also provide 'highly liquid forms of engagement' because they need to be continually updated to stay relevant and appealing.[58] The necessary focus of Kiva staff on maintaining the distinctiveness and user-friendliness of the website is clearly visible in its three major redesigns since 2005, in addition to innumerable background tweaks. Some of these changes seem to be responding to academic critiques, although they probably aren't. For example, the second version of the website featured on its homepage a wall of 33 mainly non-White faces of women, men, couples and groups, arranged in 2 x 2 cm squares. The effect was striking, turning Kiva borrowers into a mass of Third World entrepreneurs that confirmed Wilson's observation that 'through a process of repetition and accumulation of images, an overwhelming sense of "the South" as a single, though endlessly diverse, place where poor women are constantly, diligently and happily engaged in small-scale but productive labour for the market is created'.[59] Now, the homepage features a rolling band of five close-up shots of smiling entrepreneurs at their places of work, closely resembling conventional microfinance images that draw on traditional tropes of development representations. To keep attracting the support of lenders in the increasingly crowded marketplace of online lending platforms means that Kiva has to keep reinventing itself.

Financial clicktivism

What most of the online do-good platforms have in common is that action is only one click away and, in addition to donating money, includes forwarding links, liking a cause, sharing a tweet or adding one's name to a petition. The online nature of these actions condenses the time between knowing and acting and thereby lessens chances of 'implicatory denial' in the form of 'arguments, reasons or rationalizations for not responding sympathetically to distressing information'.[60] Because action is simple, often routinised, clearly defined and requires minimal effort, it is easy to undertake. This form of online, everyday social engagement is a prime example of Haskell's ordinary techniques; its fit with people's daily online practices explains the reach of campaigns such as Kony2012, the ice-bucket challenge or indeed Kiva's US$1billion in loans. Many of these campaigns have also attracted controversy.

For its critics, internet action can slide into clicktivism that is too easy, passive and singular. Online action is carried out by individuals first and foremost, partly because of online platforms' architecture and pop development's emphasis on individual action. Most importantly, clicktivism results in the decoupling of action from understanding the causes and contexts of suffering.[61] In the case of Kiva, lenders learning about the challenges and complexities, never mind critiques, of microfinance is foreclosed. On the one hand, this is the result of the continued appeal of what I have called 'microfinance's obligatory success story', originating with Yunus' insistence that simply giving a woman a small loan will allow her to enterprise herself and her family out of poverty, because poor women are innate entrepreneurs and 'know that credit is their only way to break out of poverty'.[62] This story appeals to everyday humanitarians precisely because it is so simple and commonsensical, reinforced by Kiva's tagline of 'loans that change lives'. On the other hand, the dearth of information about microfinance results from Kiva's own 'diminutive narrative frame' animated by short, simple, feel-good narratives.[63] The first two versions of the Kiva website did have an About Microfinance page, which only reiterated rather than challenged conventional misinformation about the success and impact of microfinance. Such meta-information has now disappeared altogether and instead impact is conveyed through numbers: repayment data, total loan amount as well as numbers of borrowers and lenders. In this way, according to Shameem Black:

> Kiva might be seen to contribute to the larger cultural project of repressions since its ability to spark vivid feelings of responsibility potentially allows lenders to forget how large-scale development aid has worked to produce the uneven topographies of capitalism across the world that microfinance ostensibly seeks to alter.[64]

These uneven topographies have been sharpened since the commercialisation of microfinance beginning in the early 2000s, when mainstream banks discovered that lending to the poor can be a lucrative and relatively low-risk niche investment, based on expectations that 'the poor always pay back'.[65] This commercialisation has been linked to aggressive lending practices by microfinance organisations and subsequent over-indebtedness of borrowers.[66]

The changing terrain of microfinance now includes online lending platforms and their mobilisation of affective investments. The latter are technologically hyper-mediated through organisations such as Kiva and their affective architectures promoting sentiments of affinity, agency and pleasure among everyday humanitarians, which in turn shape their connections with the recipients of their actions.[67] In the case of Kiva, that means lenders and borrowers and their financial relationships.

Financial mediations

Yunus' repeated appearance in this article is not only warranted because he is an embodiment of Mazzarella's dictum that 'one must be affective in order to be effective',[68] but also because it was a talk he gave at Stanford University in California that led to Jackley working for a microfinance organisation in East Africa. It is here where the idea of Kiva as 'sponsoring a business' by lending to its owner was born, inspired by the co-founders' own experiences of child sponsorship.[69] Sponsorship of an individual, be it a child or an entrepreneur, is a prime example of the mobilisation of affective investments via financial contributions. In this section, I show how such contributions first give rise to and then continue through mediated affective relationships between sponsor and sponsee. This is especially the case for making loans, which also leads to particular risks that are invisibilised by Kiva's affective architecture.

Person-to-person?

Child sponsorship is one of the oldest and most prominent modes of caring and sharing aimed at everyday people. Through the use of 'highly emotive tactics', it is also a very successful fundraising strategies of Northern non-governmental organisations (NGOs), using images of children that produce sympathy and compassion.[70] The focus of these representations is the lone child's face, resulting in an abstraction that is reinforced through sponsorship's impersonal, monetary exchange and children's commodification. They lend their faces and stories so that money can be raised for the development of 'their communities'. This instrumentalisation stands in marked contrast with the personal, close relations promised by child sponsorship, which manifest in letters and tearful encounters.[71] Moreover, the presumed one-to-one relationship of intimate correspondence is heavily mediated by NGO staff who manage the proper flow of documents, translate and censor mail and often help children write return letters.[72] Similar dynamics take place in the case of Kiva.

Central to the organisation's success has been the illusion of a person-to-person (p2p) connection established via lending through the website. It was the promise of a personal connection, heavily promoted during Kiva's early days, which attracted lenders in the first place.[73] Kiva was explicit in setting itself up against conventional charities and their large administrative overheads, where it is difficult to track the impact of donations, and against impersonal microfinance organisations, where impact is measured in financials rather than personal stories. For everyday humanitarians who wanted to learn exactly where their money went and what difference it made in the lives of individual beneficiaries, Kiva seemed to offer a user-friendly solution. To reinforce this message, an early promotional video showed Grace, a peanut vendor in Uganda, sitting down in front of a computer to write a message to Nathan, her borrower in San Francisco who likes chunky peanut butter. Grace is thanking Nathan for the equipment she was able to purchase with the help of his loan while Nathan replies that he is glad to be able to help her improve her business.[74] This staging of 'benevolent microlending' produces the immediacy, connectivity and affinity that is at the heart of processes of mediation.[75]

While this p2p connection might have been an accurate representation of how Kiva worked in the very beginning, it was quickly lost as the organisation expanded. A widely-read blog post in 2009 exposed that the loans lenders thought they were making to the individuals on whose pictures they had clicked on the website did in fact go to similar borrowers at the local Kiva partner, which in all likelihood had already given a loan to the person on the website.[76] The revelation that Kiva used intermediary microfinance organisations caused much controversy and debate. In the end, while many lenders said that Kiva was doing so much good, they understood this backfilling of loans to be an operational necessity and just asked for it to be clearer on the website, other lenders felt betrayed precisely because they had invested so much in the personal connection. The website now has a more accurate graphic of how the funding process works and also shows the disbursement date of each loan. Nevertheless, the all-important but illusory p2p connection is maintained through the visual dominance of individual borrowers' photos and their stories on the Kiva website as part of its affective architecture, which in turn is critical to the Kiva business model because of the depersonalising effects of the organisation's central medium – money.

As a form of sponsorship recast in the neoliberal language of business investments, lending on Kiva is subject to the tension between the intimate connections fostered by everyday humanitarianism and the generic nature of the monetary donations by which they are most often made manifest. According to Marx, 'the exchange of money indiscriminately for all qualities and objects seems to make all of our particular human essential powers indifferent, thus distorting our relationships to each other and the world and undermining our powers to create social bonds'.[77] In the humanitarian realm, money therefore negates the singularity of the donor and the recipient, who as undifferentiated abstractions stand in the way of humanitarian affect. This does not mean that money is a non-affective entity, as it evokes strong positive and negative sentiments.[78] Nevertheless, as an impersonal medium, money obscures donors and their commitments, opening the door for accusations of superficial engagement. It also hides the recipients and, as a result, 'the bond created between the donor and the unfortunate is minimal and abstract'.[79] The circulation of affective objects, such as letters from children or business updates from Kiva entrepreneurs, aims to counter this flattening. There is, however, one important distinction between child sponsorship, which consists of charitable donations, and Kiva, which makes loans. This distinction, while contributing to maintaining connections, also carries risks.

Risky connections

Lending via Kiva is not only a financial transaction, but also an exchange. On the one hand, working in the microfinance space allows Kiva to capitalise on the wider financialisation of poverty and the continued popularity of microfinance at the beginning of the twenty-first century. As a result, the financial relationships between Kiva lenders and borrowers are clearly primary. On the other hand, the unidirectional charitable impulse becomes a two-way interchange. That loans have to be repaid creates ongoing interactions different from one-time donations; on Kiva, loan repayments flow back into lenders' accounts and most of them are reinvested in new loans. According to Jackley, 'loans are a very interesting tool for connectivity', by which she meant the human connections the co-founders hoped to build through Kiva lending.[80] The co-founders had also envisioned these loans to build 'dignified, intellectual and equitable relationships',[81] which 'can promote respect and hope … and blur the lines between the traditional rich and poor categories'.[82] Such visions ignore the persistent critiques of microfinance I have laid out above, which are linked to entrenched, structural inequalities that no amount of Kiva loans can eradicate.[83]

As I have already indicated, these critiques are absent from the Kiva website, whose latest version has also adopted the more palatable language of financial inclusion, following a discursive move by the wider microfinance industry to distance itself from the problematic connotations of microfinance. This change in language is connected to arguments that providing marginalised people with financial products and services is of value in and of itself, irrespective of whether it reduces poverty.[84] Correspondingly, Kiva's mission has changed from 'connecting people through lending to alleviate poverty' to 'expand[ing] financial access to help underserved communities thrive'.[85] Further references on the website to 'reinventing microfinance with more flexible terms … or lowering costs to borrowers' could be seen to address some of the critiques of microfinance without actually mentioning them. One of these are the high interest rates charged by microfinance organisations, which they justify by the larger cost of servicing very small loans to borrowers who are often difficult to reach. Because Kiva lenders cannot receive financial interest on their Kiva loans due to US regulations, initially they might not have been aware that borrowers have to pay interest on their loans to Kiva's local partners that administer the loans. Kiva has been forced to make that fact more explicit on the website, opting for a minimalist approach that does not actually show how much interest borrowers are paying.[86] Instead it claims that it 'will not partner with an organization that charges unreasonable interest rates'[87] – a purposely obtuse statement that helps to mask that credit relationships are also debt relations, with corresponding risk.

These riskscapes are very different for lenders and borrowers and are also differently communicated on the website. While lenders are informed on the home page (arguably in very small font) that 'lending on Kiva involves risk through principal loss', what is less clear is the risk to borrowers. This is in line with the general tendency to ascribe microfinance risk to lenders rather than borrowers.[88] But not only can the consequences of a bad loan be devastating to vulnerable borrowers in precarious circumstances, the commercialisation of microfinance has been shown to create cycles of over-indebtedness that in extreme cases can lead to borrower suicides.[89] Even in less severe situations, getting into debt entangles borrowers in complex relationships of kinship, obligation and consumption that shape how loans are being used, by whom and to what effects. These relationships are situated in culturally-specific, gendered norms of honour and shame that can have detrimental social and materials in addition to financial consequences for borrowers.[90] Practices such as peer surveillance, seizing of property and house breaking can result from women being unable to make repayments, leading to material deprivation and social ostracism.[91] However, Kiva's virtual relationships channel the emotions of lenders in such a way that they can both distance themselves from any potentially harmful effects on the borrower at the same time as they can feel a connection to that individual borrower ... the experience of kinship by the lender in the Global North to the borrower in the Global South works to neutralize or erase the finalization aspects of the transaction.[92]

In other words, the asymmetry of risk, and the financial relationships from which it arises, are invisibilised by the social and emotional connections forged via Kiva. In a way, the growth of online affective connections masks the reconfiguration of borrowers' offline affective connections, for example when kinship relations become relations of usury.[93] Financial mediation, based on simplified and fictitious stories of microfinance's impact on individual borrowers' lives, results in a sense of efficacy that by lending on Kiva, everyday humanitarians can contribute to positive change. To uphold this sense, which is vital for the continued popularity of Kiva, non-existing p2p connections are highlighted while existing risks are hidden. These dynamics operate in a spatially-mediated geography of care.

Spatial mediations

Kiva promises its over one million users connections to distant others and the opportunity to improve their lives through Kiva loans. The extent to which digital technologies affect everyday humanitarians' abilities to assume responsibility at a distance as a form of 'disinterested care' has been linked to questions about the 'proper distance' they establish in relationships with others.[94] While proper refers to a sense of genuine, fitting and socially appropriate, distance has geographical, social and moral dimensions. For Roger Silverstone, simply searching for connections is insufficient to ensure ethical relationships, which instead must 'navigate a precarious territory[:] against the logic of sameness, it must reflexively assert the irreducibly distinct quality of the other whilst, against the logic of difference, it must sustain an empathetic sense of the other as a figure endowed with her own humanity'.[95] In this section, I explore how tensions between proximity and distance manifest on Kiva and then show how the organisation's digital mediations are enabled by the physical immediacy of Kiva volunteers.

Proximity and distance

Kiva's mediated connections capitalise on proximity and distance in ways that allow lenders to draw on their own imaginations regarding borrowers' similarities or differences. Several quantitative studies of Kiva have found that lenders prefer 'culturally similar and geographically proximate borrowers'.[96] Often, lending choices are also made on the basis of shared professions, a country travelled to or a touching story that might resonate with a lender's own life journey. By contrast, the co-founders realised early on that lenders' preferences often corresponded to stereotypes about poor others, so that loans to rural African women were funded the fastest while those to Bulgarian taxi drivers went unfilled for weeks.[97] Such loans allow lenders to not only help those they see as most needy and deserving, but also to fulfil nostalgic, premodern fantasies.[98] Some of these shifts might have arisen when Kiva started making loans to US borrowers in 2009, amidst initial accusations of selling out on its original goal of alleviating poverty in the Global South. However, for the co-founders this expansion went some way towards the original goal of 'leveling the playing field' by enabling not only loans from US lenders to borrowers in the

Global South, but also from Kenyans to US entrepreneurs and from Cambodians to each other.[99] While such loans do indeed happen now, larger aspirations of global equalities have not been fulfilled.

The tensions on Kiva between proximity/similarity and distance/difference can be traced to older ideas introduced in the beginning of this paper. Ideas of similarity stem from eighteenth century cosmopolitan notions around a common humanity. Difference, on the other hand, results from more recent theories of the irreducible difference produced by linguistic practices of representation.[100] On Kiva, the balancing act between both is open-ended, which enables lenders to establish their preferred connections by picking and choosing among hundreds of borrowers to find the ones that suit them. Together with the aforementioned algorithmisation, ever more sophisticated categorisation and search capabilities on the website have made this process easier and faster, manifesting that connections are made on lenders' terms. Borrowers can be as close or as distant as lenders like, giving rise to an improper distance that 'mistake[s] connection for closeness and closeness for commitment and confuse[s] reciprocity for responsibility'.[101] In its promise to establish connections, Kiva generates affective investments in a compromised way that produces self-gratification and digital asymmetries. While searching for pure connections would yield very little in any domain, lenders' control over these connections negate Kiva's own claims of levelling the playing field. In addition, digital mediations are themselves enabled by practices grounded in spatial proximity.

Geographic immediacy

While the overwhelming majority of lenders use the Kiva website to make their investments from afar, a few, such as Bob Harris, go and visit borrowers and my family as part of this research.[102] Then there are the so-called Kiva Fellows who volunteer to spend six months with Kiva partner organisations on the ground. They are mostly young professionals in business, finance, technology or management consulting who work with partners to implement Kiva infrastructures and procedures and to train local staff as Kiva coordinators. As Kiva's 'eyes and ears on the ground', Fellows are also an important part of Kiva's due diligence apparatus.[103] This happens mainly through borrower verification visits to randomly selected Kiva borrowers to check their details, trips during which Fellows also produce many of the photos and updates that sustain Kiva's connections. It is in these various ways of managing partner organisations, verifying their work and producing representational artefacts, that Fellows are a critical part of Kiva's digital mediations.

All Fellows write posts for the Kiva Fellows blog, which is a rich source of information about their experiences. Elsewhere, I analysed Kiva Fellows as 'deep voluntourists', whose favourite activities are the borrower visits.[104] The blog posts show that these visits produce intense affective investments through emotional encounters that often leave Fellows transformed. The description of one Fellow in Guatemala is typical: 'as I came home after the day of interviewing, the women's stories, tears, smiles and laughter stuck deep in my soul. I will never be the same, and I am so thankful for being able to have a day like this'.[105] In addition, it is in the blog posts that more nuanced accounts of microfinance can be found. One Fellow wrote 'I so badly want to see the extreme transformations that I have to make sure I am not fabricating it. Progress is so incremental, often non-existent'.[106] Another Fellow described his reaction to meeting his first Kiva borrower in Vietnam, who empathically told him that her loan had not brought about any positive changes in her life, as getting a 'gut punch ... I felt confused and frustrated. I knew that as a Kiva Fellow I wouldn't be hearing dramatic stories every time I met a client, but I didn't believe that I would have a client tell me that their loan hasn't helped much'.[107]

These writings speak to affective investments of a slightly different kind. Rather than investments engendered through the Kiva website, Kiva Fellows are emotionally invested in the idea of doing good through microfinance so strongly that it becomes difficult for them to relinquish this idea.[108] They hold on to their subject position even in the face of contradictory evidence, allowing themselves to be frustrated and impatient but not doubtful. In spite of their realisations that microfinance is not a simple solution to poverty, they never question the need for loans, also in part because of Kiva's relentless focus on generating more investments. Most of the fellows never seem to ask why borrowers are in such precarious circumstances in the first place and seem unaware of the role of structural inequalities in shaping the lives of the borrowers whose stories move them to tears. In this way, even though Fellow's physical immersion into Kiva's work stands at the opposite spectrum of financial clicktivism, their narratives from the field continuously enable lenders' affective investments in Kiva, its cause and its borrowers.

Conclusion

Kiva thrives on the double meaning of being invested in somebody financially and emotionally.[109] In this article I have shown how Kiva's institutional practices and their manifestation in the organisation's affective architecture are producing everyday humanitarians. Their affective investments in the entrepreneurship of distant others shows the entanglement of financial, social and emotional elements of everyday humanitarian practice, mediated in technological, financial and spatial ways, which contribute to Kiva's popularity. At the intersection of technology and finance are Kiva's lending practices, which fit with its supporters' ordinary forms of digital engagement, to the tune of US$1 billion in loans. They have also resulted in a form of financial clicktivism where learning about the complexities and critiques of microfinance is foreclosed by Kiva's own representational practices, which mirror conventional microfinance narratives at large. Most critical amongst the absences is the acknowledgement of the risk that microfinance recipients face when they engage in debt relationships. Kiva's technology also affords social and emotional investments in borrowers who are imagined that stand in a p2p relationship with Kiva lenders. Closer analysis shows that these connections are fictitious, as borrowers become exchangeable stand-ins for stories of imagined entrepreneurial success and connections are mediated by intermediary organisations. Everyday humanitarianism may thrive on digital mediations but falters in the face of transformative social engagements with its beneficiaries.

Acknowledgements

I would like to thank Meike Fechter for the enjoyable collaboration in organising the original workshop on Citizen Aid at Sussex and in working on this special issue. All workshop participations provided valuable comments which, together with two *Third World Quarterly* reviewers, have made this a better paper. The workshop was funded by a Sussex Research Opportunity Fund and the Department of Anthropology.

Notes

1. https://www.kiva.org/team/bobharrisdotcom, accessed November 30, 2018.
2. Harris, *First International Bank of Bob*.
3. Cited in Heim, "Web of Giving."
4. Laqueur, "Mourning, Pity," 32.
5. Flannery, "Kiva and the Birth," 37.
6. Bateman and MacLean, *Seduced and Betrayed*.
7. Mader, *The Political Economy*.
8. Roy, *Poverty Capital*, 22.
9. Ibid.
10. Khandelwal and Freeman, "Pop development."
11. Bajde, "Kiva's Staging."
12. Black, "Microloans and Micronarratives."
13. There are studies by computer scientists and business scholars on Kiva, but these tend to be more uncritical and instead concerned with understanding the organisation's technology and business model per se.
14. Roy, "Subjects of Risk," 151.
15. Vestergaard, "Humanitarian Appeal," 446.
16. Harding and Pribram, "Losing our Cool?" 879.
17. While some authors argue for the importance of analytical and linguistic distinctions between affects, sentiments and emotions, I follow the many scholars who use the terms almost interchangeably.
18. Richard and Rudnyckyi, "Economies of Affect," 63.
19. Grossberg, "Postmodernity and Affect," 285.
20. Cited in Fassin, *Humanitarian Reason*, 1.
21. Rorty, "Human Rights."
22. Fassin, *Humanitarian Reason*, 269.
23. Malkki, "Children, Humanity," 83.
24. Haskell, "Capitalism and the Origins," 358.
25. Wilson and Brown, *Humanitarianism and Suffering*, 10.
26. Sliwinski, "The Aesthetics of Human Rights," 24.
27. Bornstein and Redfield, *Forces of Compassion*.
28. Wilson and Brown, *Humanitarianism and Suffering*.
29. Fassin, *Humanitarian Reason*, 272.
30. Haskell, "Capitalism and the Origins."
31. Calhoun, *The Idea of Emergency*.
32. Rozario, "Delicious Horrors."
33. Feldman, "Ad Hoc Humanity," 201.
34. Brainard and LaFleur, *Making Poverty History?* 9.
35. Chouliaraki, "The Theatricality of Humanitarianism."
36. Richey and Ponte, *Brand Aid*.
37. Boltanski, *Distant Suffering*, 100.
38. Cohen, *States of Denial*.

39. Sontag, *Regarding the pain of others*.
40. Fassin, *Humanitarian Reason*.
41. Rozario, "Delicious Horrors."
42. Wright, "Emotional Geographies of Development"; Clouser, "Nexus of Emotional."
43. Arrillaga-Andreessen, *Giving 2.0*.
44. Braund and Schwittay, "Scaling Inclusive Digital Innovation."
45. Flannery, "Kiva and the Birth," 31.
46. Gillespie, "The Politics of Platforms," 359.
47. Ibid., 349.
48. https://www.kiva.org/about, accessed April 15, 2019.
49. Black, "Microloans and Micronarratives"; Black, "Fictions of Humanitarian Responsibility."
50. Flannery, "Kiva and the Birth," 40.
51. Bajde, "Kiva's Staging," 96.
52. Ibid., 100.
53. https://www.kiva.org/teams, accessed April 15, 2019.
54. Quoted in Bajde, "Kiva's Staging," 97.
55. Flannery, "Kiva and the Birth," 34.
56. Büscher, "Conservation and Development 2.0," 164.
57. Ibid., 166.
58. Ibid.
59. Wilson, "'Race', Gender," 323.
60. Cohen, *States of Denial*, 211.
61. Madianou, "Humanitarian Campaigns."
62. Yunus in Schwittay, "Muhammad Yunus," 77.
63. Black, "Microloans and Micronarratives."
64. Black, "Fictions of Humanitarian Responsibility," 108.
65. Dowla and Barua, *The Poor Always Pay Back*.
66. Guérin et al., *Microfinance, Debt and Over-Indebtedness*.
67. Vestergaard, "Humanitarian Appeal."
68. Cited in Schwittay, "Muhammad Yunus," 71.
69. Flannery, "Kiva and the Birth."
70. Suski, "Children, Suffering," 213.
71. Bornstein, "Child Sponsorship."
72. O'Neill, "Left Behind."
73. Flannery, "Kiva and the Birth."
74. https://www.youtube.com/watch?v=MXk4GUGXNTQ, accessed April 16, 2019.
75. Bajde, "Kiva's Staging," 99; Vestergaard, "Humanitarian Appeal."
76. Roodman, "Kiva is not Quite."
77. Paraphrased by Hardt, "For Love or Money," 679.
78. Konings, "Financial Affect."
79. Boltanski, *Distant Suffering*, 18.
80. Jackley, "*Poverty, Money – and Love.*"
81. Flannery, "Kiva at Four," 40.
82. Jackley, "*Poverty, Money – and Love.*"
83. Guérin et al., *Microfinance, Debt and Over-Indebtedness*.
84. Mader, *The Political Economy*.
85. https://www.kiva.org/about, accessed April 15, 2019.
86. Bajde, "Kiva's Staging."
87. https://www.kiva.org/lend/1735943, accessed April 15, 2019.
88. Moodie, "Microfinance and the Gender."
89. Guérin et al., *Microfinance, Debt and Over-Indebtedness*.
90. Brett, "We Sacrifice and Eat Less"; Hayes, "The Hidden Labor"; Schuster, *Social Collateral*.
91. Karim, *Microfinance and its Discontents*.
92. Moodie, "Microfinance and the Gender," 280–1.

93. I thank one of the article's reviewers for this observation.
94. Silverstone, "Proper Distance."
95. Chouliaraki and Orgad, "Proper Distance," 343.
96. Burtch et al., "Cultural Differences," 773.
97. Flannery, "Kiva and the Birth."
98. Black, "Microloans and Micronarratives."
99. Flannery, "Kiva at Four."
100. Chouliaraki and Orgad, "Proper Distance."
101. Silverstone, "Proper Distance," 476.
102. US lending has led to more meet-ups between lenders and borrowers in the same area, sometimes enabled by Kiva.
103. Schwittay, *New Media and International Development*, 143.
104. Ibid.
105. Ibid., 162.
106. Ibid., 148.
107. Ibid., 148.
108. I thank one of the article's reviewers to pointing out this nuance to me.
109. Black, "Microloans and Micronarratives."

Bibliography

Arrillaga-Andreessen, Laura. *Giving 2.0: Transform Your Giving and Our World*. San Francisco, Hoboken, NJ: John Wiley & Sons, 2011.

Bajde, Domen. "Kiva's Staging of 'Peer-to-Peer' Charitable Lending: Innovative Marketing or Egregious Deception?" M. Bateman and K. Maclean (eds.) In *Seduced and Betrayed*. New Mexico: University of New Mexico Press, 2017.

Bateman, Milton, and Kate MacLean (eds.). *Seduced and Betrayed: exposing the Contemporary Microfinance Phenomeno*. New Mexico: University of New Mexico Press, 2017.

Black, Shameem. "Microloans and Micronarratives: Sentiment for a Small World." *Public Culture* 21, no. 2 (2009): 269–292.

Black, Shameem, "Fictions of Humanitarian Responsibility: Narrating Microfinance." *Journal of Human Rights* 12, no. 1 (2013): 103–120.

Braund, Paul, and Anke Schwittay. "Scaling Inclusive Digital Innovation Successfully: The Case of Crowdfunding Social Enterprises." *Innovation and Development* 6, no.1 (2016): 15–29.

Brett, John A. "'We Sacrifice and Eat Less': The Structural Complexities of Microfinance Participation." *Human* 65, no. 1 (2006): 8–19. doi:10.17730/humo.65.1.6wvq3ea7pbl38mub.

Boltanski, Luc. *Distant Suffering: Morality, Media and Politics*. Cambridge: Cambridge University Press, 1999.

Bornstein, Erica. "Child Sponsorship, Evangelism, and Belonging in the Work of World Vision Zimbabwe." *American Ethnologist* 28, no. 3 (2001): 595–622. doi:10.1525/ae.2001.28.3.595.

Bornstein, Erica, and Peter Redfield, eds. *Forces of Compassion: Humanitarianism between Ethics and Politics*. Santa: School for Advanced Research Press, 2010.

Brainard, Lael, and Vinca LaFleur. *Making Poverty History? How Activists, Philanthropists, and the Public are Changing Global Development*. Brookings: Global Economy and Development, Brookings Institution, 2008.

Burtch, Gordon, Anindya Ghose, and Sunil Wattal. "Cultural Differences and Geography as Determinants of Online Pro-Social Lending." (November 21, 2013). MIS Quarterly, Forthcoming; Fox School of Business Research Paper No. 14-021. Available at SSRN: https://ssrn.com/abstract=2271298 or http://dx.doi.org/10.2139/ssrn.2271298.

Büscher, Bram. "Conservation and Development 2.0: Intensifications and Disjunctures in the Politics of Online 'Do-Good' Platforms." *Geoforum* 79 (2017): 163–173. doi:10.1016/j.geoforum.2016.05.002.

Calhoun, Craig. *The Idea of Emergency: Humanitarian Action and Global (Dis) Order*. New York, NY: Zone Books, 2010, 29–58.

Chouliaraki, Lilie. "The Theatricality of Humanitarianism: A Critique of Celebrity Advocacy." *Communication and Critical/Cultural Studies* 9, no. 1 (2012): 1–21. doi:10.1080/14791420.2011.637055.

Chouliaraki, Lilie, and Shani Orgad. "Proper Distance: Mediation, Ethics, Otherness." *International Journal of Cultural Studies* 14, no. 4 (2011): 341–345. doi:10.1177/1367877911403245.

Clouser, Rebecca. "Nexus of Emotional and Development Geographies." *Geography Compass* 10, no. 8 (2016): 321–332. doi:10.1111/gec3.12275.

Cohen, Stanley. *States of Denial: Knowing about Atrocities and Suffering*. Cambridge: Polity Press, 2001.

Dowla, Asif, and Dipal Barua. *The Poor Always Pay Back: The Grameen II Story*. USA: Kumarian Press, 2006.

Fassin, Didier. *Humanitarian Reason: A Moral History of the Present*. California: University of California Press, 2011.

Feldman, Ilana. "Ad Hoc Humanity: UN Peacekeeping and the Limits of International Community in Gaza." *American Anthropologist* 112, no. 3 (2010): 416–429. doi:10.1111/j.1548-1433.2010.01249.x.

Flannery, Matt. "Kiva and the Birth of Person-to-Person Microfinance." *Innovations: Technology, Governance, Globalization* 2, no. 1–2 (2007): 31–56. doi:10.1162/itgg.2007.2.1-2.31.

Flannery, Matt. "Kiva at Four." *Innovations: Technology, Governance, Globalization* 4, no. 2 (2009): 31–49. doi:10.1162/itgg.2009.4.2.31.

Gillespie, Tarleton. "The Politics of 'Platforms.'" *New Media & Society* 12, no. 3 (2010): 347–364. doi:10.1177/1461444809342738.

Grossberg, Lawrence. "Postmodernity and Affect – All Dressed up with No Place to Go." *Communication* 10, no. 3 (1988): 271–293.

Guérin, Isabelle, Marc Roesch, G. Venkatasubramanian, and S. Kumar. *Microfinance, Debt and Over-Indebtedness: Juggling with Money*. London: Routledge, 2013.

Harding, Jennifer, and E. Deidre Pribram. "Losing Our Cool? Following Williams and Grossberg on Emotions." *Cultural Studies* 18, no. 6 (2004): 863–883. doi:10.1080/0950238042000306909.

Hardt, Michael. "For Love or Money." *Cultural Anthropology* 26, no. 4 (2011): 676–682. doi:10.1111/j.1548-1360.2011.01119.x.

Harris, Bob. *The International Bank of Bob: Connecting Our Worlds One $25 Kiva Loan at a Time*. USA: Bloomsbury Publishing, 2013.

Haskell, Thomas L. "Capitalism and the Origins of the Humanitarian Sensibility." *The American Historical Review* 90, no. 2 (1985): 339–361. doi:10.2307/1852669.

Hayes, Lauren A. "The Hidden Labor of Repayment: Women, Credit, and Strategies of Microenterprise in Northern Honduras." *Economic Anthropology* 4, no. 1 (2017): 22–36. doi:10.1002/sea2.12070.

Heim, Kirstin. 2006. "Web of Giving." *Seattle Times*.

Jackley, Jessica. "*Poverty, Money – and Love.*" *TED Talk* (2010). https://www.ted.com/talks/jessica_jackley_poverty_money_and_love?language=en

Karim, Lamia. *Microfinance and its Discontents: Women in Debt in Bangladesh*. Minnesota: University of Minnesota Press, 2011.

Khandelwal, Meena, and Carla Freeman. "Pop development and the uses of feminism." In M. Bateman, and K. Maclean (eds) In *Seduced and Betrayed*. New Mexico: University of New Mexico Press, 2017.

Konings, Martijn. "Financial Affect." *Distinktion: Scandinavian Journal of Social Theory* 15, no. 1 (2014): 37–53. doi:10.1080/1600910X.2013.864689.

Laqueur, Thomas. "Mourning, Pity, and the Work of Narrative in the Making of 'Humanity.'" In R. Wilson and R. Brown (eds.) *Humanitarianism and Suffering: The Mobilization of Empathy*. New York: Cambridge University Press, 2009.

Mader, Philipp. *The Political Economy of Microfinance*. Basingstoke, United Kingdom: Palgrave Macmillan, 2015.

Madianou, Mirca. "Humanitarian Campaigns in Social Media: Network Architectures and Polymedia Events." *Journalism Studies* 14, no. 2 (2013): 249–266. doi:10.1080/1461670X.2012.718558.

Malkki, Liisa. "Children, humanity, and the infantilization of peace." In I. Feldman and Miriam Ticktin. (eds.) *In the Name of Humanity: The Government of Threat and Care*. Durham, NC: Duke University Press, 2010.

Moodie, Megan. "Microfinance and the Gender of Risk: The Case of Kiva. org." *Signs: Journal of Women in Culture and Society* 38, no. 2 (2013): 279–302. doi:10.1086/667448.

O'Neill, Kevin. "Left behind: Security, Salvation, and the Subject of Prevention." *Cultural Anthropology* 28, no. 2 (2013): 204–226. doi:10.1111/cuan.12001.

Richard, Analiese, and Daromir Rudnyckyj. "Economies of Affect." *Journal of the Royal Anthropological Institute* 15, no. 1 (2009): 57–77. doi:10.1111/j.1467-9655.2008.01530.x.

Richey, Lisa Ann, and Stefano Ponte. *Brand Aid: Shopping Well to Save the World*. Minnesota: University of Minnesota Press, 2011.

Roodman, David. "Kiva is not quite what it seems." *Center for Global Development*. http://blogs.cgdev.org/open_book/2009/10/kiva-is-not-quitewhat-it-seems.Php (2009).

Rorty, Richard. "Human Rights, Rationality, and Sentimentality." *Wronging Rights? Philosophical Challenges for Human Rights* (1993): 1–34.

Roy, Ananya. "Subjects of Risk: Technologies of Gender in the Making of Millennial Modernity." *Public Culture* 24, no. 1 (2012): 131–155. doi:10.1215/08992363-1498001.

Roy, Ananya. *Poverty Capital: Microfinance and the Making of Development*. London: Routledge, 2010.

Rozario, Kevin. "'Delicious Horrors': Mass Culture, the Red Cross, and the Appeal of Modern American Humanitarianism." *American Quarterly* 55, no. 3 (2003): 417–455. doi:10.1353/aq.2003.0026.

Schwittay, Anke. *New Media and International Development: Representation and Affect in Microfinance*. London: Routledge, 2015.

Schwittay, Anke. "Muhammad Yunus: A Bangladeshi Aid Celebrity." In L. Richey (ed.) *Celebrity Humanitarianism and North-South Relations*. London: Routledge, 2015.

Schuster, Caroline E. *Social Collateral: Women and Microfinance in Paraguay's Smuggling Economy*. California: University of California Press, 2015.

Silverstone, Roger. (2003). "Proper Distance: Towards an Ethics for Cyberspace." In *Digital Media Revisited*, edited by Gunnar Liestol, Andrew Morrison and Terje Rasmussen, 469–491. Boston: MIT University Press, 2003.

Sliwinski, Sharon. "The Aesthetics of Human Rights." *Culture, Theory & Critique* 50, no. 1 (2009): 23–39. doi:10.1080/14735780802696336.

Sontag, Susan. *Regarding the Pain of Others*. New York: Picador, 2003.

Suski, Laura. "Children, Suffering and the Humanitarian Appeal," In *Humanitarianism and Suffering: The Mobilization of Empathy*, edited by Richard Ashby Wilson and Richard D. Brown, 202–222. New York: Cambridge University Press, 2009.

Vestergaard, Anne. "Humanitarian Appeal and the Paradox of Power." *Critical Discourse Studies* 10, no. 4 (2013): 444–467. doi:10.1080/17405904.2012.744322.

Wright, Sarah. "Emotional Geographies of Development." *Third World Quarterly* 33, no. 6 (2012): 1113–1127. doi:10.1080/01436597.2012.681500.

Wilson, Kalpana. "'Race', Gender and Neoliberalism: changing Visual Representations in Development." *Third World Quarterly* 32, no. 2 (2011): 315–331. doi:10.1080/01436597.2011.560471.

Wilson, Richard, and Richard Brown, eds. "Humanitarianism and Suffering: The Mobilization of Empathy." Cambridge: Cambridge University Press, 2009.

Index

Tables are denoted by bold text and notes by "n" and the number of the note after the page number e.g., 131 n.15 refers to note number 15 on page 131.

Abed, Sir F.H. 126
Accord **69**
accountability 5, 6, 7, 21, 73; Cambodia 55–6, 59; Kenya 85, 87, 92; Philippines 136, 141, 142, 144, 145, 149
Achana, J. 20, 22–3
Action Against Hunger 122
Active Learning Network for Accountability and Performance in Humanitarian Action (ALNAP) 15
activism 2, 4–6, 8, 13, 16–20, 22–3, 107–8; Bangladesh 124, 126–7; light touch 102
administration costs 34, 36, 40, 83
advocacy work 6, 8, 67, 108, 111, 123–4
affective investments 154–5, 160, 163, 164–5
affinity 153, 154, 157, 160, 161; groups 73
Africa 14, 15, 20–4, 65, 85
agency 2, 5, 104, 109–12, 117, 141, 148, 154, 160
Aldrich, D. 136, 138
Algeria National Front (FLN) 19; war of independence 18–19
Allama Fazlullah Foundation 127
altruism 15, 32, 34–5, 41–2, 147; liberal 50, 139
amateurism 5, 6, 67, 71, **75**, 121
American Cultural Solutions 22
Appe, S. 6, 86
army involvement (Bangladesh) 119, 123
Arnold, K. 120
Arslan, T. 78 n.17
Asia 65, 85
Asian tsunami 118
Athens blockade by British navy 17
Atlani-Duault, L. 15
Australian Strategic Policy Institute 132 n.17
authenticity 52–3
autonomy 6, 14, 50, 65; Philippines 138, 142, 144–5, 147, 148

Balkans 13
Bangladesh see civil society and Rohingya refugee crisis in Bangladesh
Bankoff, G. 136

Barford, A. 49, 60
Bateman, M. 154
Belgium 3, 103
beliefs 32, 35, 83
Bengal famine 14
Berman, N. 87–8
Biafra 20
bilateral agencies 31, 82, 84, **88**, 90–1, 94–5, 103
Black, S. 157, 159
blog posts and seminars 108, 111, 161, 164
BoardSource **69**, 72
Boltanski, L. 156
Bornstein, E. 50, 56, 57, 117, 124–5
Boston Network for International Development **69**, 74
BRAC 122–3, 126
Brand Aid 156
brand reputation 149
Brittain, V. 16
brokerage 1, 7, 39, 55; see also social media and brokerage after Typhoon Haiyan in Philippines
Brønnøysund Register Centre (Norway) 36–7
Brown, L.D. 67, 75
Brun, C. 110
budgets 3, 15, 32, 89, 117; GINGOs 64–5, 67, 70–1, 75; Kenya 84–7, 91–2, 94–5
Bulgaria 101
bureaucratisation 7, 24, 33–4, 49; Kenya 86, 91–3; Lesvos (Greece) 104, 109; Philippines 144–5, 148
Büscher, B. 158

Calais migration crisis 13
California Association of Nonprofits **69**
Cambodia 3, 13, 164; see also Cambodia: development and the search for connection
Cambodia: development and the search for connection 48–60; accountability 55–6, 59; authenticity 53; friendships 49; loyalty 56; meaning of 'make a connection' 52–6; personal connections/relationships 49–50,

54–5, 56–7, 58, 59; quality of relations 49; real experience, quest for 53; research context 51–2; similarity and difference, connections across 56–9; support for others 56; 'thick' connections 52, 54, 56, 59; 'thin' connections 52, 54; trust 56, 59
Canadian women development workers in sub-Saharan Africa 50
capacity building 88, 91, 92; *see also* grassroots international NGOs (GINGOs): capacity building
CARE 20
cash donations 17, 137–8
cash relief 117, 119
celebrity humanitarians 84, 103, 104, 156
Central and Eastern Europe 101
centrality of sentimentality 66
Charity Commission 3, 15, 21
Charity for Life, Sydney 116
child sponsorship 33–4, 38, 53–4, 55, 160, 161
China 17
Chouliaraki, L. 102, 121, 154
Chowdhury, M. 120, 121, 123
Christian African Relief Trust (CART) 13, 14–15, 20–4
citizen initiatives for global solidarity (CIGS) in Lesvos: crisis management during refugee influx 6–7, 101–12; activities 104; actor identities 110; advocacy work 108, 111; biological life/biographical life distinction 110; bureaucratisation 104, 109; civil society communication and engagement 102; comparative advantage 103; context 105; critical concerns 103–4; culturally appropriate clothing 106, 108; dehumanising actions 107, 110; duplication 106; education initiatives and basic needs 104, 109; emergence of CIGS 105–9; emotional encounters 102, 105–6, 109; empowerment by similarity 109–10; environmental concerns 106, 109–10; field research notes 105; flexibility 109; funding 104, 106; human dignity 109–10; immediate needs 104; knowledgeability 104; local government 104; mimesis 109–10; 'Mini Lesvos dialogues' 105; motivations 103; power and agency: resistance as transformative act 104, 109–12; pragmatism 109; private donors 106; recycling 107; religious factors 107; resistance 104; solidarity 104, 111–12; tourism 101–2; United Nations Refugee Agency (UNHCR) 101–2, 104, 106–7; xenophobia 109
civil society 13, 15, 18, 33, 102, 135–6, 139; organisations 2, 6, 84, 88, 94–5, 104, 148; *see also* civil society and Rohingya refugee crisis in Bangladesh
civil society and Rohingya refugee crisis in Bangladesh 4, 6, 116–30; advocacy 124; amateurism 121; army involvement 119, 123; Awami League (AL) 118, 128; BRAC 122–3, 126; Buddhists 119; cash relief 117, 119; change over time 118; charity 117, 126; clothing and relief goods 117, 119, 121–2; common characteristics 118; community groups ('bondhu sabha' or friends' clubs) 121; continuity and change 123–9; coordination 129; corruption 124; Cox's Bazar Government College 121; diaspora organisations 123; District Commissioner (DC) 121, 122; diversity 118; emotional responses 119; food 117, 119, 120, 121, 122, 123; formal organisational responses 117, 121, 123, 128, 129; fundraising 121; government involvement 121–2, 123; groups and associations 121; Head of Sub-Office (HoSO) Group 122; health care 122; Hefazat-i-islami religious movement 127; historical, cultural and performative aspects 124, 129, 130; housing materials 119; identities 116, 117, 118, 125, 129; income-generation skills-training projects 123; International Crimes Tribunal (AL) 127; Liberation War (1971) 6; *madrasa* support 123, 127; market-based approaches and service delivery 124; mental health counselling 122; Ministry of Disaster Management and Relief 122; Ministry of Foreign Affairs 122; motivations 118; Mukhti Cox's Bazar 116; Muslims 118–20, 124, 125; national generosity 118; National Strategy on Myanmar Refugees and Undocumented Myanmar Nationals 122; National Task Force 122; NGO Affairs Bureau 127; person-to-person informal responses 117, 120–1, 123–7, 129, 130; political factors 127, 130; process 118; *Prothom Alo* newspaper 121; reciprocity 125–6; Refugee Relief and Repatriation Commissioner (RRRC) 122; religious dimensions of actions 123–7, 130; religious piety 118, 128; religious solidarity 117; representation 128; responses to crisis 118–23; Seagull Hotel 121; selflessness 125–6; Senior Coordinator (SC) 122; shelter 119, 120, 122, 123; social concerns 117; solidarity 119, 126; Strategic Executive Group (SEG) 122; Tangail and Cox's Bazar Rotary Club 116; visibility 128, 129; water, sanitation and hygiene facilities 120, 122
civilateral aid 31, 84, **88**, 91
Clifford, D. 3
clothing and relief goods 117, 119, 121
co-working model 75
Coast Trust 121
Collovald, A. 23
Colorado Nonprofits **69**, 74
Combinido, P. 137
commercialisation 154, 160, 162
commodification of beneficiaries 22
community exchange 72

community fatigue 92
community groups ('bondhu sabha' or friends' clubs) (Bangladesh) 121
community-led protection 131 n.15
Comoros 109–10
competitive humanitarianism 4
connection 6, 15, 157; *see also* Cambodia: development and the search for connection
conspicuous giving 127–8
constructions of heroism 129
contextual factors 42
control 38–41, 42
Cook, K. 136
corruption and fraud 21, 40, 86, 124, 138
credibility 93
credit services 123; *see also* microlending
crimes against humanity 131 n.14
crisis management *see* citizen initiatives for global solidarity (CIGS) in Lesvos: crisis management during refugee influx
crisis mapping platforms 7
crowd-sourcing platforms 7, 157
crowdfunding 7, 106
cultural capital 138

Danish International Development Agency (DANIDA) 82
Darfur 118
De Bruyn, T. 31
de Jong, S. 35, 41
de-bureaucratisation 34
de-professionalisation 34
decentralisation of voluntarisation 3
democratisation 3, 85
demotic humanitarianism: historical perspectives on global reach of local initiatives (1940–2017) 13–24; Christian African Relief Trust (CART) 13, 14–15, 20–4; Ghana Outlook (GO) 14–15, 21–4; Hudfam 13, 14–15, 16–20, 23–4; Wilson, E. 13–14, 16, 18–20, 23–4
Department for International Development (DFID): Amplify programme 7
Development Studies 136
Develtere, P. 31, 83
diaspora organisations 123
differences 59, 60
digital actants 148
digital humanitarianism 7, 136; *see also* social media and brokerage after Typhoon Haiyan in Philippines
digital media 1, 5
digital mediations: Kiva and microlending 7, 153–65; affective investments 154–5, 160, 163, 164–5; algorithmisation 164; borrower risks 162; categorisation of loans 158, 164; commercialisation 154, 160, 162; competition 158; confidence, conscience and know-how 155; continuous change producing continuous consumption 158; differences 163–4; distance 163–4; distinctiveness and user-friendliness of website 158–9; due diligence 164; emotional dimensions 155–6, 164, 165; empathetic identification 156; exploitation 154; financial clicktivism 153, 157, 159–60, 165; financial mediations 160, 165; gamification 158; gender dynamics 154; geographic immediacy 164–5; house breaking 162; hypermediacy 154; immediacy, connectivity and affinity 154, 161; institutional practices 165; interest rates 162; intermediaries 161; kinship 162–3; Kiva 'addicts' 158; Kiva Fellows 164–5; 'Kivaholics' 158; lending teams 158; loan repayments 162; materiality of Kiva 154; membership of lending teams 158; neo-liberal policies 154; online do-good 2.0 platforms 157–9; over-indebtedness 162; peer surveillance 162; person-to-person mediations 160–1; property seizure 162; proximity 163–4; relationships 155; risky connections 161–3; sentiments 155; shared humanity 156; similarities 163–4; social elements 165; spatial mediations 163–5; structural inequalities 162, 165; technological, financial and spatial aspects 157–9, 165
digital technologies, role of 7
Disaster Risk Reduction Management plan 144
domination 7
due diligence 17
Duffield, M. 14
Dunkirk migration crisis 13
duplication 7, 83, 92, 95, 106
Dutch Private Development Initiatives (PDIs) in Kwale County, Kenya 7, 82–96; accountability 87, 92; awareness 89, 90–1; 'being' PDIs 85; Bureau of Statistics (Kenya) 87; bureaucracy 86, 91; capacity building 91; civic education 88; cooperation with local government 82, 86, 88, 89–96; coordination and alignment 88; corruption 86; County Integrated Development Plan (CIDP) 86–7, 88, 90, 92, 93–5; current status of Kwale County 86–7; development architecture 87, **88;** 'doing' PDIs 85; financing projects 88; findings 89–95; geographical focus 94; government response 91–3; government signature as proof of consent 91; historical origins 89; institutional donors, influence of 92; intervention areas 89, 94; Memorandum of Understanding 86; new government structure 91–2; number and diversity of actors 90, 95; perception 93; policy formulation process support 88; power play 95; Public Benefit Organisations (PBO) Act 92, 94; qualitative research 89; quantitative research 89; regional focus 92; regulatory framework 95; 'relating' PDIs 85; research approach 89; research context 84–8;

resource mobilisation 88; size of organisations 89; thematic orientation 89, 92, 94; tourism 87–8; watchdog roles 88; *see also* legitimacy

East Africa 160
education 65, 89, 123
educational capital 138
Eggen, Ø. 40
emotional aspects 32, 37, 66, 76, 119, 155
empowerment 65, 158; by similarity 109–10
Engineers Without Borders 70b
environmental concerns 6, 106, 109–10
established actors, relationship to 6–7
ethics 2, 7–8, 16, 35, 50, 117; Kiva 155, 166; Philippines 145, 147–9
Ethiopia famine 20
Europe and European Union 1, 8, 13, 15
everyday humanitarianism 117
evidence base 3
exploitation 147, 149, 154
expressive perspective 67
Eyben, R. 49

Facebook 40, 106, 120, 137, 140–1, 143–4, 148–9, 157
faith-based initiatives 32–3, 123, 126–7
Farré, S. 20
Fassin, D. 127, 155
feelings 32, 37; *see also* emotional aspects
Field, J. 18
financial clicktivism 153, 157, 159–60, 165
Finland 14
first-generation development strategies 65
Flannery, M. 155, 158
Flyvbjerg, B. 111
folk-to-folk aid 33–4
Food for Life project 53
food relief 117, 119, 120, 121, 122, 123
ForeFront **69**, 72–3
form of events 129
formalisation 2, 6, 121
Forrest, S. 136
Foucault, M. 111
fragility of initiatives 41
fragmentation 1, 2, 7, 67, 71, **75**, 76
French Declaration of the Rights of Man and of the Citizen 156
friendships 49, 59, 155
'fun factor' 38, 66
funding 14–15, 22, 104, 106, 161; Bangladesh 127; Cambodia 56, 59; GINGOs 65–6, 70, 74–5; Kenya 83, 91; Philippines 139
fundraising 1, 7, 17, 18, 22, 32, 37, 51, 52, 54–5, 139; *see also* crowdfunding
Fylkesnes, J. 6

Gambia 3, 88; *see also* Norwegian initiatives in the Gambia
Gatrell, P. 17

genocide 131 n.14
Germany 65
Ghana 13, 85, 88
Ghana Outlook (GO) 14–15, 21–4
Gillespie, T. 157
global citizenship 2
global networks 145, 154
Global PDX **69**, 71, 73
global solidarity *see* citizen initiatives for global solidarity (CIGS) in Lesvos: crisis management during refugee influx
Global Washington **69**, 70, 74
GlobeMed 22
Good Samaritans identity and motivation 34–5; interdependency and identity 40–1
Google 157
governance structures, strengthening of 92
government involvement Bangladesh 121–2, 123; Philippines 144–5
governmentality 5, 8
grassroots international NGOs (GINGOs): capacity building 64–77; amateurism 67, 71, **75;** background 66–8; characteristics 66–7; critiques 66–7; fragmentation 67, 71, **75**, 76; information sharing 73–4; material scarcity 67, 71, **75**–6; national-level international development support organisations 68, **69**, 71; national-level nonprofit support organisations 68, **69**, 73; networking 72–3, 74, 76, 77; paternalism 67–8, **75**–6; peer-building programmes 72–3, 76–7; potential sources of building capacity 67–8; research approach 68–9; restricted focus 67, **75**–6; state-level international development support organisations 68, **69**, 71; state-level nonprofit organisations 68, **69**, 70; support organisations 65–6, 67, 68, **69**–74; training programmes 72
grassroots interventions 1–8; digital technologies, role of 7; established actors, relationship to 6–7; origins and motivations 6; themes and contributions 5–6; 'unstable category', citizen aid as 1–5; *see also* grassroots international NGOs (GINGOs): capacity building
Greece 13; *see also* citizen initiatives for global solidarity (CIGS) in Lesvos: crisis management during refugee influx
Grossberg, L. 154
Guatemala 88, 164

Haaland, H. 6, 33, 35, 66
Haiti 7, 65
Harris, B. 153, 164
Hasina, Sheikh 119
Haskell, T.L. 155, 159
Hayed, A. 120
health care 89, 122, 123
Healy, B.F. 78n.17

Hefazat-i-islami religious movement 127
Hénon, S. 5
Heron, B. 50, 58, 60
Hilhorst, D. 118, 121, 129, 136
Hilton, M. 18
historical perspectives 1, 6
Honduras 3
Hopgood, S. 18
horizontal flow of aid 145
housing materials 119
Hudfam 6, 13, 14–15, 16–20, 23–4; localisation 16; Oxfam 17–18; Quakers 17; *see also* Wilson, E.
human dignity 109–10
Hungary insurrection (1956) 17
Huq, S. 124
Hurricane Katrina (United States) 4

iDE 70b
identities 32, 34–5, 37, 38, 42, 50
in-person workshops and conferences 72
income-generation and skills-training projects 5, 89, 123
independent development volunteers 2
Independent Sector **69**, 70–1, 72, 73, 74
India 17, 19, 50, 56, 57, 65, 85
Indian Ocean tsunami (2004) 4
individual-level membership 71
individualism 33, 35
Indonesia 85, 88, 155
inequalities 7; *see also* structural inequalities
informal aid organisations 3–5, 8, 15, 49, 103; Bangladesh 117, 120–1, 123, 129–30; Philippines 135–7, 145, 148–9
information sharing 73–4
insider forms of helping 117
institutionalisation 109
instrumental assessment 66–7
InterAction 69–70, **69**
International Network for Education in Emergencies (INEE) **69**, 72–3; Minimum Standards on Education in Emergencies 73; Working Group on Standards and Practices 73
international NGOs (INGOs) 15, 24, 122–3, 144; *see also* grassroots international NGOs (GINGOs): capacity building
International Organisation for Migration (IOM) 122, 123
internationalism 16, 20
Islamic Relief 123, 127
Italy 101

Jackley, J. 155, 160, 162
Jackson Cole, C. 17–18
Jansen, B. 118, 121, 129
Jung, K. 19

Kapucu, N. 78n.17
Kelagor (Playroom)(Bangladesh) 121

Kelegaonkar, A. 67, 75
Kenya 65, 85, 164; *see also* Dutch Private Development Initiatives (PDIs) in Kwale County, Kenya
Kinsbergen, S. 7, 31, 32, 38, 65
kinship 57
Kiva *see* digital mediations: Kiva and microlending
Kiva Fellow 52, 54, 164–5
Korean War 14, 17
Korten, D.C. 65
Kosovo 118
Krause, M. 22
Kristof, N. 2

Laos 13
Latin America 65
legitimacy 1, 83, 93, 94–5, 96, 128, 148; cognitive 82, 83, 94, 95; normative 82, 83–4, 94, 95; pragmatic 82, 83, 94, 95; regulatory 82, 83, 94
Lewis, D. 2, 6
Lichtenberg, J. 35
lifestyle evangelism 124–5
Lisbon earthquake 155–6
Lister, S. 83, 94
local government units 6, 144–5
localisation 13, 14, 136
locating citizen aid 136–40
Lom, C. 123
loyalty 56

McCabe, A. 2
McIlwaine, C. 136
McKay, D. 7
Madge, C. 49
Malkki, L. 14, 22, 35, 38, 50, 155
Marx, K. 161
material scarcity 67, 71, **75–6**
Mawdsley, E. 49
Médecins Sans Frontières 122
media coverage 4
mediated citizen aid 143; *see also* digital mediations: Kiva and microlending
medical clinics 65
mental health counselling 122
mental models 83
Mexico 65, 155
microlending 54, 126; *see also* digital mediations: Kiva and microlending
micro-mentorship program 72
Middle East 127
Millennium Development Goals 103
mimesis 109–10
Minnesota International NGO Network (MINN) **69**, 72
MONGOs (my own NGO) 2
moral capital 148

moral sentiments 156
morals *see* ethics
Morocco 19
Mostafanezhad, M. 66
motivations 1, 3, 6, 19, 23, 103, 118, 129; Cambodia 48, 50, 52, 56, 57, 58, 60; Gambia 31, 32, 33–5, 37–42
Mujib, S 124
multilateral aid 31, **88**, 90–1, 94–5
Muslim Aid 123, 127
mutual recognition 57
Myanmar 118–19, 120

narratives of suffering 129
National Strategy on Myanmar Refugees and Undocumented Myanmar Nationals 122
national-level international development support organisations 68, **69**, 71
national-level nonprofit support organisations 68, **69**, 73
Nepal 85
Netherlands 3, 42, 65, 103; *see also* Dutch Private Development Initiatives (PDIs) in Kwale County, Kenya
networking 5, 36, 37, 51, 64; grassroots international NGOs (GINGOs): capacity building 70–4, 76–7
new development actors 84
new development goals 84
new development instruments 84
New York Council of Nonprofits (NYCON) **69**, 72
NGOs 2, 5, 16, 32, 33, 38–9, 84, 160; Bangladesh 117, 122, 123–4, 126, 132; Cambodia 49, 51, 52, 53, 55, 58; Gambia 31, 34; Kenya 83, 91; Lesvos (Greece) 102–3, 104, 108–9; Philippines 136, 137, 144
norms 35, 83
North America 15
Norway 3, 65, 105; *see also* Norwegian initiatives in the Gambia
Norwegian initiatives in the Gambia 6, 31–42; administration costs 34, 40; altruism 34–5, 41–2; Brønnøysund Register Centre 36–7; concrete projects 33–4; control 38–40; folk-to-folk aid 33–4; Good Samaritans, interdependency and motivation 34–5, 40–1; identities 34–5, 40–2; initiatives as continuity and change 32–3; motivations 33–4, 37–42; ownership 38–40; personal involvement 42; power 39–40; research methods and context 35–6; self-interest 34–5, 41–2; selflessness 41–2; social media 33, 42; structural characteristics 33–4; travelling and transformations 33, 38; 'warm glow' effect 35, 41–2
Noxolo, P. 49

Office of the Scottish Charity Regulator (OSCR) 15

Olive Leaves 107–9
Ong, J. 137
online do-good 2.0 platforms 157–9
online platforms 66, 74, 76, 157
organisational factors 42
organisational independence 66
origins 6
Ossewaarde, R. 83, 94
outsider forms of helping 117
overlap 83, 92, 95
ownership 5, 6, 38–42
Oxfam 17–18, 122, 144

participation 24, 39; Bangladesh 124; Cambodia 52–3, 59; demotic 14; GINGOs 68, 70–1; Lesvos (Greece) 102; Philippines 136, 149
paternalism 67–8, **75–6**
Pedwell, C. 49
peer-building programmes 66, 72–3, 76–7
Perez, P. 7
performance dimension 126
personal connections/relationships 1, 6, 66; Bangladesh 117, 120–1, 123–7, 129, 130; Cambodia 49–50, 54–9; Gambia 38, 39, 40, 42
Peru 65, 88
philanteral aid 31, **88**
philanthropy 8, 33, 104
Philippines *see* social media and brokerage after Typhoon Haiyan in Philippines
Phillimore, J. 2
physical presence and participation 52–3, 59; *see also* personal connections/relationships
Plan International 95
Polish model of social resistance to oppression 15
Polman, L. 2
Porter, G. 49
Posner Center for International Development 69, **69**, 70b, 71, 73, 74, 75
power 39–40, 56, 60, 86, 93, 95, 130; imbalances 1, 4, 8, 49–50, 53, 60; Lesvos (Greece) 101, 104, 109, 111; play 95; relations 33, 66, 76, 112; *see also* empowerment
private aid initiatives 2, 3, 5, 48, 51
private development initiatives (PDIs) 3, 65, 103; *see also* Dutch Private Development Initiatives (PDIs) in Kwale County, Kenya
private foundations 84, 103
professionalisation 1, 6, 14, 33–4
profiteering 149
protest 8
Putnam, R. 15, 18, 23

Quakerism 15, 17, 18

Raghuram, P. 49
real experience, quest for 53
recipient entrepreneurs 39
reciprocity 125–6, 136

recycling 107
Red Cross 14, 20, 144, 146; Finland 14, 50
Redfield, P. 117
refugees *see* citizen initiatives for global solidarity (CIGS) in Lesvos: crisis management during refugee influx; civil society and Rohingya refugee crisis in Bangladesh
regime of goodness analysis 34, 40
relational empathy 50
relief goods 121, 122
religion 15, 23; *see also* faith-based initiatives
religious dimensions of everyday humanitarian action 123, 124–5, 126–7, 130
religious piety 127
religious solidarity 120
religious values 16
resistance 5, 6, 7, 8, 15, 16, 104, 109–12
responsibility and care, practices of 49
restricted focus 67, **75–6**
Richey, L.A. 121
Rotary International 22
Rozakou, K. 111

Saban, L. 135
Salvation Army 18, 22
Save the Children Fund (SCF) 13, 108, 122
Schnable, A. 3, 6, 85
Schuller, M. 2
Schwittay, A. 52–4, 58
Scott, J. 110
Scott-Smith, T. 128
self-interested aid 34–5, 41–2, 83
self-transformation 38
selfless aid 35, 41–2, 125–6, 147
services and resources 71
shared experiences 57
shared humanity 5
shelter 89, 119, 120, 122, 123
Shopna Shiri (Ladder of Dreams) (Bangladesh) 121
Shulpen, L. 31
Silverstone, R. 163
similarities 57, 59, 60
Six-Day War refugees 19
slavery abolition 155
Smith, A. 155, 156
social capital 15–16, 138, 141
social dimensions 155
social justice 5
social media 51; Gambia 33, 42; Lesvos (Greece) 102, 106, 107, 109, 111; *see also* Facebook; social media and brokerage after Typhoon Haiyan in Philippines; Twitter
social media and brokerage after Typhoon Haiyan in Philippines 4, 7, 135–50; accountability 136, 141, 142, 144, 145, 149; audit measures 145; autonomy 138, 142, 144–5, 147, 148; brokers and brokerage 138–9; capacity 135; case study approach: EcoTrek 139–47; cash donations 137; credibility 143; dysfunctional systems 139; efficacy 142, 145; expansion up and out 143–4; flexible informality 145; frustration and mistrust 138; fundraising 139; government involvement 144–5; hierarchy of organisations 135; horizontal flow of aid 145; images as brokers 141–3; immediate community needs 140, 145–7; in-person and material responders 137; influence 135; informal aid organisations 136–7; (in)visibility 143–5; layered brokerage 143; Local Government Units 144–5; locating citizen aid 136–40; methodology 137–8; novelty and reach of aid-delivery model 139; online aid workers 137; personal relationships 135; reciprocity 136; refusal 146–7; resource flows 139; responsiveness 148; social capital 148; social media reshaping citizen aid 147–8; structural holes 135–6, 139, 149; transparency 136, 141–2, 146–9; trust relationships 136–8, 141–9
social networks 37, 51
Society for International Development - Washington Chapter **69**
solidarity 4, 5, 14, 15, 20, 21, 66, 104, 111–12, 155; *see also* citizen initiatives for global solidarity (CIGS) in Lesvos: crisis management during refugee influx
Sou, G. 136
South-South initiatives 2, 136, 142, 148
spiritual quality of charity work 23
sponsorship of individual 160; *see also* child sponsorship
spontaneity of inception 4
spontaneous associations 15, 57
standardisation 109
state-level international development support organisations 68, **69**, 71
state-level nonprofit organisations 68, **69**, 70
Stoler, A. 50
structural holes 135–6, 139
structural inequalities 60
support organisations 65–6, 67, 68, **69–74**
sustainability of initiatives 39, 41–2, 65
Sustainable Development Goals 103, 112

Taithe, B. 6
Talpalaru, M. 127–8
Tanzania 88
Telch, F. 86
themes 5–6
Thompson, J. 118, 126, 129
Ticktin, M. 7–8
Townsend, J. 49
training programmes 72
transaction costs 83
transformations 38

transparency 5, 136, 141–2, 146–9
travelling as motivation 33, 38
triple revolution 84
trust relationships 15, 23, 155; Cambodia 49, 55, 56, 59; Kenya 93; Philippines 136–8, 141–9
Tunisia 19
Tvedt, T. 34, 40
Twitter 137
Typhoon Haiyan *see* social media and brokerage after Typhoon Haiyan in Philippines

Uganda 85
United Kingdom 13, 15, 85, 103
United Nations 84, 112; 2030 Agenda for Sustainable Development 103; Development Programme (UNDP) - Human Development Index 2018 35–6; Freedom from Hunger campaign 17; High Commissioner for Refugees (UNHCR) 101–2, 104, 106, 122; Relief and Rehabilitation Agency (UNRRA) 15; Relief and Work Agency for Palestine (UNWRA) 15; Security Council 19; World Refugee Year 17
United States 3, 65, 66–8, 70, 76–7, 85, 103, 155, 163; Agency for International Development (USAID) 82; Declaration of Independence 156
'unstable category', citizen aid as 1–5

values 35, 83; cultural 16
Vestergaard, A. 154
Vietnam 13, 164–5
visibility 2, 3, 34, 49, 143–5

Walker, J. 109–10
Wallevik, H. 6, 33, 35, 66
war crimes 131 n.14
'warm glow' effect 35, 41–2, 66
water, sanitation and hygiene facilities 65, 89, 120, 122
web-based campaigns 157
Wieters, H. 20
Wilson, E. 6, 13–14, 16, 18–20, 23–4; activism 18; Quakerism 18–19; spirituality 18
Wilson, K. 159
Wilson, P. 18
World Bank 84, 95

Yunus, M. 154, 159, 160